Praise for *The Co*

"*Fear of snakes makes sense. After all, snakes bite! On the other hand, fear of public speaking is worth overcoming. This book is an excellent place to start.*"

—SETH GODIN, SPEAKER AND BESTSELLING AUTHOR OF *PURPLE COW* AND *FREE PRIZE INSIDE*

"*Your ability to speak confidently on your feet will impress more people and open more doors than you can imagine.* The Confident Speaker *shows you how.*"

—BRIAN TRACY, BESTSELLING AUTHOR OF *THE PSYCHOLOGY OF SELLING*

"*Eureka! This book is exactly what every beginning speaker needs, and every advanced speaker will want, because it is packed with simple, enjoyable, workable ways to overcome speaking fear and project a strong persona to every audience member. Bravo!*"

—DOTTIE WALTERS, CSP, AUTHOR OF BESTSELLING *SPEAK AND GROW RICH*

"*When we speak in public, we convey our knowledge, our interest in others, and our value. Not being able to communicate with confidence and skill can barricade the door to success. Now, thanks to Monarth and Kase, their book* The Confident Speaker, *opens that door to successful public speaking.*"

—SUSAN ROANE, BESTSELLING AUTHOR OF *HOW TO WORK A ROOM*®

"*Speaking before a group stresses many otherwise capable people, and as a result their anxiety cripples their careers. Monarth and Kase offer the antidote in their highly readable book. Much easier and safer than taking a Valium!*"

—DIANNA BOOHER, BESTSELLING AUTHOR OF *SPEAK WITH CONFIDENCE* AND *COMMUNICATE WITH CONFIDENCE*

"*I've trained some of the finest speakers in the world. This book will make that process a lot easier in the future.* The Confident Speaker is the single finest book I've ever read on the subject. Even for those of us who do this for a living, there are a lot more than just a few gems here. This book is packed solid and will soon be acknowledged as the authority and go-to book in the field."

— KEVIN HOGAN, PSY.D, AUTHOR OF *SCIENCE OF INFLUENCE* AND *THE PSYCHOLOGY OF PERSUASION*

"If you want to build confidence, persuade others with your ideas, and greatly improve your presentation skills, The Confident Speaker is a MUST READ!"

— DEBBIE ALLEN, AUTHOR OF *CONFESSIONS OF SHAMELESS SELF-PROMOTERS*

"Harrison Monarth and Larina Kase have created the blueprint for giving high-impact presentations and overcoming the anxiety that stops careers in their tracks for even the most competent professionals. The bottom line remains, 'If you can't speak confidently before groups, you're going nowhere.' The Confident Speaker is a powerful tool that will help speakers and business professionals go places."

— SHERRON BIENVENU, PH.D., AUTHOR OF *THE PRESENTATION SKILLS WORKSHOP*

"Monarth and Kase get right to the point exploding speaking myths that fool even seasoned presenters … pick it up, listen to the experts, and it won't be long before you become 'The Confident Speaker!'"

— T. SCOTT GROSS, AUTHOR OF *POSITIVELY OUTRAGEOUS SERVICE*

"The Confident Speaker is the best book of its kind. By following its wisdom, even 'nervous speakers' will be able to command the room."

— MARK LEVY, FOUNDER OF LEVY INNOVATION AND COAUTHOR OF *HOW TO PERSUADE PEOPLE WHO DON'T WANT TO BE PERSUADED*

"This book is essential for readers who want to improve their presentation skills and conquer their anxiety over public speaking once and for all. It is very well written, full of practical advice, and based on proven strategies. I will certainly recommend it to my clients, students, and colleagues."

— MARTIN M. ANTONY, PH.D., ABPP, PROFESSOR OF PSYCHOLOGY, RYERSON UNIVERSITY, TORONTO, AND AUTHOR OF *10 SIMPLE SOLUTIONS TO SHYNESS* AND *THE SHYNESS AND SOCIAL ANXIETY WORKBOOK*

THE CONFIDENT SPEAKER

Beat Your Nerves and Communicate at Your Best in Any Situation

HARRISON MONARTH

AND

LARINA KASE

MCGRAW-HILL

NEW YORK   CHICAGO   SAN FRANCISCO   LISBON
LONDON   MADRID   MEXICO CITY   MILAN   NEW DELHI
SAN JUAN   SEOUL   SINGAPORE   SYDNEY   TORONTO

1 2 3 4 5 6 7 8 9 0   FGR/FGR   0 9 8 7

ISBN-13: 978-0-07-148149-6
ISBN-10: 0-07-148149-4

McGraw-Hill books are available at special quantity discounts to use as premiums and
sales promotions, or for use in corporate training programs. For more information,
please write to the Director of Special Sales, Professional Publishing, McGraw-Hill,
Two Penn Plaza, New York, NY 10121–2298. Or contact your local bookstore.

This book is printed on acid-free paper.

◆ ◆ ◆

To my mother, Roswitha Krems, who was my best friend and the love
of my life.

H. M.

To my parents, to whom I owe my creativity, courage, and confidence.
To my sister, Nicole, who has helped me in more ways than she knows.

L. K.

Contents

Part III: Toolbox for the Nervous Speaker

Part IV: Using the Tools in the Real World

Contents

Part III: Toolbox for the Nervous Speaker

Part IV: Using the Tools in the Real World

Acknowledgments

Without our outstanding literary agent, Rita Rosenkranz, this work would not have been possible. We thank Rita for her thoughtful comments, fine-tuned eye for editing and improvement, and belief in our project. We also extend our gratitude to our editor at McGraw-Hill, Donya Dickerson. In addition to her contagious enthusiasm, Donya provided us with considerable support and excellent suggestions, significantly improving the quality of our book. We also appreciate the efforts of others associated with the production of this book, including Ruth Mannino, Janice Race, Peter Weissman, Laura Starrett, and Kay Schlembach.

Harrison would like to extend heartfelt gratitude to all of his teachers, mentors, and role models who continuously inspire him to become a better trainer, coach, and communications expert. He especially credits Prof. Richard E. Vatz of Towson State University, speaker and author Fergus Reid Buckley, and fellow speech coach Lt. Col. Larry Tracy, as major sources of inspiration for his work. Their research, writing, and contributions in the areas of persuasive communication, critical thinking, and high-impact presenting have helped students and professionals across the world become better orators and communicators.

Harrison feels that the love and unwavering support of his wife, Asli, and the memory of his beloved mother, Roswitha, have provided him with the inspiration and energy to pursue his life's passions and dreams. Harrison also thanks all of his wonderful friends who make him laugh and think, lend an ear, and give advice when needed. They are, in no particular order: Rachid Baligh, Chris Rahbany, Stuart Geshgoren, Todd Weiss, Larina Kase, and Michael Zimmerle. A special hello goes to Scot Hopps and Dave Craig, who would have paid good money to be mentioned here. Harrison thanks all of them for their friendship and support.

Because Harrison's family deserves most of the credit for how he turned out, much of his love and gratitude belongs to his mother, Roswitha; his stepfather, Janusch; his father, Charles; his little sister, Tanja; his uncle Roland; his aunt Monika; his uncle August; and many other members of his extended family who care and love him with all of his faults. Jack, the cat who is Harrison's shadow, is the other love of his life. And dachshund sisters Peanut and Butter have a special place in his heart.

✦ ✦ ✦

Larina would like to thank her teachers, professors, mentors, supervisors, and her dissertation chair, all of whom have filled her with knowledge and a desire to share it with others. She appreciates the faculty and staff at the Center for Treatment and Study of Anxiety at the University of Pennsylvania who helped her to hone her skills with regard to helping people overcome anxiety. She particularly appreciates Edna Foa, Deborah Roth Ledley, Jonathan Huppert, and Miles Lawrence for the supervision of and consultation on the treatment of social and speaking anxiety. She is also thankful to key contributors to the field of social anxiety and public speaking phobias, including Martin Antony, Richard Heimberg, and David Clark, whose research has benefited not only countless professionals specializing in anxiety research and treatment but also clients across the world.

Larina is also grateful to the meeting planners (who took a chance on her when she entered the field of professional speaking) for giving her the opportunity to share her ideas with their audiences and experience the fulfillment and joy public speaking provides. Larina greatly appreciates her virtual manager, Cindy Greenway of Victoria Business Solutions, who has been a key player in the growth of her business, Performance & Success Coaching. She also thanks her Web designer, Angela Nielsen of www.OneLily.com, who designed this book's Web site, www.TheConfidentSpeaker.com. Larina is honored to count people such as Harrison Monarth, Sam Rosen, Joe Vitale, Terri Levine, Milana Leshinsky, Max Vogt, and Tom Beal as joint venture partners.

Larina believes her professional accomplishments stem from her strong support network of family, including her parents, Eric and Carol Kase; her sister, Nicole; her grandparents, Moraima, John, Earl, June, and Cesare; her aunt and uncle Arnelle and Roger Kase; and all her wonderful friends. She appreciates the celebratory dinners and time with Donna, Chuck, and Jen. Larina is unendingly grateful for her love, John, without whom she cannot imagine being as focused, inspired, and happy as she is, and who serves as a great chief technology officer. And she has to acknowledge her canine assistant, Portuguese water dog, Maggie, for her great paper-shredding skills and for the smiles she brings throughout the work day.

Introduction

THE MOMENT YOU'VE dreaded is here. The murmur is slowly dying down as seats are taken, voices become hushed, and one pair of eyes after another begins to focus on you. Some faces are smiling in expectation, while others stare blankly at you, waiting for the show to start. You feel your throat closing, your heart pounding out of your chest, and your tongue drying up in your mouth.

You try to smile, but your face feels as if it's paralyzed. Your rehearsed opening statement seems to have vanished from your memory, and all you can focus on is the feeling of panic that once again has taken complete control over your body and mind.

We've all been there—from the Fortune 500 CEO addressing share-holders, to the student giving an oral presentation to a full auditorium of peers and faculty, to the project manager who wants to share her ideas at a company meeting but is afraid to draw attention to herself by speaking up.

To one degree or another, these are stressful situations, yet many of us who *have to* speak as part of our profession somehow manage to push through the distress, for better or worse. That is, unless the naked terror this fear of speaking produces takes the upper hand. Because we cannot express ourselves confidently when it counts, some of us stare the road-block in our careers dead in the face.

This panic of speaking in public, however, doesn't just affect those climbing the corporate ladder or the entrepreneurs who have to hustle for business. It can unhinge anyone who interacts with others for a purpose. It affects some people so much that they avoid any type of meaningful social contact that requires self-presentation to groups of any size.

It is for all the sufferers of this terrible fear that we wrote *The Confident Speaker*. We know your plight because we've worked with thousands of people who suffer from the same symptoms, which keep many of them from engaging in life's social interactions and from taking advantage of professional advancement opportunities.

As social animals, we humans have to communicate confidently and effectively in order to be heard and get what we want. If fear keeps us from doing so, we are relegated to a life on the sidelines.

We want to assure you that what you're feeling is not unusual. We can help you ease your fears of speaking in public and overcome once and for all the kinds of debilitating symptoms that keep you from sharing your ideas with others. We know that you have much to contribute and that you can triumph over your fear.

PART I

IDENTIFYING THE FEARS

1

When Fear Controls You

Sarah woke up suddenly at 4:00 a.m. Oh, no! she thought as her eyes popped open. Today is the day. How in the world will I survive this? Sarah had to give a presentation in front of 50 people that day. As a marketing director with a medium-size company, she had been successful in avoiding large presentations until a recent promotion. Now, she could not fall back to sleep—all she could think about was standing in front of 50 people in five hours with all eyes focused on her. My boss is going to regret the fact that she promoted me, she thought.

Five hours later Sarah looked out at the audience from the podium. She felt frozen, as if she could not think of any words and did not know how to move. She felt weak and dizzy. As Sarah tried to gather her notes, her hands trembled, and she was afraid she would drop the pages. After a pause that felt like five minutes, she told herself: "Start talking—they are all staring at you, waiting!" She began to speak and noticed that her mouth was totally dry. All she could think about was drinking some water. *This is going to be a disaster*, she thought. Her eyes scanned the audience, and it seemed to her that people looked annoyed and bored. She shuddered. It had only been two minutes, and already it was torturous. How would she survive, standing up there, trying to talk for 30 minutes?

✦   ✦   ✦

Jon was on his way to a party that an acquaintance from work had invited him to. He was walking very slowly because he did not want to go. He only knew a few of the people who would be there. As if it wasn't bad enough to go in the first place, he was going alone, so he had no one to stand near. "I should have made an excuse to get out of this!" he said aloud to himself. Jon typically avoided office parties because he would have to make small talk with strangers, and that made him highly anxious. While he felt fine about his formal presentations at work, he felt completely incompetent when it came to small talk and socializing. He never knew what to say and when to say it. He feared that he would say something silly or embarrassing or that he would bore people.

Because Jon was successful in his career, he feared that he would be "found out" as a closet speaking-phobe, and he worried that his "charade" would be revealed. His colleagues at work seemed to like and respect him, and he didn't want to ruin the pleasant situation. As he arrived at the party, he was already thinking of ways to get out of there as quickly as possible.

- Do either of these stories describe you?
- Do you fear speaking in front of an audience?
- Does the thought of giving a presentation make you nauseated?
- Do you avoid talking to your boss or other people in authority?
- Do you get anxious and have a racing heart, blushing face, or shaky hands when you speak in front of others?

- Do you think you could be much further ahead in your career and social life if you were able to be comfortable and confident while speaking in public?
- Do you avoid telling stories and being the center of attention in social gatherings?

If you answered yes to any of these questions, this book could significantly change your life.

Do You Have Speaking Anxiety?

Since you're reading this book, chances are you already know that you have anxiety about speaking in public. You know:

> You dread getting up and speaking in front of people.
> You avoid situations where you may have to spontaneously say something.
> You try to hide so you don't get called on.
> When you need to speak, you say something as briefly and quickly as possible so you don't prolong the agony.

You know who you are. And, luckily for you, we know who you are too. We are a team consisting of a professional speaking trainer (Harrison Monarth) and a cognitive-behavioral psychologist and success coach specializing in anxiety and stress (Larina Kase). We have helped hundreds of people like you, and we've both learned how to manage our own speaking apprehension as well.

The reality is, most people have some degree of nervousness about public speaking. When people don't worry about getting up and talking in front of others, it's usually because they have had a lot of practice.

If you do have some level of discomfort, the question becomes: *How severe is your public speaking anxiety?*

Answer the following questions to find out.

Rate each item on a scale of 1 to 5:

1	2	3	4	5
Not at all True for me	A little True	Somewhat True	Very True	Extremely True for me

1. I get very anxious when speaking in front of a small group (3 to 10 people). _____
2. I worry about when I will have to talk to strangers. _____
3. My heart pounds when I think I'll have to speak in front of others. _____
4. I typically get nervous when I talk with my boss or someone in authority. _____5
5. Most of the time I avoid giving a speech or presentation. _____
6. I get embarrassed when others watch me speak. _____
7. Usually I avoid telling stories to groups at parties and other social gatherings. _____
8. I would not volunteer to give a toast. _____
9. I worry that my voice will sound strange or that I will tremble when public speaking. _____
10. I would not give a talk if I did not absolutely *need* to. _____
11. I worry that I will forget what to say during a presentation or not have anything interesting to say during casual conversations. _____
12. I have had negative consequences at work, such as not getting a promotion or not getting my point across, because I avoid speaking up._____
13. Getting up in front of a large audience is one of my biggest fears. _____
14. When I talk, I think that other people are likely to evaluate me negatively. _____
15. I try to avoid answering questions when I give a talk. _____
16. Generally, I do not speak up at meetings. _____
17. If I'm not 100 percent sure of an answer, I will not say anything. _____
18. When I speak in public, I think I'm likely to make a fool of myself or that people will lose respect for me. _____

19. When I know I need to speak, I typically get hot, sweaty, or flushed in anticipation of needing to say something. _____
20. I think it's better if I avoid speaking so people do not see my nervousness. _____

Scoring

80 to 100: Very High Speaking Anxiety

You are likely to be someone who becomes highly nervous about speaking in public and who goes to great lengths to avoid public speaking. *The Confident Speaker* will help you understand and gain control over these significant fears.

60 to 80: High Speaking Anxiety

Speaking in public is likely to cause you a significant amount of discomfort. You are likely to avoid many situations altogether and to suffer through some other ones. We will walk you through conquering your worries and developing the skills of an eloquent speaker.

40 to 60: Some Speaking Anxiety

Some speaking situations are anxiety provoking for you, while you are likely to feel more comfortable in other situations. This book will help you learn how to harness your nerves and use them to your benefit. Learning specific skills of the spectacular speaker will help you build confidence.

20 to 40: Low Speaking Anxiety

While some aspects of public speaking can make you a little uncomfortable, in general you are not too nervous about speaking. You are someone who can benefit from the chapters on more advanced skills, such as capturing an audience, polishing your delivery, and finding opportunities to speak.

The Truth About Public Speaking Anxiety

You have probably heard a lot about what causes fear and how to change it. Some of what you know may be useful information that has already helped you. Some of what you know may be inaccurate or less helpful. Our goal is to give you the specific information you need to enable you to see the nuts and bolts of anxiety—and the tools you need to overcome it.

Understanding the way nervousness functions is like having a map in unfamiliar territory: Without it, you are lost, uncertain, and frustrated. When armed with the right information, you can focus, feel safe, and go confidently in the direction of your objective.

The fear of speaking in public is only the proverbial tip of the iceberg. There is actually much more to this fear than what initially meets the eye. There may also be a fear of experiencing intense physical sensations, like the pounding chest, trembling, and sweating that can go along with talking in front of people. You may be bothered by these sensations because of the discomfort they cause you or because they could be noticeable to others.

It is also a fear of incurring negative social consequences, such as criticism, embarrassment, humiliation, and damage to one's reputation, as well as negative evaluation. The fear of speaking publicly is typically associated with *thinking that other people are likely to judge you if they see your anxiety*. People commonly fear that they can come across as rude, unintelligent, boring, offensive, unlikable, not confident, uncharismatic, or not on the same level as those they speak to or with. Are any of these concerns true for you?

The fear of public speaking is extremely common, and as we mentioned, most people experience it to some degree. Speaking anxiety is actually a form of social anxiety. Being nervous about speaking in public does *not* necessarily mean you have a social anxiety disorder or social phobia. If your fear has led to significant impairment and you think you may have a social phobia, it's a good idea to have an evaluation by a psychologist and or psychiatrist. *The Confident Speaker* does not serve as a substitute for cognitive behavior therapy for social phobia.

For most of you, your discomfort with speaking up is completely normal: Remember that the fear of public speaking is the number one fear in adult Americans. We'll guide you through the steps of becoming a confident speaker. You may also benefit from working with a coach to gain additional practice and feedback as you go through the strategies you will learn. Visit www.TheConfidentSpeaker.com for free resources to help you.

Why Speaking Makes You Nervous

A question that most of our clients ask us is, "Why am I someone who worries about speaking in public?" It is important to understand how anxiety works so that you are able to beat it. It is even more important to understand *how* to beat it, so we will devote some time now to helping you spot and understand it, and the rest of the book on how to overcome it.

Anxiety develops in response to a combination of a biological predisposition and environmental components. In other words, the way your genes are "wired" and the way you perceive the world around you have a lot to do with your susceptibility to feelings of apprehension and your ability to deal with them.

Your Biological Makeup

Some people have a physiological predisposition that increases the probability that they will respond to certain situations in an anxious manner. This capacity is genetic or inborn. If you think you are one of these people, you may notice that many members of your family tend to worry about things or show fear about various situations.

The presence of anxiety in family members may indicate a biological predisposition toward nervousness, or it may indicate the presence of a shared environment—you learn how to be anxious from observing other people. Anxiety in family members who have not lived together is more likely to indicate a genetic component. As a result of a combination of biological and genetic factors, some people are more prone than others to experiencing various forms of anxiety.

You probably are wondering why your worry is about public speaking. It can be because of your temperament, such as shyness (see below), because you strongly value how others see you, because you had a memorable negative experience speaking in public, or a variety of other reasons. Regardless of its origins, you should know that it is a natural fear. *The intensity varies, but most people are uneasy about speaking in public or about how others view them.*

Your Life Experiences

Many anxious reactions are acquired through interactions with the environment. Children learn a good deal about how to respond to situations by watching their parents and other people. When they continuously see people responding with fear, verbalizing worries, or expressing apprehension, they learn that things are not safe and should be feared.

Another way of learning anxiety from the environment is based on our own experiences. When we're exposed to a frightening situation and experience the physiological, cognitive, and behavioral responses described above, it is likely that we will develop a fear of that situation. This is particularly true if the situation is avoided the next time, because the more the situation is avoided, the more the fear grows.

Many people with public speaking fears remember one or several incidents where their speaking in public had a negative outcome. Do any of the following sound familiar?

> *I remember when I was in high school and had to give a report in front of the class. I thought I was well prepared, but when I got up there, all I could think about were the people staring at me. I froze and had to go back to my seat. My classmates teased me mercilessly. It was awful.*

✦ ✦ ✦

> *I remember that day 15 years ago like it was yesterday. I was in a college psychology course and I had to stand up and give a report on Freud. I felt embarrassed to talk about his psychosexual*

stages. I got up there and literally stumbled through 10 agonizing minutes. I couldn't get my words out and I turned beet red. I was wearing a red shirt, and I remember thinking that my face was the exact same color as the shirt. I swore I would never give another presentation.

I sat uncomfortably as everyone went around introducing themselves and saying some interesting things about themselves. I tried to think of something to say, but grew increasingly nervous as it got closer to my turn. When it was time for me to speak, I tried to make a joke and it was received with dead silence. I was mortified and couldn't think of anything else to say. I told myself I'd never recover from that first awful impression I made.

I got up in front of the others in our office meeting and my hands were shaking so badly, I could barely hold my notes. I was so embarrassed and nervous that my coworkers would notice my anxiety and think I was not competent.

A different type of negative experience occurs less frequently but can also spawn public speaking anxiety. This is when you receive an unfavorable or derisive comment about your speaking abilities or appearance. One client said that she had a supervisor who put her down after she gave a presentation. Her supervisor would tell her that she turned bright red, that she did not speak intelligently, and that her voice was difficult to understand. Of course she felt nervous the next time she had to speak up.

Shyness and Introversion

Some people who are introverted or shy experience discomfort about speaking in public. Introversion is a largely genetic personality trait, and introverts tend to have less experience talking in public. They also tend to be observers rather than participators, and more likely to be thoughtful, introspective, and quiet than the life of the party. It's not that talking with people always makes them uncomfortable. Sometimes they simply prefer solitary activities. This leads to less practice with or exposure to public speaking, which can increase anxiety.

Some scholars believe that shyness is a form of social anxiety, whereas others believe it is more similar to introversion. Shy people are often more likely to feel anxious about speaking than their less shy peers. Someone can be introverted without being shy. Like introverts, shy people often have less experience with telling stories at parties, giving presentations, and speaking up, so they are more likely to be uncomfortable in speaking situations.

However, the fear of public speaking is also quite common in outgoing and high-powered individuals. People are often shocked to discover that some of the most gregarious people are nervous about getting up and speaking in front of an audience. An extroverted, sociable person may feel fine in some situations (such as one-on-one conversations) but feel nervous in other situations (such as speaking in a group).

Avoidance Behaviors

Fears are maintained or increased based on the way that we respond to the worries. The natural response when you're nervous about a situation is to want to get out of it. We all know this feeling, where we want to be anywhere but where we are. We want to escape from the nerve-racking situation as quickly as possible—and not get into it again. While avoidance is a natural response, it is also one of the major behaviors that increase anxiety. While you may not be able to reliably determine *why* you experience discomfort, what matters most is how you *react* to it. So if you are still unsure why you have this anxiety, don't worry because you don't need to know exactly where it comes from in order to overcome it. We'll go into greater detail about avoidance behaviors later in the chapter.

The good news? You can change how you feel about public speaking by changing your thoughts and behaviors. We are going to help you do this.

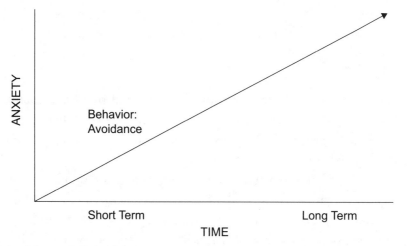

Avoidance and Anxiety

The Four Horsemen of Anxiety

Anxiety consists of the "Four Horsemen of Anxiety," or the four major components: biology, mood, behavior, and thinking. We are often not aware of the presence of all of these components when we feel anxious. We may just note, for instance, that "my heart felt like it would pound right out of my chest!" or "I thought everyone was laughing at me."

In fact, each of these components leads to and increases the cycle of apprehension. The top Four Horsemen play together to get the anxiety started, and before you know it, the anxiety can be off to the races. We'll explain them now so you can start identifying them in yourself, the first major step to beating the fear.

Biological Response: My Heart Is Pounding Out of My Chest!

Carlos felt his heart pounding in his chest as he sat in the meeting. Soon it's going to be my turn to say something, he thought. What if I'm not ready, what if I have nothing to say? His heart beat faster, and he felt himself becoming warm. Will it look bad if I take off my jacket? What if all my

*colleagues see me sweating? he agonized. Oh, no, the pressure
is on now, I'm just moments away from standing up and making a fool of myself!*

Fear has stuck around throughout history because at times it is highly
adaptive. It can get the body and mind going to protect you when you're
faced with danger. A fearful response is experienced by all people when
faced with a real or perceived danger.

The sympathetic nervous system produces a release of adrenaline,
the "fight or flight" hormone. The body has the same response when
you're facing a lion in the jungle and when you facing a crowd in a stadium. We all know this feeling; it is a rush of nervous energy. The activa-
tion of the sympathetic nervous system results in a number of biological
responses. Some of the most typical responses include:

- Your heart pounds in your chest because blood is redirected
  toward your vital organs. You may also feel a flash of heat rising
  up into your head and you may blush.
- You may feel clammy or cold, particularly in your hands and
  feet, since blood goes to major muscle groups. Your hands may
  begin to tremble and shake.
- Your breathing becomes rapid and shallow and you may feel out
  of breath or dizzy and light-headed.
- Your sweat glands become activated, and you start to sweat.

Eventually, this response is stopped either by adrenaline being
destroyed by other bodily chemicals or by the parasympathetic nervous
system kicking in. The parasympathetic nervous system serves to counteract the effects of the sympathetic nervous system. It makes you feel
relaxed. So, while fear may be intense for some time, it will be stopped
by the parasympathetic nervous system. *It is physiologically impossible
to be anxious forever.* In fact, most anxiety habituates or goes away very
quickly. This is an important point to remember as you move through
this book.

Thinking Response: I Will Never Be Able to Face These People Again!

Along with the physiological component, a cognitive component is typically present. These are the disturbing thoughts that race through your mind. You start to have thoughts that mirror the fight or flight biological response, such as:

- How will I be able to get out of here before I have to say something and I embarrass myself?
- This is going to be tough; everyone will judge me negatively.
- I'm going to make a total fool of myself and look like an idiot.

Sometimes the thoughts precede the biological response, and sometimes the body responds and the thoughts follow. *This means that the thought can set off the adrenaline response or the thought can result from noticing that your heart is pounding.*

You may also notice that you have difficulty concentrating and remembering things. You may shift your attention around and have trouble focusing. You may have noticed it was hard to remember things when you felt nervous, or that you could not pay attention to something you were reading or listening to.

Cognitive therapists such as Dr. Aaron Beck, known by many as the "father of cognitive therapy," have studied the type of thinking that occurs with anxiety and written about it extensively. Research by psychologists like Dr. Beck has shown that when people face a fear, such as speaking in public, they often show a characteristic thought pattern in which thoughts are influenced by their negative mood. Thinking becomes emotionally driven and less rational. A cyclical response results because some types of thoughts (*What if I say something stupid?*) can trigger anxiety, and once anxiety is triggered, thoughts are increasingly emotionally driven and less rational (*This is going to be disastrous!*).

Here are some of the common cognitive errors that can occur when people are faced with speaking in public. See if you experience any of them. Make a note of which ones sound like you, because we will go into how to overcome these harmful thinking patterns in a later chapter.

- *All or none thinking* is when you think your speaking is going to be either great or horrible. Thinking is black or white, and it's hard to think of things in the middle. For example: Oh no, my heart just skipped a beat, that means this is horrible!
- *Fortune-telling* as a thought pattern involves predicting that you know the future, and it will be disastrous: If I get up there, everyone will lose all respect for me, and I will never be promoted in my job.
- *Catastrophizing* is overestimating the negative consequences of the situation: People are going to fall asleep or burst out laughing and won't want to talk to me anymore, and I'll have no one to speak with at work. Catastrophizing involves an exaggerated perception of the cost or disastrous result of a situation.
- *Emotional reasoning* is thinking that because you feel anxious, things will be awful. It is reasoning based on your emotions rather than logical thought: Because I am so anxious and feel sick to my stomach, I will speak poorly.
- *Minimization* is underestimating your ability to cope with any difficulties in the situation: If I forget that point, there is no way I could recover. Of course, you forget or minimize how you have been able to deal with difficult situations in the past.
- *Tunnel vision* is focusing on the one negative aspect of the situation and ignoring all the positive, comforting, or disconfirming ones. For example: That one man in the middle is really glaring at me; I must sound like an idiot. Meanwhile you ignore the nodding, smiling people around him.
- *Probability overestimation* is overestimating the likelihood of a horrible event occurring—I will definitely pass out if I have to go up on that stage—when in fact you have never passed out in your life.

Do you ever have thoughts like these? If you're nervous about speaking in public, you probably do, even if you haven't noticed them before. These types of thoughts trigger and reinforce anxiety. When you are anxious in a situation, it's highly likely that you are interpreting the situation as more threatening than it actually is. This is why anxiety-producing thoughts are called "cognitive errors." They come about when our minds are thinking emotionally and not rationally.

Behavioral Response: Get Me Out of Here!

Anxiety also has behavioral components. The desire to flee the situation is extremely common. Along with the "fight or flight" response, we sometimes have the urge to freeze in the face of a frightening situation. Have you ever experienced this "deer in the headlights" feeling? It is as if your mind goes blank and your body is paralyzed. Here are some of the common behavioral responses that occur when people dread speaking in public.

Avoidance

Avoiding feared situations or trying to get out of them as quickly as possible are the most common behavioral responses when facing something we fear. Sometimes we fall prey to the "fight" response and respond to comments with a defensive or aggressive stance. We may say things that we later regret, or we may respond impulsively to a situation.

As is the case with anxiety in general, the most common behavior with public speaking discomfort is avoidance, that is, trying to get out of "doing the talk." We make excuses, "Oh, I'd love to, *but* I really need to take care of something," or "Unfortunately I can't make it because I'll be out of town." We can come up with all kinds of creative, elaborate excuses, right?

Sometimes you simply can't avoid the talk, so what do you typically do? You probably try to get it over with as quickly as possible. A common behavior with nervousness about talking in front of others is cutting the speech as short as possible. This often leads to people rushing through their talk, answering with as few words as necessary. One client told us that he wanted to answer a question by saying, "It really depends on the situation . . . " but instead his anxiety made him answer in the shortest way possible, and he flatly said "No."

Nervous Behaviors

These are the things you do, often without realizing it, when you are nervous. They are not the things you do to hide your nervousness—those are overcompensating behaviors (see below). Rather, these are signs of your uneasiness.

Nervous behaviors include jiggling change in your pocket, playing with your pen, wringing your hands together, fixing or touching your hair, shifting your weight around, fidgeting, or talking more quickly.

Overcompensating Behaviors

Overcompensating behaviors are a major culprit in keeping anxiety around. These behaviors occur when we try to minimize the scary aspects of the situation, try to control the anxiety, or try to hide our fear or physical symptoms from others. For example, you may hide your hands to disguise trembling, say very little so you don't say something embarrassing, or overrehearse your talk.

In reality, these behaviors *actually maintain or increase the distress* we feel about talking to or in front of people. This is because we believe that we would not get through the situation without them. It's important to learn that you can get through a speech "in one piece" without overcompensating behaviors. Contrary to common belief, these overcompensating behaviors actually *maintain* anxiety. *In fact, the latest research reveals that these behaviors are largely responsible for public speaking anxiety.*

Some of these behaviors have a direct negative effect on performance. For instance, memorizing your speech may make you sound stiff and unnatural; sucking on a hard candy will make it difficult to talk; and mental overrehearsing of what you'll say will delay your responses and make them sound censored.

Other behaviors are detrimental primarily because you could become dependent on them, like a drug. You could think that you are unable to function without them and be unable to speak spontaneously. In this book, we will teach you how to speak anytime and anywhere without relying on these types of behaviors that can actually backfire and make you more nervous or perform worse.

Mood Response: I Feel Horrible! Will I Ever Feel Better?

The fourth variable in the creation of anxiety is your mood. You're probably aware of feeling anxious, nervous, concerned, frightened, scared, apprehensive, uneasy, tense, edgy, worried, jumpy, or panicky when faced with a speaking situation.

After prolonged periods of distress, other feelings often start to come into play. When you avoid situations where you would have to speak in public, you may recognize the impact of that avoidance on your career or social life. This can cause feelings of depression, dejection, frustration, hopelessness, or dread (of when you will eventually have to do it).

One of our clients, Clint, described a situation in which he came back from a meeting with the top executives in his company and felt deflated and upset. He said that he had become very anxious and did not think the meeting went well. He felt hopeless about the future of his career.

You don't want to speak in public again and experience all these negative emotions. As you learn how to change your thought patterns, behaviors, and other responses to public speaking, and as you gain more practice, polish, and confidence, these negative feelings will subside. You'll be able to use the distress of your experience to energize yourself and propel yourself forward toward excellent speaking. As Larina says, "One of the best secrets in life is how to turn distress into success."

On Your Way...

Now that you know how to recognize the four components of speaking anxiety, you are on your way to overcoming it. In the next two chapters, as you learn more about identifying your fears, we will answer all major questions about the fear of public speaking and dispel the popular myths and misconceptions about speaking in public. You will learn the most frequent ways that speaking anxiety presents itself.

In the second section of *The Confident Speaker*, you'll discover the secrets of preparation in order to beat anxiety. The third section delves into the effective tools you can use anytime you need to speak in the future, and the fourth section goes further into how to use the tools in the real world and find opportunities to practice public speaking.

By the end of the book, we trust that you will know everything you need to be an effective and confident public speaker.

2

The Top Speaking Myths Revealed

A LOT OF what you have heard or think about anxiety is simply not true. In fact, you may be doing things to overcome your fear of speaking that are actually making you feel worse, not better. The misconceptions about anxiety lead people to do things that actually maintain and increase nervousness about speaking in public.

We are here to serve as your personal coaches and dispel the myths about the fear of public speaking, and we'll give you accurate information about this fear. When you know the truth, you will be able to overcome any distress about speaking up in public. When you read this chapter, think carefully about your attitude toward each myth and you'll be well on your way to changing the beliefs that keep you feeling uncomfortable.

The Top 12 Myths and Misconceptions About Anxiety

Myth 1: Anxiety Will Continue to Increase Over Time

Many people fear that if they do not do something to control their distress, it will spiral out of control forever or until something bad happens. Some fear that the anxiety will increase until they lose control, go crazy, make a complete fool of themselves, escape from the situation, or have a heart attack. This is *not* true.

When you're agitated, the sympathetic part of your nervous system kicks in and you experience the adrenaline rush that leads to your heart racing, along with attendant sweating and trembling. This response will naturally decrease because the parasympathetic component of your nervous system acts to reduce the anxiety. This is called "habituation." Your body and mind get used to the anxiety, and it fades away.

Habituation, or getting used to anxiety, *always* occurs and makes the fear decrease over time. It is a biological response system. *Your anxiety will decrease.* Every living organism habituates. One of Larina's colleagues from the University of Pennsylvania is fond of saying, "Even sea slugs habituate."

When we are particularly nervous, it may take longer for habituation to occur. In general, the length of time for habituation is correlated with the severity of the fear. In other words, the more serious your anxiety is, the longer it will take for your nervous system to get used to it.

Another reason it might appear that we're not experiencing habituation—in other words, it feels to us that our anxiety remains high—is that our overcompensating behaviors are maintaining the anxiety. Overcompensating behaviors serve to artificially push down or push away anxiety. This disallows habituation.

Imagine that your anxiety is a ball floating in water. If you push it down, it will pop back up, right? Pushing the ball down is like avoiding something or using an overcompensating behavior. If you did not push the ball down (i.e., you did not engage in an overcompensating or avoidance behavior), the ball would slowly drift away on its own. The ball drifting away on its own is analogous to anxiety naturally decreasing over time, or the process of habituation.

Sometimes the primary form of anxiety is anticipatory anxiety. This means our fear is highest before the situation, as we anticipate it and get ready for it. Then, once we are in the situation, the anxiety decreases. Avoiding the situation keeps the worry around. When the primary distress is anticipatory, habituation occurs more quickly once you are in the actual situation.

Myth 2: Anxiety Is Dangerous

Have you ever thought that the anxiety you experience is harmful? Or that you are in danger of being hurt because you are very nervous? Have you tried to tell yourself that you'd better calm down fast or else be in serious trouble?

Many people think that the fear itself can hurt them. This is why you may be afraid of the actual symptoms of anxiety. While it is true that the *cumulative* effects of anxiety and stress can take a toll on your physical health, it is not true that being anxious will directly lead to collapse right then and there.

The fear itself is a physiological response similar to one that occurs when you engage in athletic events or run up and down stairs. You sweat, your heart pounds, you flush, you may get light-headed, or you may tremble. We do not think we are in danger after a hard run or a serious cycling class. Why do we think this way when we're nervous? Because, as we have discussed, one of the symptoms of anxiety is distorted thinking. At the time of the peak worry, it may seem reasonable that we would faint or have a heart attack, but in reality neither of these things is highly likely.

Actually, both fear and anxiety have developed over time to protect people. *The primary purpose of fear and anxiety is to help you, not to hurt you. These emotions serve to get you ready for a frightening situation.*

Myth 3: Anxiety Worsens Performance

It is very common to think that we performed worse because we were feeling anxious. In fact, this belief is a major cause and maintainer of anxiety. Overcome this belief and you are likely to overcome much of your nervousness.

With fear, it is very common to judge how the situation *went* based on how you *felt*. Do you think this is an accurate way to assess the effectiveness or quality of the performance? If you said no, you are starting to understand how fear works! There are a number of reasons why *it is not accurate to judge performance based on how we feel.*

1. Many of our feelings are not visible to others. People think that things are observable that truly are not. Some common examples of this are thinking I'm as red as a bright red tomato because I feel warm, thinking it must have been worse because my heart was pounding so much, and thinking that I must have said stupid things because my mind was racing.

2. Our thinking is distorted when we are worrying. Since thinking becomes less logical and coherent during periods of high anxiety, many of the conclusions we come to then are not valid.

3. We are our own worst critics. While we sit around dwelling on the one thing we forgot to say, our audience is actually excited about the four great points we did make.

4. It is very possible to show some nerves *and* have people rate the presentation or performance as a great one. Typically, people rate performances based on what they got out of them, the originality or uniqueness of the topics, the visual materials, and so on. Looking nervous does not negate all of these. Some expression of anxiety can actually endear you to people.

People may indeed rate you somewhat lower if you appear highly anxious, but it's likely a difference between being rated an 8 rather than a 10. Larina often has her clients with performance anxiety speak in front of others, and she asks the observers to rate the performances. Time and time again she found that high anxiety was *not related* to poor performance. Someone could be rated a 9 on anxiety (with 10 being the highest anxiety) and a 9 on performance (with 10 being the best). People often made comments such as, "I could see that Joe was nervous and was impressed with his ability to keep going and relay very interesting information."

Because so many people show signs of discomfort when speaking, audience members aren't overly surprised or disturbed if some evidence of anxiety is present. *It is the way you respond to it that is key.* Here's a hint: Responses with overcompensating (going on and on to be sure you have explained a point that you may have said incorrectly) or avoidance (leaving the room) behaviors are least favorably looked upon.

Also, raters almost always rated the anxiety they saw as being lower than the speakers rated the anxiety they felt. A speaker would give himself an 8, and the observer would give him a 3. This reinforces the idea that how we feel is not the same as how we appear.

Myth 4: People Automatically Judge You Negatively If They See Your Anxiety

Most people do not automatically judge you just because they see that you're nervous. In fact, people sometimes find others more approachable, real, and humble when they show some signs of uneasiness. The person who is overly confident, conceited, arrogant, or cocky is typically the person who turns others off. The person with a bit of nervousness, on the other hand, is often seen as genuine and trustworthy. In fact, some studies have shown that people who blush are seen as more endearing and likable.

Even if others do not judge you more positively when they see your anxiety, they will not necessarily judge you negatively. Impressions are formed on the basis of a complex collection of variables, and anxiety is only one factor. Often it is not a factor at all.

Plus, many if not most people have some level of worry about speaking in public, so when they see your nervousness, they may empathize with what you're going through. They may want to help or support you.

You may wonder: What about those judgmental jerks who *will* view me negatively? Well, it sounds like you just answered your own question. They are judgmental jerks. There certainly will be such people out there, but what you have to ask yourself is: So what? Why would you care what these people think or say? They are going to find a problem with one thing or another. If it's not your nervousness, it will be your voice, your hair, or your shoes. These people typically have their own insecurities, and they compensate by judging others.

If you must care what they think (if this person is your boss, for example), we're going to give you many tips to help you become more confident. For now, the take-away message is: *You must be willing to experience anxiety to overcome it*, and when you do experience it, the outcome is rarely as disastrous as you thought it would be.

Myth 5: Anxiety Will Decrease If You Avoid the Feared Situation

This is a common belief, and it is maintained because it's based on a natural response. Think about what happens when something causes us pain—we learn to get away and keep away from it. Did you ever burn yourself or get stung by a bee as a child? Did you stay away from flames or avoid all bees? Probably so, since this is the natural response.

Unfortunately in this case, the natural response is the least helpful response. Anxiety thrives when avoidance is present.

The reason anxiety increases with avoidance is that avoidance makes it impossible to confirm or disconfirm your feared consequence. For example, feelings of nervousness might lead you to predict that you'll make a fool of yourself if you speak in front of a large group. What happens if you avoid speaking in front of a large group? Well, you can never find out whether the anxiety-fueled prediction is right, so you're left assuming that it is right and that you better not speak in front of large groups.

The more you avoid something, the more your apprehension goes up. Imagine that you developed a fear of the dark. You left lights on for four months straight and never went out in the dark. What do you think would happen to you at night when your lightbulb blew out and you were sitting in the dark? You would be *very* scared. Bottom line: Avoidance increases anxiety. The key to beating this behavior is to *stop avoiding*.

Anticipatory anxiety (getting nervous about the speaking situation beforehand) is due to avoidance. Its reactions include:

- As soon as I know that I'll have to speak in public, fear sets in. Even if I don't have to give a talk for a couple of months, I worry about it whenever it comes to mind.

- The night before I have to give a talk, I feel tense, my stomach hurts, and I toss and turn all night long.
- The morning of a presentation is horrible. I feel jittery and nervous and my mind is racing with the problems that may occur.
- On my way to a meeting, I start to feel nervous. When I think that I may be called upon to say something, I feel a hot flush come over me.
- Right before I speak, I feel like I'm hit with a wave of terror. My heart feels like it stops, my face becomes flushed, and I think, Oh no!

Anticipatory anxiety can occur any time before public speaking. It can go on for months, or it can set in as a sense of panic right before opening your mouth. This is not the same worry you feel while you're actually speaking; instead, it's the nervousness that boils up when you *think about* speaking. The mood is often one of dread. Many people say that the fear that takes hold of them as they anticipate talking is worse than the feelings they have while actually talking.

The more you avoid a situation, the more you nervously anticipate it when it comes up. When you make elaborate excuses and stories to avoid speaking in public, the next time you need to speak, it's likely you'll have a high degree of anticipatory anxiety. Instead, you should stop avoiding and confront your anxiety. You'll find that habituation occurs very quickly because typically, once you get into the situation, you realize that it isn't as difficult as you expected.

Myth 6: Practice and Rehearse So You'll Know Everything

While it's true that you should practice any presentation so you're very comfortable not only with your material but also with talking about it, over-preparation can be too much of a good thing. When you start to overrehearse, the rehearsals can become a type of overcompensating behavior. Ultimately, you may think that if you ever have to speak without rehearsing thoroughly, which is likely to happen a lot, you won't do well. This creates a bigger problem: You soon may attribute your speech success to practicing over and over, and you may believe that you can't speak without extensive rehearsal. This actually takes away from your confidence when you have to give spontaneous or last-minute talks.

One client, Maria, said that she practiced her speech about 100 times, and it went very well *until* the question-and-answer phase. People asked her about things she was not ready for, and all she could think was, Oh no, I didn't prepare for this! Her problem was she thought she was able to speak so well because of her huge amount of practicing, and when it came to saying things that weren't rehearsed, she panicked.

Another problem that comes from practicing too much is that you can *sound* like you practiced too much. When a talk is overpracticed, it can become stiff and sound mechanical. You may come across as if you were reading off a TelePrompTer rather than speaking naturally.

Myth 7: Write Down Your Talk and Read It So You Don't Have to Worry About Remembering Things

Again, there is a partial truth to this. It's not a bad idea to take in a couple of notes to cue you during your talk; however, *never read a speech.*

Have you ever watched a speech that was written down and read? How was it? Most likely it was boring and dreadful. Since one of the keys to speaking successfully is connecting with the audience, how can you do that if you are staring at your speech? All you can connect with is the piece of paper. If you really want to read a speech, be sure that you look down to jog your memory but then look up while you speak.

People often worry about how they will remember what to say during a talk if they don't write it all down. Remember this: You will have practiced the talk, and you know what you're talking about. You don't need a written speech to remember what you want to say. Some brief notes can be helpful, but they should be kept to a minimum.

Having a written speech can also cause more anxiety. It can raise questions such as: "What if I forget it?" "What if it gets out of order?" "What if I lose my place in reading it?" "How can I read and look up at the audience?" It's better instead to write down key talking points and use those as your guide.

Myth 8: Afterward, Don't Ask People If They Have Questions

Depending on the type of presentation, skipping the Q&A session may not look so good. Audience members may wonder why they cannot make comments and ask questions. The bottom line is that this is avoidance, and you now know how unhelpful avoidance is. The more you avoid answering questions, the harder it will be when you eventually do have to answer them.

A variant of this myth is: When speaking with new or intimidating people, ask others a lot of questions so they cannot ask you questions about yourself.

Sometimes people avoid answering questions about themselves because it can be more difficult to talk about personal things than objective things. It is great to ask others questions to express interest and get to know them, but *do not avoid speaking about yourself.* Decide how much you want to reveal and get practice in speaking about more difficult things, such as yourself.

Myth 9: Sit Out of the Leader's Line of Vision in a Group Setting So You Won't Be Asked Questions

This is a popular strategy used in classes, meetings, talks, and other places. Have you ever tried to get out of the way or avoid eye contact so no one sees you and calls on you? This reminds us of how little kids put their hands over their faces and think you cannot see them anymore.

This is one of the worst tactics because it is avoidance, and it's often not successful. You can still see the kid behind the hands, right?

The solution: Even if you do not have any clue as to what the speaker is talking about or how to answer questions put to you, sit in a visible place and make eye contact. Your chance of being called on is no higher, and you will achieve greater confidence by not avoiding the situation.

Myth 10: Hide Your Nervousness By Wearing Makeup, Staying Behind a Lectern, and So On

Do you recognize what these kinds of behaviors are?

We've probably made this point clear by now, and you realize that they are overcompensating behaviors. Know that you can still speak well without doing all these special things.

Often these behaviors are even more noticeable than the signs of nervousness themselves. You think it's horrible, so you hide your face with your hands, wear makeup so people can't see that you're blushing (even some of Larina's male clients have done this), or avoid looking at people in the hope that they won't look at you. These behaviors are much worse than the blushing itself. If you cake on the makeup, you'll look odd and unattractive, which will make you feel less confident. If you try to hide your hands so people don't see them shaking, you'll look stiff and unnatural. If you wear a turtleneck to hide your splotchy red chest, your face is likely to turn crimson. *Do not become dependent on these sorts of behaviors.* These are all solutions where the cure is worse than the problem.

Did you know that some social blushing is actually interpreted as a good thing? Researchers on blushing prefer to call it "social facial vasodilation" because dark-skinned people blush too, even though it isn't seen as a blush. Researchers theorize that blushing has been preserved throughout human evolution for a reason. Facial vasodilation can help defuse tension, divert undesirable attention, and apologize nonverbally for transgressions. Instead, face your fears without any crutches. Do what you need to do to appear your best (and we'll help you with this), not to attempt to hide signs of nerves.

Myth 11: Picture the Audience in Their Underwear, Walk with Superman's Cape, and So On

These "tricks" actually take you out of the moment and raise your negative stress level.

The key to successful speaking is to focus on your number one task: connecting with the audience. Silly tricks like these that are intended to decrease anxiety actually spike distress because they prevent connecting with your audience.

These tactics also make you less focused on your topic and take you out of the moment. Essentially, they accomplish nothing except to give you a false sense of control over your anxiety. *Forget these and learn how to actually gain control over your anxiety.*

Myth 12: Analyzing What You Did After a Talk Is Helpful

Analyzing your performance can be helpful if you do it in a constructive, nonjudgmental way. But be honest: Are you nonjudgmental with yourself as you analyze how you came across after a speaking situation? If so, that's great, but when people have discomfort with speaking in public, the internal conversation often goes something like this:

- I can't believe I said that—how stupid!
- Those people must have thought that I am totally incompetent. I'm sure they saw how anxious I was and wondered how I could have made it to a director position.
- I should have said so many important things that I did not say. I got nervous and could not even think straight.
- That was so embarrassing. How in the world will I ever face my friends and neighbors again? They're sure to think that I'm weird.
- I'm sure that people were just bored to death while I was talking. I put them to sleep. I must have had the most monotone voice they ever heard.
- They definitely saw me blushing and trembling. They probably thought I was shy and uncomfortable. They will not want to talk with me again.

Have you ever had any thoughts like these go through your mind after you spoke? You finally got through speaking, and now you have to get through the part in which you beat yourself up. We call this a "postmortem." As you can imagine, it is not helpful.

A postmortem is the period after a talk when you ruminate about how horrible and miserable the experience was. During postmortems, we tend to dwell on all the negative feelings we had, what we should have said, what we said in less than perfect ways, little fumbles we made, and the horrible consequences that will follow. Do you think these types of thoughts will make you ever want to get back up in front of people again? Not likely. We'll show you how to get rid of them in the next chapters.

Using the Truths

You now know not only how these myths are false, but you've also learned some of the essential truths that will help you manage speaking anxiety. Recognizing how to redirect your thoughts and behaviors away from these misconceptions is an important step in overcoming the fear of public speaking. For some people, simply changing misconceptions and false beliefs is all they need to do to overcome speaking fears. For others, more practice and skills are needed. Throughout the book, we'll delve into how to change misconceptions and the behaviors that follow them, and also how to replace them with more confidence-inspiring beliefs and behaviors.

In the next chapter we'll identify the 10 most common situations in which nervousness about speaking arises. In each situation that applies to you, consider whether any of these misconceptions have created or sustained your fear.

3

Getting into Your Personal Fears

Is This You?

As you just learned in your self-assessment about the severity of your nervousness, the stronger your fear, the more likely that it will be pervasive in various situations. It's a misconception that people fear speaking only in front of large audiences. Many people also fear other situations that cause them to speak up. And some people have no problem giving talks in front of large groups, but they fear situations such as small social gatherings or one-on-one discussions with a boss.

There are many faces to the fear of public speaking. In this chapter we'll cover the top 10 situations that most frequently cause people anxiety. Of course, in addition to the 10 most common situations in which speaking anxiety manifests itself, there are many other circumstances where you may feel discomfort while speaking, and everyone's experience is unique.

As you read through the 10 situations, ask yourself which scenarios look like those in which you would like to gain more confidence and comfort. As you'll see, some scenarios occur in the workplace, while

33

others occur in social settings. We suggest that you read through all the categories, even if the headings don't sound like you, because they may describe feelings and situations that you do experience and would like to change. Make note of which ones sound true for you, because in the book we will be taking you through specific step-by-step solutions for overcoming fear in these situations.

Situation 1: Speaking Up at a Meeting

Yao was sitting in a meeting with other executives in his company. Some of the senior executives were present, and Yao was starting to get nervous. I'm going to have to say some intelligent-sounding things today, he thought. I don't have anything to say, and the others here speak so eloquently, I'm going to look like an idiot. My coworkers will wonder how in the world I got this position. As the meeting went on, he became more and more anxious because he realized he had not said anything yet and he needed to say something soon, or the meeting would be over. Yao was sweating, and he hoped no one could notice. He became so focused on thinking of things to say that he lost track of the conversation and what people were saying.

Have you had any experiences like Yao's? Speaking up at a meeting can be difficult for a number of reasons. First, there are likely to be authority figures present. This is another form of speaking anxiety, which we get into in Situation 4 below.

Second, the format is often unclear. For people who have some degree of nervousness about talking in front of others, it can be most difficult when they have to interject themselves into conversations or meetings. Do you know that feeling when you want to say something at a meeting but either you don't because of nervousness, or you try to but someone else has already begun talking? How frustrating is that? You actually got up the nerve to talk, but you lost your chance because someone beat you by a second or was more assertive than you.

Equally frustrating is losing your nerve to make an excellent point only to have someone else make the point and receive credit for it. If you've had this experience, you know how maddening it can feel. The good news is that it gives you the motivation and drive to beat your anxiety and make those important points.

A third difficulty with speaking up in meetings is that you have to say something spontaneously without much time to prepare. Nervous thoughts and symptoms can make it quite difficult to do this. Anxiety interferes with a rational thought process, causes attention and memory problems, and produces symptoms that are distracting in and of themselves. It's hard to think about the topic at hand when you have sweat dripping down your brow or are starting to shake, right?

Another common problem with speaking up is that you may have colleagues and coworkers who love to hear themselves talk and who dominate meetings. These people are the opposite of you and could easily go on and on and jump into a conversation at any moment. We are not trying to get you to be like this, although it would be nice to speak in a more carefree manner. It can legitimately be difficult to talk when others have not paused for one second. People can be domineering in these contexts, and that makes it much harder to get a word in edgewise, especially if you are nervous. We'll give you solutions for dealing with such situations throughout the book.

Situation 2: Meeting Someone New and Going to Parties

Maria was going to a neighborhood party on Saturday afternoon. She had just moved into the area and did not yet know many of her neighbors. Her husband was out of town, so she would need to go to her neighbor's house alone. On Saturday morning she did not feel like herself. She had a pit in her stomach and was feeling queasy. She began worrying about who she would talk to when she got to the party. As she was walking over, she began to feel nauseous.

How am I going to eat anything with this stomachache? she wondered. *People will think I'm weird to go to a cookout and not eat anything. What if they think it's rude and that I don't like their cooking, or if they feel that I'm too good for hot dogs and hamburgers? I don't want to give the wrong impression.* When Maria walked in the door, she thought, *Who should I talk to, what do I do? Everyone is already speaking to someone. Should I interrupt?* Then the host came over and introduced Maria to another neighbor. Maria said hello but then could not think of anything else to say. She thought, *They're going to think they have strange new neighbors, and this will be embarrassing for my husband too!*

Often, people who have wonderful social or speaking skills get uncomfortable about unstructured social situations such as parties. Usually people are already gathered into groups, and it can be hard for them to walk up and introduce themselves to new people. Many worry that they are being rude by interrupting the groups or that they will have nothing interesting to contribute to the conversations.

In addition to the speaking part, people worry about their appearance, eating and drinking, and how they're holding themselves. If you are uncomfortable with any aspect of your appearance, parties can be intimidating. One of Larina's clients worried that her "horrible skin" would be quite embarrassing in the "broad daylight" of an afternoon get-together. Prior to coaching, she would pile on a ton of makeup, wear giant sunglasses, and avoid eye contact with people to disguise her perceived skin imperfections.

Other people worry that they will be boring, uncharismatic, or uninteresting. Your nervousness can make you less charismatic because you're so focused on your anxiety. In this book, we'll help you reduce your self-consciousness so that your natural personality can shine through. You can also find free resources on improving your personal charisma, including the self-assessment "What's Your Charisma Quotient?" and the special report "The Ten Secrets to Magnetic Confidence—Feel Great and Attract Others Every Time You Speak" at www.TheConfidentSpeaker.com.

Food presents dozens of challenges. Many people worry about getting food on themselves or spilling something on someone else. They worry about getting food stuck in their teeth. Others worry that they'll tremble, and it will be obvious while they eat. Those who are overweight, preoccupied with bodily "flaws," or who have lost weight face another form of pressure when it comes to social gatherings, since such situations often center around food. Here are some of the common concerns that people have when it comes to eating at get-togethers:

- If I eat fattening food, people will think, No wonder she's overweight—look at what she's eating!
- If I don't eat the food that is prepared, people will think I'm rude, but if I do, I may overeat and go back down an unhealthy path.
- How will I balance food, eat food, and talk to someone at the same time?
- What do I do if someone talks to me while I have food in my mouth?
- What if I try to tell a joke or smile or laugh and I have food stuck in my teeth?
- I don't want to speak up and draw further attention to my bulging tummy, which can't be disguised in a T-shirt—I'd rather just try to blend into the crowd.

Ever experience any of these worries?

There is a lot of pressure to say the right thing when we meet someone new. We all know that a first impression is vital in personal or professional relationships. Many fear that they will not recover if they don't say the right thing when they first meet someone. Nervousness when speaking with someone new is further heightened when the person is someone who can be very influential in your life. You may notice that it's uncomfortable to talk about yourself with a complete stranger, such as when someone asks you what you do for a living. Parties entail multiple first impressions, so it makes sense that they can be pretty intimidating.

Situation 3: Talking to an Authority Figure

Petra felt her legs shake as she was walking down the hall to have a meeting with her boss. She felt like she was going off to battle or some other horrible fate. She disliked meeting with her supervisor. Petra did not realize that she was anxious; she just thought that her boss was not very nice and that's why she did not like meeting with her. Today was different. After the meeting, Petra realized that she truly did have anxiety about meeting with authority figures. At the meeting, Petra choked and could not come up with any good answers to her boss's questions. She shook and was embarrassed that her boss saw her nervousness. She became distracted by trying to hide her shaking and could not think of anything to say.

Petra realized that she became nervous around people in authority because she recognized that in addition to being nervous when meeting with her boss, she also used to be nervous around professors in college. Are you uncomfortable around people in authority as Petra was?

If we think of public speaking anxiety as the result of being afraid of a negative evaluation, it makes sense that this fear would be present around authority figures. These are the people, after all, who often evaluate us. Whether they're giving us a grade in a class, writing an evaluation for us, deciding whether we're the right match for their son or daughter, determining our fitness for inclusion in a club or group, or deciding about giving us a promotion, these people hold some power over us. These are the decision makers, and we need to help them make the best decision for us by saying the right thing. So we feel that we have to be very careful about what we say around them in order to create the best impression possible. That is a lot of pressure.

Fortunately, most bosses do not evaluate their employees negatively. And if your boss is supercritical, it may not be because of your poor performance—some people find fault more than others. If you're like Petra and worry about speaking with authority figures, we'll have many tips to help you.

Situation 4: Giving a Presentation or Leading a Workshop

Jorge was a relatively new salesperson who really wanted to make it in sales. The main problem was that his job required many presentations of his company's products to potential customers. Jorge dreaded this aspect of his job and feared that he would not make his numbers and would be fired because he was so poor at giving demonstrations and presentations. At his last presentation, his main goal was simple: survival. He just wanted to get through it. He told himself, "Just focus on showing them the product, do it quickly and get out of here!" So Jorge rushed through the presentation, took off his jacket because he was so hot, and stared at the product or the table the whole time. He looked up briefly to see people looking away or down, appearing bored. It did not go well.

Presentations, demonstrations, and workshops require a good deal of interaction with the audience. When people like Jorge worry about balancing the content of the presentation with the discussions with the audience, they often neglect important aspects. In his case this led to a poor outcome because a vicious cycle ensued. When you become more anxious, you do things like Jorge did (rush, look down, and so on), and the audience reacts negatively, so you become more anxious, and on and on.

Many people make mistakes in the way that they prepare their presentations. They don't want to think about preparation (because thinking about preparation feels uncomfortable, since it reminds them of doing it), so they avoid it. As a result, the presentation does not go well. On the flip side, in an attempt to ensure a great performance, others overprepare. This can also be problematic and lead to stiff or artificial presentations. Another common response is to prepare ineffectively by focusing on inconsequential aspects of the performance or by avoiding portions that increase nervousness.

Another potential problem is that you may evaluate your presentation skills more negatively than others do. You think that you're doing a horrible job as you go along, but this is not the case. Frequently, your presentation or workshop actually goes much better than you think. We will tell you why this is and give you some great solutions in later chapters. Keep reading!

Situation 5: Being Interviewed

Jennifer had a major interview coming up for her dream job. As the interview got closer, she became more and more anxious. She dreaded interviews because she did not like to talk about herself. She always felt that she was bragging if she said something laudatory about her accomplishments, but at the same time, that she was not selling herself adequately if she did not. As she sat in her interview, she agonized about the answer to the question: Am I saying what she wants to hear? The interviewer wasn't smiling, so it seemed that she did not like her answer. I'm blowing this, she thought. I'm not saying the right things. I've said "um" about 100 times. The more Jennifer worried, the more she felt the blood rush to her face. Now I'm red as a tomato, she thought. Who would want to hire someone who gets embarrassed like this?

When interviewing for a new position, there's a good deal of pressure. Not only do you worry about what you're saying, you worry about how you're saying it, how the interviewer is responding, and how it's all going to impact the likelihood of your being hired. Many people put a lot of pressure on themselves because they think that they worked very hard to get where they are, so they need to seal the deal with the interview. "Don't blow it!" they tell themselves.

Other types of interviews can also be anxiety provoking. Being interviewed for your expertise for an article or some other form of media can be nerve-racking. You need to think about how to appear professional, knowledgeable, interesting, and so on. The thought might well come to mind that you have come that far, so you don't want to ruin it by what you might say.

Interviewing others can induce speaking anxiety in people for similar reasons. You may feel you have a certain image to uphold to ensure that others respect you. This can lead to the belief that you have to ask all the right questions in the right way. You may feel that if you show any speaking anxiety, you'll never be taken seriously. Keep in mind that interviews make most people nervous—you are definitely not alone. And there are specific ways to combat these feelings during an interview.

Situation 6: Being Called Upon

Daniella sat in the back of her large lecture class. "Please don't call on me. Please don't call on me," she prayed to herself. She was so distracted by her nervousness and by trying to blend into the crowd and look inconspicuous that she had no idea what the professor was lecturing about at that point. Now I have no idea what's going on, she thought. It will be so embarrassing if he calls on me and I just say, "Uh, I don't know." There are people I know in this class, how could I face them again? Daniella's muscles were so tense that she sat stiffly in her chair.

Being called upon creates so much speaking anxiety because it also brings on a sense that you lack control. Throughout this book we are going to help you learn how to control your anxiety rather than have it control you.

Many people with nervousness about public speaking feel that they need to be "ready" to talk. When they're called on out of the blue, a surge of anxiety often ensues. "Being called on" speaking anxiety is common in classroom settings, in meetings, and in social interactions.

One client, Susan, described a situation at a social function at which she was aware that she wasn't contributing to the conversation. This knowledge made her feel tense, and she was trying to think of something to say. She became engrossed in her own thoughts, trying to come up with something that would be interesting to contribute. Just then one of her friends said, "Oh, that happened to Susan! Susan, tell everyone that story, it's so funny." Susan felt like she was put on the spot. She didn't even know what her friend was talking about, and she did not want to tell the story or say anything. She just wanted to run and hide.

Another common situation where you may be called on is in meetings. You hear your boss bellow your name and ask for your opinion about the topic of conversation. You become instantly nervous if you have nothing to say or if you were zoning out, thinking about what you would eat for dinner that night. Or, you might completely disagree with your boss's point of view and not want to contradict her in front of everyone.

Situation 7: Answering Questions After a Speech

> *Martin breathed a sigh of relief. Whew, I got through that talk and survived! he thought. Just as he was thanking his lucky stars, a hand shot up in the audience. "I have a question," someone announced. Uh-oh, Martin fretted. He had no idea what he would be asked, and he thought, What if I have nothing to say? He tentatively responded to the audience member, saying, "Yeah?" and the man proceeded to ask him a question of moderate difficulty. But Martin was so distracted by his anxiety symptoms spiking up that he didn't pay attention to the question. Instead, he was noticing his brow becoming moist with sweat and his mind racing. He fumbled through a response and prayed that there would be no more questions so that he could get out of there quickly and save face.*

When a question is asked of you, you feel as if you're in the spotlight. You don't want to appear unknowledgeable and say "I don't have any idea," and you don't want to make up an answer, so it can be tricky to navigate these tough waters. Many people are like Martin in that they can get through the relatively structured part of a talk because they know what they're going to be talking about. But the question-and-answer part can be intimidating because the audience members can ask anything and everything they feel like. Sometimes the questions are only peripherally related to the topic, so they're outside the speaker's area of knowledge.

Another common problem is being caught off guard by a question and not listening to a question. Then you have to ask yourself whether you should have the question repeated or whether it's better to try to answer. Sometimes audience members also feed off one another. If one person asks a difficult question, that may spur another audience member to ask a similar question, and before you know it, the conversation has taken a turn to an area about which you know nothing. This can also feel as if the audience is being hostile and ganging up on you. We'll help you answer questions—even when you have no idea what to say—with eloquence and poise.

Situation 8: Introducing Yourself to a Group

It was Latoya's first day in a new women's group. The leader of the group asked everyone to go around and introduce them-selves. She asked that they all say where they were from and tell an interesting anecdote about themselves. An interesting anec-dote? Latoya thought. What in the world am I going to say? She watched as everyone went around the room and seemingly enjoyed talking about themselves until there were just a couple of people left. Soon it was her turn. She felt as if a wildfire was spreading and coming right at her. Her time came. "Um, my name is Latoya," she said, "and I'm from Brooklyn and, uh, I guess what's interesting is that I, uh, I don't know, I like to cook." Afterward she was so embarrassed that she beat herself up and spent the rest of the time thinking about what she had said and what she could have said instead.

Does anything from Latoya's experience sound familiar to you? Introduc-ing yourself to a group is difficult because you know that what you say will frame everyone's first impression of you. One of the hardest things to do is tell an interesting story about yourself. Many people worry about appearing to brag or seeming conceited or snobbish. At the same time, they do not want to say something boring or uninteresting.

Sometimes people become so nervous about introducing themselves that they blank out and can't think of anything to say. What? My name, uh . . . they think as they feel their hearts pound in their chests.

Part of what's difficult about introducing yourself is the order of introductions. If you go first, you don't have an example of how others introduce themselves. If you go last or later in the process, you have a while for your anxiety to build as you get ready to go, and meanwhile you compare yourself to the others.

Situation 9: Participating in a Group Conversation

Phillip did not like all of the team-based projects at his job. Why can't I just get projects and do them on my own? he asked himself. For Phillip, the problem was speaking up in the group. He disliked how talkative everyone else in the group was and how difficult that made it for him to say anything. The worst part was that he often had things he did want to say. He was a bright, creative, and insightful person who could contribute to the group, but his fear kept him quiet.

Phillip had the same experiences in social situations. He felt comfortable having conversations with people one on one, but he dreaded social engagements that required group conversations. His fiancée, an extremely extroverted, talkative woman, loved going to and hosting dinner parties. Phillip felt nauseated during most of these dinners because he was so preoccupied thinking about what to say and the fact that he was so quiet. People must think there's something wrong with me because I'm not contributing to the conversation, he frequently thought. Sometimes he couldn't think of anything to contribute to the conversations. Other times he had ideas but was unsure about when to interject them and second-guessed his potential comments before he made them, worrying that they would come across as dumb or uninteresting. His fiancée could not understand why he was like this at dinner parties because he was so comfortable and talkative with her.

Many of Phillip's experiences are common for people who become nervous about speaking in public. The fear about participating in a group discussion comes up in situations such as team projects at work, group seminars, projects in college or graduate school, and in social situations, such as group conversations at parties, bars, or restaurants. Does any of this sound familiar to you?

A common experience for Phillip was to sit amidst the group, thinking about how he could add something and say it in a way that would hide his nervousness about speaking in public. He often had the extremely frustrating experience of watching someone else in the group say something he was going to say. It's disappointing to have the same idea as someone else and yet have that person be the one to express and receive the accolades instead of you. Other times it seems that people are publicly taking credit for your work. In fact, if you don't speak up and people know this, they might take advantage of the situation and indeed take credit for your ideas. This is one reason why your fear of speaking up can negatively influence your career.

Sometimes people are afraid that they don't have anything of value to contribute to the group. Other times people realize that they have good things to say, but anxiety interferes with their saying them because either they cannot think clearly when they're anxious or they avoid talking because of their nervousness.

Situation 10: Giving a Talk to a Large Audience

Sarah could not believe she had agreed to do this talk. In 10 minutes she'd have to get up in front of all these people! She looked at her watch and thought, I don't know if I can do this; maybe it's better if I just leave and say that I got sick or something. Ten minutes turned to five, and then one, and she was tentatively walking up to the podium. Oh my gosh, there must be at least 100 people staring at me, she worried as she looked out over the audience. She picked up her note cards and her hands started to shake. She quivered and thought that this could be the end of her professional career.

Giving a talk in front of a large audience is typically one of the most feared speaking situations. All eyes are focused on you, which of course is extremely intimidating. People are taking time out of their busy schedules to listen to you, and you don't want to disappoint them. All of the pressure is on you to make sure that everything goes well, and there are usually a ton of things to consider, from audiovisual materials to your notes to making eye contact with the audience.

These types of presentations are also sometimes lengthy, and it is common to wonder how you're going to speak for that long without saying something stupid, or how you're going to get through such a long talk. Many people say that in the first minute or two they think about how much time is left and about how they will never make it through, or that they'll be a total mess by the end. Because speaking in front of large groups is such a major fear, we'll devote a whole chapter to it. You might decide to tackle the fear of large presentations even if you don't need to speak before large audiences to be successful. When you tackle this fear, everything else may feel easy.

Some people, on the other hand, are completely comfortable with formal presentations because they can prepare for them, but they worry about speaking spontaneously when in a meeting, when encountering new people, or when participating in group conversations.

Whichever type of scenario causes you discomfort, we'll give you several tools to overcome it. You'll even want to put yourself into these situations to get more practice and show yourself that you can do it—imagine that!

In the next section of the book we'll help you prepare for various speaking situations to reduce anxiety and gain self-assurance. You'll learn how to organize a talk, prepare to reduce anxiety, relax before speaking up, and what to do and not do before you speak in public.

PART II

PREPARING TO BEAT YOUR ANXIETY

4

"O" Is for Objective and Organization

The First Step: The Objective

One of the most powerful aids for a reluctant speaker is also one of the most misunderstood. It isn't alcohol. It isn't an anti-anxiety drug. And it most definitely isn't picturing the audience naked. It is something so easy and obvious that everyone can use it immediately. In fact, our coaching clients are often shocked at how powerful this "tool" is in helping them reduce their anxiety. This power tool is called the "objective."

While the objective gets plenty of lip service in everyday conversation, few know how to effectively form an objective. Often when we ask people about their objective before a talk or public speaking event, they describe the "process" rather than the "result" they are pursuing. Here's a typical example of a "false" objective:

> *Lisa put together the slides for her presentation to a potential new client, complete with handouts and collateral material from her company. When asked about her objective for this*

meeting, she responded: "I want to show this prospect that we can provide a better service than our competitor, while saving them money."

Close, but no cigar. What Lisa is describing here is what she is going to do during the meeting, not where she intends to end up. And that is the key to forming an objective — the clear definition of one's destination. In other words, it's where you want to end up and what you want to have happen.

What Makes a Good Objective?

Before we can answer what makes a good objective, we should understand that whenever we interact with others, we typically want something from them, particularly where business is concerned. In countless daily encounters with peers, subordinates, or bosses, we either directly or indirectly request something from them or respond to a request they have of us. There are few truly neutral interactions where one party isn't trying to get the other to comply with a request. This does not mean that you're selfish or rude; it's just human nature.

Knowing this concept, and being comfortable with it, we can now easily craft our objective based on what we want from those we're dealing with. Let's go back to Lisa's presentation to understand how to use this knowledge to create an objective for her meeting. The objective of her presentation could be to have the prospect ask for a proposal following her speech. It could also be to get the prospect to sign a purchase order following her talk. Another acceptable objective might be to have the prospect invite her for another meeting with a higher-level executive decision maker.

All these possible objectives have one thing in common: They are actionable. They require a specific action from someone. They demand a result based on something you are doing or saying. By crafting such a clear objective, you now have a firm, unwavering goal line in front of you that determines everything you do to accomplish this objective.

And once you know where you're going, it will be much easier to know whether you're getting closer to or further from your target.

Why You Need It

But what, you might ask, does having a clear objective have to do with reducing anxiety prior to a public speaking situation?

First, it anchors you. It allows you to focus all of your (nervous) energy and language on one firm goal. By nature, you can only focus on one thing at a time. By taking the focus from how nervous you are and directing it with all of your mental faculties and physical resources toward your simple objective, you will naturally feel less anxious.

Second, a clear objective also helps motivate you to confront a speaking situation that arouses anxiety, because with an objective, you'll have a significant potential payoff.

Based on what we discussed above, give these quick exercises a try to help you determine if you're ready to form a clear objective:

1. You are entering into a salary negotiation session with your potential new boss and the VP of Human Resources, where you've applied for a management position. Write your objective on the line below.
   My objective is: _____.

2. You are giving a humorous toast at the wedding of a good friend.
   My objective is: _____.

3. You have been falsely accused of misplacing important files that were later found. You are confronting the accuser.
   My objective is: _____.

4. You are giving a sales pitch to a new client who could be very important for your firm's business objectives.
   My objective is: _____.

5. You have a new idea that you know would enhance productivity at the office and save the company money over the long term. You're going to present your idea at the next staff meeting.
   My objective is: _____.

Remember in these quick exercises that an objective is a clearly defined actionable result that you want from those you are presenting to.

Here are some options for clear objectives you could have for each of the situations above:

1. Your objective could be *to get a written commitment for a starting salary of no less than 70,000 including a year-end bonus tied to my performance.*
2. Your objective could be *to elicit tears of joy from my friend and laughter and applause from the other guests present.*
3. Your objective could be *to get an apology from the accuser and a verbal commitment to be more careful with her assumptions in the future.*
4. Your objective could be *to get a request for a formal proposal.*
5. Your objective could be *to get my boss to agree to a private meeting with me to discuss the details of the idea and the feasibility to have me spearhead the project.*

The beauty of a clear objective is its simplicity and its role as a beacon in your communication efforts. A guiding objective helps you to stay on track with your message and to focus on the parts of the presentation that are necessary to reach the objective.

Next, we'll focus on the objective of proper organization and how it helps you gain confidence quickly.

The Quickest Way to Becoming a Confident Speaker: Proper Organization

Most people faced with the task of having to speak on a particular topic have a favorite crutch they lean on again and again. It's called Power-Point, and it is the antidote to interesting and inspiring presentations the world over. Particularly in the hands of the anxious speaker, PowerPoint becomes the security blanket that organizes (quite rigidly), suggests (predictably), decorates (clip-art*fully*), and provides the nervous speaker with an excellent physical barrier to hide behind when the glazed-over eyes of bored executives search for structure and meaning in a presentation.

While the content wizard of PowerPoint can have its value if used intelligently, you don't want to rely on it for the effective organization of your talk. You want to actively organize your talk with your objective firmly in mind and supply a structure that makes sense for your particular topic.

Proper organization isn't brain surgery. To stick with the medical analogy, it's more like removing an appendix. Easy and routine once you know how to do it, after which you'll do it over and over again without breaking into the sweat of nervous agony. But before you can organize your talk, you'll have to identify what kind of presentation you are giving. Let's look at a few common formats your talks could have.

1. The Speech

One of the main types of speeches is the persuasive speech. Throughout life we either give or are an audience for persuasive speeches: to students at colleges on the dangers of binge drinking and hazing rituals, at business schools to convince professors of the validity of our ideas, to venture capital firms to obtain start-up funding, and to juries in courts of law in order to create doubt on issues of guilt and responsibility. We speak to persuade when we need or want something, and we are making a deliberate and strategic effort to get it with our language and nonverbal communication.

Another type of speech, the entertaining speech, is often in the form of the keynote. It uses anecdotes, storytelling, humor, and personal experiences with the objective of delighting an audience. Skilled performers of this type of speech use their personalities and animated deliveries, as well as mental imagery and word pictures, in order to connect with their audiences. For example, the purpose of a speech at a benefit or an awards ceremony would most likely be to entertain the audience.

Yet another classic type of speech is the speech to inform, which can have a number of applications. We often speak to inform at corporate gatherings, or to a group of shareholders during the annual meeting when CEOs present earnings and losses to corporate investors. We also speak to inform when we share information with neighbors on new developments in the community, or with parents at the monthly PTA meeting in school.

Our advice is to not get too caught up in these classifications, because any time you get up and speak to an audience, unless it is for an executive summary (see below), every speaking attempt needs some or all of the elements of the above. All speeches are persuasive (remember, we always want something from our audience, even if it's simply approval or feedback in the form of head-nodding or smiles); can use a touch of humor; in one way or another intend to inform people of something; and will benefit from the use of illustrative word imagery.

Clearly, every time you speak you should have mastered your material, know your audience, and be aware of their biases, attitudes, motivations, needs, and wants. You should know how the audience thinks of you and of your topic. You should know whether the audience holds you in high regard or thinks very little of you based on your reputation. Persuasion is ubiquitous. This deserves repeating; even if your speech or talk or presentation is not meant to be persuasive per se, you still are trying to influence the audience—to pay attention, to listen, to understand, and to think a certain way.

2. The Executive Summary

Executive summaries are by definition designed to be succinct and entirely based on the facts that you've gathered and that you feel are critical for your audience to know. The main objectives of the summary are to provide crucial information to a select audience of key players and to report on a specific issue or project. The executive summary can have a variety of other purposes, such as influencing an audience to adopt a new way of doing something, to approve a request, or to change their perspectives on a contentious issue.

When an audience asks for an executive summary, they want the facts without the frills. Stories, anecdotes, and metaphors would be out of place during this type of presentation. Key characteristics of the effective executive summary are attention to relevant detail, complete focus on a key issue, and the ability to keep the summary short and sweet.

Smart presenters remember these three keys to executive summaries when presenting their information to senior management, the board, a group of colleagues, or a panel of interviewers.

Remember the golden rule of executive summaries: Make sure your information is complete, your message is on point, and your presentation is as succinct and short as possible.

3. The Instructive Presentation

Many presentations in business and corporate environments are in the form of training, explaining, and instructing. Seminars and workshops are commonplace in millions of offices and conference rooms across the globe. The instructive presentation requires an expert in a particular field or on a specific topic to present new information in the most compelling way possible to a group of learners. For new material to "stick," a presenter has to consider the learning styles of the audience as well as circumstances such as prior knowledge of the issue and personal motivation, among others.

Remember the golden rule for the instructive presentation: If your audience doesn't get it, they can't apply it. Make sure you ask for feedback every step of the way to make sure that whatever knowledge or skills you want to impart are easily understood and can be put into practice by all participants—the fast learners as well as the slower ones.

How to Structure Your Talk

Now that you've determined the specific format of your talk, let's look at the body of your talk. Then we'll go into how to organize the information you want to share.

The Body

The body is the part of your talk where your main ideas and any subordinated points need to be organized so the entire structure makes sense. Structuring these components with some serious thought about the overall message you want to convey will give you a mental road map, enabling you to hit on all of your major points in the planned order, and providing your listeners with a clear path to follow. This is one of the key remedies against rambling. We've all been there, and it's a good place to get lost (pun intended).

One of Harrison's clients, Garrett, was a smart young development manager who was passionate about his job. Whenever he gave presentations, however, he invariably packed way too much information into his talks, drowning the audience in data they could have gotten in writing before or after his talks. Garrett felt that all of the information he gathered to make his points was important, and he had a difficult time determining what was critical for the talk and what was nonessential in driving home the message. His audiences would often end up tuning out emotionally, as they tried to process the flood of information that washed over them.

A good piece of advice to post on your computer prior to organizing your talk is that the average audience of adults typically processes three key points fairly well, providing there aren't too many subpoints attached that allow the message to get off track. So, three is the magic number. If you have more than three major thoughts to share, be sure to at least keep the subpoints to three, at most, and use clear language supported by effective nonverbal communication to keep your audience focused. You don't want to drone on and on and give your audience any reason to mind-drift toward grocery lists, past-due bills, and faraway vacations.

The Organization

One of the top reasons many presentations amount to a colossal waste of time for speakers and audiences alike, without achieving the desired results, can be attributed to ill-prepared presenters who create talks that lack effective structure and organization, two things that would greatly benefit their audience's understanding.

If you want to achieve your intended results with your talk, you have to empathize with your audience, logically and emotionally; in other words, what you're telling them has to make sense, but it also has to move them somehow. This is critically important for reaching your objective. Also crucial for your success is the necessity to arrange your presentation with the needs, wants, fears, and biases of your audience in mind.

It is virtually impossible to think of any powerful story, presentation, speech, or talk—be it formal or informal—that doesn't have a strong beginning and a compelling ending. Whether you call them opening and closing statements, as in the field of law, or the introduction and the conclusion, as in business and academia, the point is that they are critically important components of any talk. Often, you won't even get an audience's attention if you don't have a strong, interest-arousing opening. If people are forced to sit through your talk for any reason, you may have their bodies present, but you can count on their minds wandering freely across their vast individual agendas.

Some say that equally important to having a strong beginning—perhaps even more important—is having a powerful conclusion that influences the way the audience thinks, feels, and acts based on all they've heard during your talk.

Depending on how you like to work, you can prepare the introduction and the conclusion after preparing the body of the talk, which can be your guide to the beginning and end. Or you can prepare your conclusion first, working your way backward to support it with a well-researched body and a riveting opener or lead-in to your talk.

There are a number of ways to organize your talk, and it's up to you to find the one that works best for the speaking opportunity you have. It may take some trial and error to figure out which method of organization works best and is most effective to your cause. Generally, starting with the introduction and then working your way to the conclusion can seem overwhelming, and it can be dangerous too, since it's easy to lose your focus and end up at a conclusion different from the one you intended. (If this happens during the preparation stage, it might actually be a benefit because it tells you that perhaps you should use that different conclusion.)

Methods of Organization

So what, you ask, are your options when it comes to organizing your ideas, points, and key information for your next talk?

To answer this question, we go way back to the classics. Because the methods that build the foundation for almost any effective talk these days are the same ones the ancient Greeks and Romans used a couple of millennia ago. And incidentally, they are the same mix of organization methods that Anderson Cooper uses when giving a report on CNN or that the president uses when delivering the State of the Union address or that any good speaker follows when presenting a message to his or her audience. Unlike Anderson and the president, however, most of us mere mortal orators don't have ambitious producers and presidential speechwriters to craft our message and organize our talk for us. But with the following methods, even the most inexperienced speaker can structure an effective talk for maximum impact.

The methods of structure we're talking about are easy-to-use three-step patterns that can be applied to many different speaking purposes. They include patterns where the subject matter is arranged chronologically, spatially, by cause and effect, by problem and solution, topically, as well as by comparison and contrast. We'll explore each of these in the next section.

So what is the best way to determine which methods and strategies of organization will work for you? Listen to your intuition first. By simply listening to your gut, you may find the most appropriate way to make your information flow in a talk. You'll find, however, that by looking at the various methods of organization, one will stand out more than the others and will make the most sense. Below we'll present some examples of effective organization methods, including a quick three-step formula that will give you a very good idea of how the various methods and strategies can be used to organize your key ideas.

Spatial Method

The spatial method can serve as your talk's structure whether you're discussing the allied occupation of Iraq and its various areas of military installations or the geographic expansion of a corporate franchise and the regional territories each of its individual franchisees "owns."

Likewise, if you were to describe certain structures or physical objects, such as an architect talking about a new office building project, you might detail the project from the underground garage to the penthouse, while an artist, in contrast, may start at the focal point of her painting, leading to the surrounding areas of her work.

The spatial method lends itself to a convenient three-step process that looks like this:

1. *Location* A. You'll use phrases like, "This is the area where they . . . " or "From here we expand to . . . " or "Right next to it you can see . . . "
2. *Location* B. You'll use phrases like, "If you look at where we've come from . . . " or "Moving the entire structure to this area . . . " or "Ending up here . . . "
3. *So what.* You'll use phrases like, "The result of this configuration presented us with . . . " or "By building it like this . . . " or "This will give us the space . . . "

To create the desired response in the audience when choosing this type of arrangement, you have to make sure that the audience can clearly follow your train of thought as you illustrate your talk. Whether you design your talking points from left to right, top to bottom, or here to there, you should always help the audience understand how the individual points relate to one another and why you've chosen a particular sequence. In other words, tell the audience what the connection is between the various points you're making, or you might lose them at one of your stops.

Cause-Effect and Effect-Cause Method

This is a common structuring method where you talk about a set of circumstances (effect) that resulted from a previous set of circumstances (cause). Effect and cause can of course be reversed, depending on the objective of your talk. In that case you might be describing a certain situation (cause) that has resulted in a new set of conditions, desirable or not, depending again on your objective.

We use our three-step method to illustrate how you could quickly structure a talk with this method.

1. *Effect.* You'll use phrases like, "The problem we are facing today is . . . " or "What we've experienced over the last quarter was . . . " or "This is what we're dealing with right now . . . "
2. *Cause.* You'll use phrases like, "Recent cost-cutting measures by several of our key customers . . . " or "Because of our

existing relationship with . . . " or "A relentless onslaught of negative publicity has . . . "

3. *Course of action.* You'll use phrases like, "What we need to do now is . . . ", or "Therefore I want us to implement an immediate . . . " or "That's why I propose an alternate . . . "

Let's have a look at how this method of organization could be used to make your point convincingly. Say you're preparing a speech about your desire to see an increase in the number of women in the executive suite and on corporate boards in America. You start by asserting that women can make progress by being more proactive in pushing for positions responsible for profit and loss, in order to get in line for corporate leadership positions. You further state that women already in leadership positions should foster a culture of mentoring in order to prepare more women for jobs in the executive suite.

What could be a desired effect of such initiatives? Perhaps that more women would be promoted to corporate P&L positions, effectively preparing for C-level or executive leadership posts where traditionally there are many more men than women.

In another example, the reversed method of effect and cause can be used effectively in a presentation on increased domestic layoffs, unemployment, and corporate offshore outsourcing. As one of your key ideas, you may illustrate the effects of corporate outsourcing to offshore countries on U.S. employment statistics, and job cuts in various services and manufacturing industries.

Another point you could assert is that likely causes for increased outsourcing are ever-increasing competition, price wars, and pressure from shareholders on corporations to cut costs and perform with more efficiency and lower overhead.

Before you use the method of cause and effect for organizing your presentation, make sure you feel comfortable about the relationship between the alleged cause and effect you're trying to illustrate. It's a rookie mistake to automatically assume that a certain effect was produced because of a set of conditions that existed prior to the effect. Future legal eagles learn this in law school, and successful speakers need to be aware of it as well: the trap of false causes. As a speaker, it's critically important to your credibility and the validity of your message that you be absolutely clear on the relationship between the cause and effect you are presenting.

Here's another example. A person who was a heavy smoker all her life develops lung cancer in her late fifties. Most people would automatically assume that a lifetime of heavy smoking resulted in the woman's cancer. While smoking could certainly be a likely cause for her illness, it would be false to conclusively assume it is without knowing the results of a medical diagnosis. That's because statistics show that even people who have never smoked in their lives have developed lung cancer, eliminating smoking as a guaranteed cause. Research into the soundness of the relationship between cause and effect is critical in order to give your claims and points solid credibility.

Another misconception as it relates to cause and effect, and one for a presenter to look out for, are effects that on the surface seem to result from a single cause. In fact, a particular set of circumstances often results from more than one definitive cause.

Here's an example. Ask yourself: "Are porous borders between Mexico and the United States the only cause for increasing numbers of illegal immigrants in certain parts of the United States?" Not likely. However, a lack of opportunity at home, the promise of a better future north of the border, quality health care for oneself and one's family, plus the presence of many friends and family already in the United States, may certainly all contribute to the rising number of illegal aliens in parts of this country.

To round off this pattern of cause and effect or effect and cause in your talk you'll have to propose a course of action; otherwise, there would be no real benefit in pointing out the conditions you illustrated during your speech. Steer your audience in the direction you want them to go by letting them know what you want them to do and how you want them to think, using the new perspectives they gained as a result of your talk.

Chronological Method

Past. Present. Future. The human being is the only animal that measures life in chunks of time. Our language reflects this vividly. "What worked yesterday, won't work today," or "Time is money," we say, or "Time will tell." We make plans for tomorrow, next week, or next month. We tell stories of things that happened yesterday, a few weeks ago, or last year. The concept of time is a constant in our communication with others.

The chronological three-step is an easy-to-remember structure that looks like this:

1. *The Past.* You'll use phrases like, "Last year we all agreed to . . ." or "A week ago we celebrated . . . " or "When I assumed leadership of this project a couple of months ago . . . "

2. *The Present.* You'll use phrases like, "Now it's come to this . . . " or "Today we are looking at . . . " or "Currently the attitude seems to be . . . "

3. *The Future.* You'll use phrases like, "This year we'll prove that . . . " or "What we have to do from now on . . . " or "Tomorrow will show that we . . . "

Other ways to structure a talk chronologically include presenting certain pieces of information in their order of occurrence, such as, "Jack gave me the papers around 10:00 a.m. yesterday, after which I immediately faxed them to the client. I did not get a response until 9:00 a.m. today, which gave us little more than two hours to adjust our proposal before our scheduled 11:00 a.m. meeting."

Another example would be to give an audience instructions based on the units of time in which they should be carried out. Suppose you're giving instructions to a group of learners during a workshop you are conducting. You might say, "Right now I would like you to write down 10 ways of demonstrating 'active listening' during a conversation. You have five minutes to do this. After that you'll choose a partner and take turns of three minutes each to tell your partner a personal story utilizing the techniques you wrote down. After you've told your stories, we will debrief and discuss."

Organizing your talk chronologically also lends itself well to topics such as "How to Prepare PowerPoint Slides," "Planning the Annual Shareholders Meeting," or "How to Prepare for the Media Interview."

Whichever chronological arrangement you choose as you structure your talk, make sure that time units and sequence make sense to your listeners and that they are easily able to follow your talk from point to point.

Problem-and-Solution Method

An organizational method often used for persuasive presentations, the problem-and-solution pattern illustrates a certain problem for the audience, refers to its source or cause, and subsequently offers at least one possible solution that will eliminate the problem. The key when using this method of organization is to outline the problem in detail and discuss its negative fallout if an effective solution is not found. Don't neglect this step, because research has shown that fear of loss is a powerful motivator for most people. Then, when offering the solution, you have to be able to show that your antidote to the problem is exactly what the audience needs, either completely eliminating the severity of the problem or at least reducing it.

Here's our example of the three-step method when using this technique:

1. *Problem and source.* You'll use phrases like, "The increase of the homeless population in our inner city is a direct result of . . . " or "Criminal activity in our neighborhood has become commonplace mostly due to . . . " or "We've lost our top two salespeople to the competition simply because . . . "
2. *Fallout.* You'll use phrases like, "If we can't stop this situation from escalating . . . " or "The horrific consequences of this will be . . . " or "What our kids will end up with is less than . . . "
3. *Solution.* You'll use phrases like, "The only way to prevent this in the future . . . " or "Our next step should be . . . " or "The obvious choice for us is therefore . . . "

This method of organization can be especially effective in sales presentations, where clients are looking for solutions to their various organizational challenges, including increasing sales, reducing expenses, developing human resources, and so on. It can also be very effective in presentations to senior management, where smart solutions to critical problems are often a key rung on the ladder toward the executive suite.

Let's examine what the problem-and-solution method can look like in practice when you speak to a group.

Assume you identify a number of problems for which you have the fitting solutions. For example, training and development of staff is always a concern in big organizations. The issue of getting people trained in various job-related competencies could present the specific problems of high travel expenses to training sites, loss of productivity, staffing shortages, and implementation of newly learned skills. If you approach each of these problems as a main point and offer a solution for each one, you will be in a better position to convince the audience of the power of your solutions than if you had grouped the problems as one big issue and offered a single blanket solution.

Topical Method

When organizing your talk with the topical method, you need to group your main points into specific sections within your topic. This is less complex than it sounds. In fact, the division of a topic into smaller categories can be accomplished quite easily, particularly if you are well steeped in the subject matter.

Our quick three-step formula illustrates the types of phrases that characterize this method of organization.

1. *Topic A.* You'll use phrases like, "First we'll look at the expenses that we're incurring . . . " or "Let's look at the profile of a typical customer . . . " or "To the question whether we have the necessary resources . . . "
2. *Topic B.* You'll use phrases like, "Next, we'll look at the design of . . . " or "Moving forward, I'm concerned about staffing of . . . " or "Another issue that complicates this project is . . . "
3. *Topic C.* You'll use phrases like, "Finally, the budget . . . " or "Coming to the issue of training for . . . " or "During the fourth quarter we saw . . . "

For example, a talk about a typical public relations campaign could be broken down into the main points of branding, graphic design, and media exposure, with each area of competency serving as a key idea.

Employee training and development could be discussed in terms of in-house and off-campus training. A department manager's presentation on the soon-to-be-installed systems network could be arranged according to the main points of software, hardware, staff training, and production downtime.

Another look at how a topic can be broken down into its main points is the example of an outside corporate trainer's talk on a long-term training and development initiative. This talk would begin with the Assessment of Current Staff Performance, then move to a Training Needs Assessment Questions for Management, Calculation of Training Costs, and, finally, Calculation of Training ROI. As usual, however you choose to arrange your main points, remember that the audience's understanding of your message has to be your guiding standard whenever you set out to organize your presentation.

Compare-and-Contrast Method

Comparison and contrast is another popular organization method that speakers and presenters often use to highlight the similarities and differences of two objects, issues, or situations. Political opponents often employ this method during a debate, trying to impress their message upon an undecided audience. For instance, Candidate A may point out that he served in the military, just as Candidate B proudly claims he did. That's the comparison. Next, Candidate A discloses that Candidate B served "safely" in the National Guard, at a U.S. base, whereas he, Candidate A, served in an overseas conflict zone as part of an elite unit that saw combat on a number of their missions. That's the contrast.

In using this method of arranging your talk, you would chose two items that on the surface may seem to be very much alike, or have much in common, until you point out significant differences that contribute to the objective of your talk. Similarly, you may take two seemingly unrelated items and point out the commonalities that exist between them, again leading the audience to your perspective on the talk you are giving.

Before we give you specific examples, we'll demonstrate the three-step method again on how such a talk could be constructed quickly by using certain phrasing.

1. *Similarities.* You'll use phrases like, "I have no doubt that my opponent, like I, means well, but . . . " or "We all want this company to succeed, yet . . . " or "Both drugs work equally well in treating the symptoms, but . . . "

2. *Contrast/pointing out differences.:* You'll use phrases like, ". . . but in spite of the similarities, if you look closer at his record, compared to mine, you'll see that . . . " or ". . . yet that's where the similarities end, because the inevitable consequence of their plan as opposed to ours . . . " or ". . . whereas our competitor does not offer any warranties for the same product."

3. *Consequences.* You'll use phrases like, "Knowing this, you'll want to . . . " or "Considering that you'll get the same benefits, why would you . . . " or ". . . the result of Option A will prove disastrous for . . . "

As we mentioned before, this scenario can be flipped by pointing out differences first and then outlining the similarities that lead the audience to your desired conclusion.

Here's an example of how you can use this arrangement for one of your talks. Say you're a parent who is fighting for custody of a child. By first pointing out the actions that seem to show that the other parent also has the best interest of the child at heart, you are acknowledging the obvious. Yet, in structuring your talk toward your objective, you must illustrate the crucial differences that show that you are the better choice as parent, ending your talk with a conclusion that your audience automatically infers from your argument.

Another example could be a manager who is working hard to build a cohesive team within her department in order to reach certain organizational goals. What she might do initially during a talk she is giving to the entire department is point out the individual differences everyone feels that might hamper a true team effort. Then she would start listing all of the similarities the team members share and their common goal within the department. She'll conclude that, in spite of the differences, the common interest and the similarities among the team members make a strong point for the effective collaboration of all individuals involved.

The key here is that you want to acknowledge what your audience likely feels and perceives as far as differences or similarities are concerned before pointing out one or the other, leading the audience to agree with your point of view on the issue.

Combining Organization Methods

You can of course combine methods of organization. However, it will be to your and the audience's benefit if you stick with the single most appropriate one.

Focusing on one particular method of organization will work for the audience, because each method is designed logically to appeal to their internal sense of organization. It also gives you, the presenter, a solid structure to follow during your talk.

Remember that when constructing your rough outline, you should always keep your audience's needs and motives foremost in mind. The most experienced and effective speakers edit and revise their outlines several times before they're satisfied and before finalizing them for their critical presentations.

Organization and Casual Conversations

You may be someone who does not do a lot of public speaking but who gets anxious in casual conversations with one or several other people. If this is you, forget everything we have said about organization in this chapter!

When people try to overly plan and organize a casual conversation, it comes across as stiff and scripted. It makes you feel more self-conscious and nervous. The rule of thumb for casual conversations is the opposite of the good planning that can help you with public speaking. Instead, it's "Go with the flow."

Let the conversation lead you. Do not try to force the other person into the topics you have in mind; rather, think of the conversation as a tennis match going back and forth. You cannot plan exactly where the ball goes, so you take it as it comes. When you spontaneously respond, you're not only dropping the unhelpful overcompensating behavior of mental preparation, you're also teaching yourself that you are quite capable of a great conversation, especially when you go with the flow.

As you can see, there are a number of ways to structure your talk, speech, or presentation. With some practice, you will be increasingly skilled in choosing the most appropriate organization for your talks and, most important, the one that gets your message across to your audience with the greatest clarity and impact. For more tips on how you can use speaking to accomplish your personal and professional objectives, go to www.TheConfidentSpeaker.com and download our free report "How to Use Speaking in Public to Attract Clients, Friends, and Unlimited Business Opportunities."

5

Getting Ready to Succeed

IMAGINE A PILOT whose plane is suddenly engulfed in a thunderous storm at 30,000 feet, and several of the gauges and instruments in the cockpit are malfunctioning. If the pilot cluelessly pushes all kinds of buttons and randomly flips a few switches without knowledge of the mechanics and the technology under his feet, he and his passengers would surely be doomed. Trial and error is not a good strategy when lives are at stake, nor is it particularly useful in critical communication situations we face with colleagues, bosses, employees, friends, and strangers on a daily basis.

Just as a pilot learns about all of the intricacies of flying—from the theoretical in the classroom to the practical rehearsal in the flight simulator to the many hours of actual flying time with an instructor—in this chapter you will learn about all of the tools you need in order to master every part of a presentation. These tools include reading people and interpreting their actions, knowing your material and preparing like the pros, crafting powerful openings and closings to your talks, responding confidently during Q&A sessions, and effectively rehearsing your newly developed skills, physically and mentally.

Tool 1: Learning to Read People

If in our interactions with others we don't have a basic knowledge of human nature and the things that underlie and motivate human behavior, we are like the rookie pilot who flies into the storm without proper training. We're destined to crash.

Without an ability to read and understand people on at least a basic level—to anticipate their reactions, respond with empathy, and influence their behavior—we're bound to struggle in our quest for building relationships, unable to rely on our communication skills to succeed in our professional and social lives. Effective communication with others requires that we first learn about the people we're communicating with. This includes knowing how they make decisions, how they think about major issues in life, and how they prioritize their values. Equally important, if not more so, is learning how people feel and what moves them on an emotional level so that we can empathize with them and strengthen our relationships with them.

This level of understanding requires us to move beyond the powerful first impressions that so often determine how we feel and think about people. First impressions are inevitable, as we can't help but form an immediate string of judgments about those we meet. This is normal and even helpful, since, in order to process the many thousands of stimuli that we perceive all day from many directions and audiovisual channels, our mind has to somehow sort them into categories that make sense to us. These categories are determined by our perceptual filters, such as experience, attitudes, values, culture, environment, and so on. For instance, our perceptional filters often protect us from people we shouldn't trust: the fast-talking car salesman with excessive jewelry and the scripted questions; the success coach who drives a beat-up 1985 Honda Civic; or the financial consultant who, upon further research, turns out to have a bankruptcy in his record.

But negative first impressions can deceive as well. Many happily married spouses say that when they first met, they couldn't stand each other. We often hear descriptions of people's first impressions of each other that sound something like, "He was so arrogant and self-centered when we first met, I couldn't stand him," or "At first I thought she was incredibly high maintenance, and there was no way I could put up with that." These and other individual perceptions are ones that could have stopped these relationships dead in their tracks. Luckily, these people decided to move beyond their first impressions, either because they intuitively felt that there was more to the other person or because they had no choice; perhaps they worked together and were thus forced to learn more about one another.

Our perceptions of others are gained from the moment we're born and someone tends to our needs as we scream our lungs out for attention pertaining to such things as positional discomfort, hunger and thirst, or pain and boredom.

We continue to learn about people's behavior and reactions as we grow up, our own behavior and thinking perpetually influenced by our environment, parents, siblings, schools, teachers, friends, the media, and so on. We learn by observing and listening, by trial and error, by experiment and experience, and through academic study. Some of us—such as psychologists, trial attorneys, hostage negotiators, jury consultants, personnel managers, sales executives, investigators, educators, and trainers—go on to study human behavior as an integral part of our professions, which require a knowledge of the human psyche in order to achieve our jobs' objectives.

By reading this book, you have shown an interest in improving the way you come across to others, in influencing their thoughts and behaviors, and in wanting to better understand what others' intentions are by what they communicate with their words as well as with their sounds and nonverbal signals.

Below, we've listed strategies for improving your ability to read people and interpret their behavior as you look beyond first impressions. While science has not yet made it possible for us to read each others' minds, you can get a head start by paying attention to the telltale signs people constantly send during social interactions and in a solitary state, sitting or standing by themselves. Being able to read people, that is, to perceive their nonverbal clues and messages accurately, is critical to communicating effectively. This skill will enable you to tailor your messages to their preferred modes of perception, give appropriate feedback when listening, and otherwise watch for signs of your message meeting its target.

1. *Look for consistency.* People whose communication appears to be consistent with their values and beliefs are easier to read than those who display "wishy-washy" attitudes and communication styles. Inconsistency in communications may be a sign of deception or other issues that need to be taken into consideration before trust can be established. To become a confident speaker, you must develop confidence in your ability to recognize the signs of deception.

2. *Do actions follow words?* We often determine people's credibility by how well they keep their promises. Confident speakers know that people who don't follow up on their commitments or who seem to be "all talk" are not a reflection of our communication style but are most likely dealing with issues outside of our control. Perceiving and recognizing their communication styles accurately helps us adjust our feedback to them and prevents us from being taken advantage of.

3. *Tune in to the "History Channel."* What behaviors have people demonstrated in the past? Learn what you can about them by reading bios, articles they've written, schools they've gone to, positions they've held, and important decisions they've made. Past behavior is a good indicator of future actions, and knowledge of past behavior allows the confident speaker to appropriately adjust his or her communication style to that of others.

4. *Look at the big picture.* People may display certain characteristics that you perceive one way. But if you take the bigger picture into consideration, your perceptions may shift as you become aware of a different context. Just because people display short tempers at certain moments doesn't necessarily make them inconsiderate jerks. Have you ever tried to talk to a corporate CPA during the weeks leading up to April 15? Another example is a person who dozes off during your talk. You may doubt your ability to hold an audience's attention until you learn that the snoozer just returned to the office after a 23-hour direct flight from New Zealand and was succumbing to a severe case of jet-lag.

5. *Keep your perceptive channels open.* When we first meet people, they communicate certain information to us whether they intend to or not. We quickly assign labels to people we observe. They're rich, poor, organized, sloppy, good listeners, easily distracted, abrupt, considerate, cheerful, conceited, and so on. What's important is that we keep letting new and possibly conflicting information in. In order to get as complete a picture as possible, we can't reject additional information just because we've made up our mind or feel that we already know them. People are complex, and the more signals our perceptive filters can process, the more complete a picture we get. By keeping an open mind, our perceptions may eventually shift away from those first impressions.

6. *Check your perceptions.* Considering how easily we can make inaccurate assumptions about people, we need a technique that allows us to check our perceptions against other points of view that may provide more accurate descriptions. This involves a quick four-step process that includes looking at people and situations from three perceptual positions. As an example, we'll use the situation of someone in your audience who keeps talking to her neighbor, interrupting your train of thought and disrupting the talk. Using the four-step perception-checking process, do the following:

   (a) First, observe and describe what's going on. You are now looking at the situation from the *first perceptual position*—yours. What you see is one of your audience members talking to a neighbor, and from your perspective she's disruptive.

   (b) Now, look at the situation from the *second perceptual position*, which is always that of the other person you're dealing with. Try to come up with at least two interpretations of that person's behavior. It's important to look at the situation from her perspective and to get out of your own perspective. One reason for the disruption could be that the person in the audience can't hear you well and is asking her neighbor to catch her up with your talk. Another reason could be that she doesn't agree with something you said and is voicing her disagreement with her neighbor. Looking at her facial expressions and body language may give you further clues as to which may be more likely. You now have two possible explanations for the person's disruptive behavior.

(c) The third step is to get into the *third perceptual position*. Take the perspective of an impartial third party, which is the position of unemotional analysis. Is the person's talking actually disrupting the concentration of others, or do others not even seem to notice her? Would it be more disruptive if you stopped the talk to address the person's behavior, or would it help the group get back on track?

(d) In the fourth step, use all the information you just gathered and take action. Depending on what you determined in the third step, you can either continue your talk because you decided it would be counterproductive to address the situation, or you can ask the talker for an explanation of her behavior. For instance, you might ask if clarification is needed for a point you made, or if she can hear you all right. The person may now confirm your interpretations of the situation or clarify by giving a different reason for her behavior.

The major benefit of this four-step process is that it gets you to look at the situation from three different perceptual positions: yours, the other person's, and the impartial one. By looking at any interpersonal situation from the two perspectives outside of your own, you may gain a better understanding of the situation, as well as resolve potential conflict more quickly.

7. *Ask questions.* And listen with all of your senses. To get people to talk about themselves, you'll have to ask open-ended questions that cannot be answered with a simple yes or no. For example, don't ask, "Are you the VP of Business Development?" Instead ask, "What is your area of responsibility within the organization?" The more you can get other people to talk about themselves, the more you can learn about them.

8. *Interrupt as little as possible.* To achieve your objective, it's important that you interrupt as little as possible and give encouraging nonverbal feedback, such as nodding, appropriate eye contact (be careful not to stare), and vocal feedback sounds like "hmm" or grunting approval. Don't think of your next question as you listen; rather, give other people an opportunity to express themselves. Let there be moments of silence, especially when it looks like the other person may be pausing and about to say something else. Don't pester them with endless questions; rather, look for "hooks" in their responses that you can use to keep the conversation moving. For example, if the person tells you he moved into the finance department from an executive position in Human Resources, ask what made him take such a different career path. Showing sincere interest in others is flattering, and their disclosure gives you insights into their personalities that you wouldn't get by plainly asking, "What do you do?"

Tool 2: Know Your Material; Prepare Without Overpreparing

There is no such thing is being too rich, too beautiful, or too smart. Neither can a speaker or presenter be too prepared. After all, being ready to give your audience 110 percent of your heart and mind is a good thing.

Yet, as you remember from our discussion of common myths in Chapter 2, there is such a thing as overpreparing. It's when you fret and worry that you just can't have enough material, and you check your PowerPoint slides 15 times to make sure they haven't dissolved into thin air overnight, and you memorize every single word of your talk, including exactly the way you want to deliver it. Wow, just writing this is exhausting.

We're going to make your preparation a little easier and give you the scoop on what's important about the right amount of preparing and what is too much. And what is too much is likely to be counterproductive for you, since it will cause you to become unduly anxious and worried as to whether you've prepared enough or not.

Platinum Rules for Preparing

1. *Know the audience.* Clearly, you have to know who you're speaking to in order to adjust your content, language or jargon, audiovisuals, and delivery style for maximum impact. You'd address a group of investors at the annual shareholder's meeting differently than the attendees at the monthly PTA assembly. The strategies in the first section of this chapter can help you learn more about your audience.

2. *Research your topic.* If you're an expert on what you're talking about, good for you. Otherwise, research the heck out of your topic. On most issues there are usually many sides to a topic. Study the arguments for and against and the ones in the middle. Know what experts are saying and what's written in the popular press. More often than not the two are at odds. Utilize the Internet and all of its wonderful search engines. Read industry magazines and newspapers. Call experts on your topic and get their input. Only once you've fully immersed yourself in all of the grist of what's out there can you confidently state your own conclusions and defend them against hecklers.

3. *Know the place.* If you're from Littleton, Colorado, and next Tuesday you're scheduled to give a keynote in Montreal, Canada, it may be a bit difficult to scope out the place beforehand. You can, however, get the necessary specs and details from someone who works there. Ideally, the person who invited you to speak can send you a layout of what the speaking venue looks like, including electrical outlets, seating arrangements, doors, exits, podium, stage, and so on. If that person doesn't have a layout, he or she can at least describe the setting for you. The more you know the environment you're speaking in, the better you can visualize yourself there during your presentation, and thus the more comfortable you'll be. Also, when you're planning to use PowerPoint or film during your talk, it's foolish not to get information on connectivity.

4. *Rehearse your talk.* While there are better ways to rehearse than in front of your mother-in-law and her bridge partners, it will do in a pinch. What's important about rehearsals is that they're realistic. That includes a perceptive audience that will give you honest and constructive feedback. Harrison advises our clients to never get feedback from someone who's ever seen them naked or in diapers. They'll think the clients are golden no matter what the clients do. U.S. presidents don't rehearse in front of the White House poodle before an important debate; they have speech coaches like yours truly throwing hard-hitting questions at them. Why should you shortchange yourself by practicing with softballs when your going to give a talk where the stakes are high? Most of us don't speak for fun, as there is always a career, a contract, or a relationship on the line. Make it as realistic as possible. The mirror is also a helpful tool, but to see what you really look like, a video camera is better. So rally your colleagues, your peers, your bosses, even your enemies to do you a favor and critique your rehearsal speech. You'll learn more from their observations as to what works and what doesn't than you would in a room by yourself.

5. *Get enough rest.* Life doesn't stop just because you have to give a presentation. We get that. But if you truly wish to become a compelling and powerful speaker, you have to think of yourself the way athletes think of themselves. They don't go out for drinks the night before an event, nor do they study or practice until four in the morning prior to the competition. In sports it's about winning. And part of that is getting your body into an optimal state for performance. Your talk tomorrow may be about getting a million-dollar contract or about getting a job offer, neither of which may be any less important to you than a sporting event is to an athlete. So treat your body with the same care and respect professional athletes do. Get enough rest. Stay hydrated. And eat healthy for optimal performance.

6. *Analyze but don't dwell.* The best time to start preparing for the next talk is when this one is over. The feedback you get from your audience will give you great clues as to what worked about your presentation and what didn't. Note which adjustments you need to make. If you have a chance to interview some people from the audience and get their impressions of your talk, do so. Anonymous surveys are good too, because people are more apt to tell you the truth about your performance if it doesn't expose them as being mean or harsh. Most people, believe it or not, want to be nice. Get every piece of input you can and make important changes that will improve your impact. If you feel your talk didn't go very well, learn from the specifics and move on. Don't dwell on it, because you'll have a chance to do better next time.

7. *Enjoy the process.* We can see your eyes rolling right now. Your stomach churns when you have to give a talk, and we're telling you to have fun? The truth is, when you learn to speak well and express yourself to others, you are entering a distinct group of people who change other people's lives, as well as their own. And that's exciting. When you eventually get the courage to speak up to people you want to meet, or you can compellingly persuade a group of executives to adopt one of your suggestions for a new product, you'll experience a power within yourself that will alter the way you look at yourself and the world. Because communication is possibility. And just imagine how much more you'll enjoy life when all of these new possibilities open up before you.

Tool 3: Creating Powerful Openings and Closings

Part of your preparation will be to create a compelling opening for your talk, as well as an equally compelling closing. You might be asking: "What's the big deal with those two? It's not like you cannot have a beginning or an ending, right? Naturally, our talks will begin with the opening and end with a closing, duh!"

The reason why these two components of a structured, perhaps more formal, talk are so important is that they carry the most weight. Not so much in terms of content. That's where the body, or the middle, comes in. That's the Clydesdale of the talk. The meat and potatoes. The beef.

Opening Your Talk

The beginning, or the opening, of your talk is like the opening ceremony at the Olympic Games. It's designed to whet your audience's appetite and get them interested in what's to come. It gets their attention and makes them sit up. After all, it's hard to get people to listen if we don't first capture their attention, right? It isn't all pomp and circumstance, however. It has to be designed to be more than just a loud bang that makes you look.

A beginning has to be relevant. It must somehow lead to the points you'll make in the body of your talk. Since there are many types of communication events, talks, and speeches, it's impossible to give you a specific guideline on how to structure a beginning that will apply to all. We can, however, give you some powerful ideas that will be effective in starting your talk on the right foot and in putting everyone at the edge of their seats. Some of these ideas are tried-and-true approaches; others are new and bold. Try them all and modify them the way you want. You'll soon figure out what works for you and what doesn't.

1. *The anecdote.* This is simply a story that either happened to you or someone else. It makes a point and can be poignant, tragic, amusing, sad, hysterical, or any other catalyst for human emotion. Make sure it has a point that relates to your topic, however. Talking about your great-grandfather rescuing *Titanic* survivors must somehow fit in with the benefits of aluminum siding in new construction. If it doesn't, you'll lose your audience.

2. *The joke.* Don't.

3. *The startling fact.* Something in the long history of your topic is startling, meaning unknown and surprising to people in your audience. Use it. This is where research becomes important. Call the Bureau of Statistics in Washington, D.C., and ask for

data on your topic. Most likely you'll find that little nugget that will make people's jaws drop. Something along the lines of: "The average American eats approximately 400 pounds of ice cream per year," or "One million babies are born every minute in India." We made these up, but you can see what effect they'd have if they were true.

4. *The demonstration.* Not the one where you clash with the riot police, but the one where you show something like a trick or an experiment or a procedure of sorts. People love performances, and the more interesting you can make a demonstration, with props or without, the more their attention is guaranteed.

5. *The question.* When we hear questions, we feel compelled to answer. If you ever overhear someone asking someone else, "What time is it?" don't you feel compelled to look at your watch and answer the question yourself? Even if it's just an impulse, we're conditioned to answer questions, so an effective speech opener may start with one. It doesn't even have to be one where you expect someone to answer. A rhetorical question will do just fine. A rhetorical question is a question that doesn't need an answer, but one that makes a point in question form. In any case, the question as opener is a classic opening technique and can be used repeatedly.

6. *Stand and stare.* This one takes courage. If you can just stand there and stare at the audience until they're squirming in their seats because of anticipation, you know you're in the big league as a speaker. This can be a very effective way to get attention, especially since most audiences expect a speaker to labor into a talk while still walking up to the podium. No drama there. Just ho-hum.

7. *The conversation.* We're all eavesdroppers. We're always curious about what two people are talking about, which is why we lean in to lovers' quarrels, husband-and-wife conversations, or the whispering between colleagues across the cubicle wall. We don't want to miss anything. Especially, God forbid, if it's

about us. So why not start a conversation with someone in the audience with whom you can have good eye contact? Make it more interesting than just banter. Ask a sincere question and wait for the answer. Keep your tone somewhat low so that the rest of the audience leans in a little more. Before a minute is over you'll have your listeners craning their necks to see who you're talking to and why.

With some creativity you can probably come up with some of your own ideas on how to get a talk started in an interesting, relevant way.

Closing Your Talk

Now that we've discussed the opening of a talk, let's have a brief look at the closing. We say brief because if you've done your work at the beginning and the middle of your talk, the closing will determine itself. But, we won't leave you hanging with this gem—we'll go into it.

The closing pretty much sums up what you stated at the beginning as the main thesis or message of your talk and what you fleshed out and backed up with evidence in the middle. If you made your points well, all you want to do in closing is draw the audience's attention to one major objective. Depending on your talk, that may be to either take the action that is now required, or to stop doing something that you discussed in your main message (to stop littering, for example), or to take an important step that you explained in the body of your speech. Whatever it is, be brief. You've already sold your message to your audience, and now you're just reminding them briefly of what you drummed into their hearts and minds for the last hour or 20 minutes or whatever: "This is what we talked about. Go do it. You'll be glad you did."

The trick is to rev up your enthusiasm again and let your passion carry your conclusion until your very last word. You have to let your audience *feel* how much you want them to do what you discussed in your talk. Don't just let them *know*, let them *feel*. It'll go much, much deeper that way.

Tool 4: Handling Q&A with Confidence

"Any questions?"

Who hasn't heard this charmer of an attempt at Q&A? In the interest of self-disclosure, Harrison confesses that he too asks this two-word question several times throughout a seminar in order to catch whoever may have been snoozing or using the bathroom during an important part of the talk. In this case, however, we're talking about the presenter who thinks Q&A means asking the audience the same question, secretly hoping that nobody raises his or her hand.

Effective Q&A, or question and answer, means giving the audience an opportunity to get clarification, take issue with a point you made, get answers to points that weren't sufficiently discussed, and, overall, clear up any misunderstandings from what may have been said.

So why would some speakers prefer to drink a cup of bleach rather than face a Q&A? The answer is because it can put them even more on the spot than merely speaking and presenting do. A Q&A can be like a job interview, but instead of answering to one interviewer, you're answering to many.

The truth is, the Q&A is a great opportunity to profile your knowledge and expertise by showing attendees that you know your stuff even when challenged on an issue related to your talk. Naturally, it helps to know your stuff.

The key to success for the speaker is to listen to the questions. This is where our advice on focusing outward, toward the audience, is critically important. It's hard to get all of the nuances of a question and its underlying motives when you're focusing on your anxiety.

Let the audience know when you'll have the Q&A session during your talk. In other words, will it be at the very end or will you take breaks for questions throughout? It will help them focus on you when they know they can get clarification on any points later. As far as fitting it in—make the time. Even three minutes of interacting with the audience in this way can tremendously boost your status and credibility.

Now that you've prepared and rehearsed, you're more than ready to answer questions from the audience. In fact, you know your material so well that you can use your answer to reinforce your message. If the question, for instance is, "Where can I learn how to speak in public?" you can of course give an answer. But what you ought to do is reinforce your message from your talk on public speaking, for example, by replying along the lines of:

> *Where can't you learn how to speak in public? While you can get more formal instruction at universities and debate clubs, there are hundreds of opportunities each day where you can sharpen your skills and hone your speaking techniques with innumerable test audiences, from peers to bosses to family members and strangers in a elevator.*

Now you've not only answered the question, but you've maximized the impact of a point you made during your talk. This is an often missed opportunity that the Q&A session affords the presenter. It's a chance to reinforce your own credibility and the validity of your message. Don't waste it.

Tool 5: Rehearsal — The Right Way

Basically there are two ways to rehearse: an ineffective way and an effective way. Here's what to do and what not to do.

When you rehearse, your purpose is *not* to negatively scrutinize yourself, dwell on all the things you did wrong, and tell yourself that you're not a speaker. These critical ways of viewing yourself are going to make you more anxious and are unlikely to improve your skills. Instead, view yourself objectively. Expect that there will be parts that you'll be naturally great at, as well as areas that you'll have to work on. Focus on both. Don't overlook your strengths, because you want to play those up and capitalize on them.

Getting feedback from others can be very beneficial in your rehearsal. Ask someone to observe your talk and give you some impressions, both favorable and less favorable. Learn to accept and appreciate constructive criticism, realizing that even the best speakers in the world are not perfect. Speaking in front of another person or, even better, several people, is also quite helpful in gaining comfort with being observed by an audience.

Another key to effective rehearsal is the right amount of rehearsal. We've discussed how nervous speakers tend to put off rehearsing because it's unpleasant for them, and how other anxious speakers over-rehearse in an attempt to get everything just right, which can create additional stress. If your life revolves around your talk and you become completely obsessed with rehearsing up until the last minute, you're likely to be more nervous and perform worse than if you rehearse the right amount. The right number of times to rehearse depends how long it takes you to have a good command of the material, if you have ideas for what to say, and if you possess confidence in knowing that you have mastered your subject matter and can deliver it in a compelling fashion. You don't even have to rehearse out loud each time . . . which brings us to our next point.

Mental Rehearsal

Read this and then close your eyes and try it.

> *Imagine yourself up in front of your audience, delivering a powerful presentation. You're enjoying yourself up there, delivering the message that is important to you to share, and the audience is getting a great deal of benefit out of your talk. They're engaged and are learning some powerful information. You feel relaxed, natural, and confident. You gesture and smile appropriately and connect with the audience by making eye contact. You finish to a booming round of applause and you feel great! Afterward, people are lined up to speak with you, and many of them tell you that they enjoyed your presentation.*

Did you picture this scene in your mind? Were you able to get a good mental picture? Could you feel the energy and see the supportive faces of your audience members? Could you feel your body moving in a relaxed, natural motion? You may need to practice this exercise a couple of times to get good at it. A small minority of people are unable to get mental images in their minds, but most people can, sometimes with a bit of practice.

When you did the exercise, how did it feel? It probably felt different than the way you normally think about yourself when you speak. Typically, your thoughts are filled with apprehension and trepidation, so they're more likely unpleasant.

Olympic athletes and other top performers use mental imagery to improve their performances. Mental imagery trains your brain to perform the way you want to, and it helps you to expect success, which makes it more likely that you *will* be successful.

Mental rehearsal—where you go through your presentation, conversation, or other speaking engagement in your mind as practice—can be very effective if you follow a few simple guidelines.

First, you should do it ahead of time as practice. You may need to practice several times to get to the point where you see yourself as polished and poised. Initially, it may be hard to see yourself speaking in that light, but once you get used to it, your images will guide you to being a confident speaker. You don't even need to believe your positive image for the technique to be effective. You can also use a quick mental image of yourself to get energized right before you begin speaking. Just make sure you aren't getting caught up in your mind and out of the moment.

Second, you should not use mental rehearsal as a way to critique yourself or imagine the worst. The point of it is to help you picture yourself, and later act, as a successful speaker. If you catch yourself "messing up" in your mental image, start over. This is not the time to get a negative or self-deprecating image of yourself.

Third, you never want to use mental rehearsal as an overcompensating behavior, which is a very different type of mental rehearsal that is likely to increase your anxiety and diminish your performance. During a conversation when you find yourself practicing what you're about to say before you say it—that is an overcompensating behavior. If you find that you go over and over the right way to introduce yourself to a group while the others are introducing themselves, that's overcompensating. One of the best ways to tell if you're overcompensating is if you're mentally rehearsing in the moment—and therefore not fully engaged in the conversation or situation. Instead, practice ahead of time by mentally visualizing a positive outcome as described above.

The pilot in the example at the beginning of this chapter would never take to the air without learning all there is to learn to become confident. Similarly, the presenter who is looking for positive feedback from an audience should carefully study the tools we presented above in order to become the confident speaker he or she wishes to be.

6

Relaxation and Managing Anticipatory Anxiety

To attempt to feel more comfortable in public speaking without practicing is like trying to learn how to swim without going in the water. When you put the strategies we've discussed (and the ones yet to come) into practice, you're likely to significantly reduce anxiety about speaking. Use the strategies regularly and gain a lot of experience by speaking in public as much as possible: We recommend at least a couple of speaking experiences per day. This means not only speaking when it comes up, but also going out of your way to find opportunities. As you do this, your discomfort will decrease, and it's likely that the physical symptoms of anxiety—pounding heart, sweating, shaking, and trembling—will be reduced as well. The horrible physical sensations you experience will diminish automatically as you gain experience.

We can appreciate how uncomfortable and distressing these feelings are, and we want to give you some great strategies to help you deal with them as you're preparing to get into a professional or social speaking situation. In this chapter, we'll also reveal techniques to help you relax as you anticipate a speaking engagement. Many people say that the anticipation is the worst part, so we'll help you deal with it.

Before getting into specific tactics to help you relax, a word of caution: These tools can become crutches if you let them. Our goal is for you to use these strategies as tools and confidence-building strategies, but not to depend on them. For example, deep breathing can be a wonderful relaxation tool, but it can become a crutch if you're about to speak up and you tell yourself, "Deep breathe—now!"

Obviously, breathing deeply won't be effective if you force yourself to do it or if you depend on it. What happens if you aren't able to breathe deeply? You may think, Oh no, I'm doomed! The message to take with you as you learn relaxation strategies is that they are helpful but not necessary. They're particularly useful when you use them before speaking rather than only when you're in the midst of the situation.

You must learn to relax just as you would do if you were learning a new sport. If you were learning how to play competitive tennis, you'd need to practice your serve and your swing many times before a big match. Similarly, it's important to practice relaxation regularly. With practice, you'll get good at it, and it will become second nature to you. You'll find that you start to use relaxation strategies without really trying to. Just as you don't have to be in a tennis match to practice your tennis serve, you don't have to be in a speaking situation to practice relaxation. You can start by practicing at a certain time of day, such as before dinner. After you gain some practice with the skills, you can effectively use them in stressful circumstances and speaking situations.

In summary, relaxation strategies are great as long as you do not depend on them and think that you *need* them, and they work best with regular daily practice. As little as five minutes per day can make a big difference in becoming more relaxed with speaking. But, again, do *not* use the ideas you're about to learn as crutches and assume that you'll only speak well if you've done them. If you find that you are starting to think this way, practice some speaking situations without using the tools to show yourself that you can perform well anytime and do not need to rely on them.

The Deep Breathing That Works

"Take a deep breath and you will relax."

Have you ever heard this? Guess what, this does not work. Do you feel automatically relaxed after taking in a big gulp of air? Probably not. Not only does this not work, but it is the opposite of what does work. This is because most people do not breathe in correctly, and the way they take their deep breath can actually increase the physical arousal associated with fear.

Remember the discussion about the biological responses to the adrenaline rush that kicks in when the sympathetic nervous system activates? One symptom of anxiety is initially taking a deep breath (and later breathing shallowly). The initial deep breath is as if to prepare for danger. If you were going to try to sit very still or starting running, what would you do first? You'd take in a deep breath. Like a racing heart, this deep breath is a signal to the body that it's in danger. The deep breath tells the body, "Uh-oh, something is threatening!"

Shallow breathing, sometimes referred to as "chest breathing," is also a symptom of fear. It is a symptom that can start the anxiety cycle and make you feel more nervous. Shallow breathing is what leads to the breathlessness that results when you're speaking in front of people. You can tell you're breathing shallowly because you can often see your chest rising and falling as you breathe in and out. In contrast, deep breathing moves the abdomen up and down. When you do the deep breathing exercise we describe below, you'll see your stomach rising as it fills with air and falling as you exhale.

The solution to breathing problems like shallow breathing is to take deep, diaphragmatic breaths. Before we describe how to do this, first try what *not* to do so you can see the difference. Take a fast, big breath in through your mouth. This is how most people attempt deep breathing. Did it feel relaxing? Probably not, because it's like a gasp for air. Often this form of "taking a deep breath" increases anxiety. Now that you know what not to do, here's the right way to take a deep, relaxing breath:

1. Place your right hand on your stomach and your left hand in the middle of your upper chest.

2. Take a slow breath in through your nose. Inhale for the count of four seconds (time yourself to see how long a second really is). Do you feel your chest or your stomach rise? Deep breathing should result in your stomach rising on the inhale, and your chest should not move much. You can tell you're engaging in shallow breathing if your left hand (on your chest) rises and falls. If this process is not clear, exaggerate shallow breathing by panting like a dog (breathing out quickly over and over). You will see and feel your chest move. Then slow your breathing down and focus on your belly filling with air like a balloon.

3. Continue to practice slowly breathing in through your nose for a count of four seconds, making sure your stomach is rising and you're doing it most effectively.

4. Once you have the hang of the four count inhale, begin to practice the exhale. This is the most important part, and the part that brings about the feeling of relaxation. Slowly exhale for four seconds, feeling your stomach sink back in as the air goes out.

5. Pick a word that describes how you want to feel as a result of this breathing training. Choose a relatively short word, preferably with two syllables or less. For instance, "calm," "poised," "relaxed," "ready," or "smooth." When you exhale for the four counts, say this word to yourself slowly over the four counts. Feel the feeling that the word connotes take over your body and allow the tension to melt away.

6. Practice this breathing for about 10 to 15 minutes per day while you're feeling relatively calm. You want to learn it well before you try to use it in stressful situations. As we discussed, the practice is like the athlete's drills and practices before he or she is in a packed stadium and the pressure is on. If you haven't prepared ahead, it will be hard to perform in the heat of the moment.

7. After you have practiced this breathing for 10 to 15 minutes per day for a week, start using it before, after, or during stressful or anxiety-provoking situations and observe the effect.

Breathing training can have a huge impact on distress for some people. It can have a minimal impact for others. It depends on whether respiratory symptoms are among the key features of anxiety for you. Some people do not have any respiratory symptoms (breathing difficulties), so the breathing does not make a huge difference. But whether or not you're prone to feeling breathless when you're nervous, these deep breathing exercises described should produce a general sense of relaxation for you. This is important as you prepare a presentation, because if you can stay calm for the days or weeks before it, you are more likely to feel calm while giving the presentation.

Melt Away Muscle Tension

Another way to relax your body and beat both stress and anxiety is through muscle relaxation. John, our client who became uptight and nervous when he had to speak up in social situations, benefited greatly from muscle relaxation. His body would become so tense when he was uncomfortable with speaking up in parties and social gatherings that he would look like a statue. The tense muscles also made him shake, and he'd become nervous because his shaking hands were visible to others. As a result he wouldn't hold anything (such as a glass or food) at parties because he was afraid people would see his hands shake. When John relaxed his body and used some of the other strategies described in this book, he was able to comfortably eat, drink, and socialize at parties.

It is difficult to relax your muscles on cue. Try it—as you're sitting there reading this, try to relax your quadriceps (thighs). Try to relax your shoulders. It's tough, right? It's like trying to feel warm when you feel cold. It is not so easy. There's a better way to get relaxed.

The best way to relax your muscles is to progressively work through different muscle groups, first tensing them and then relaxing them. It sounds strange to tighten your muscles to get them relaxed, but it works very well. Have you ever felt that Jell-O-like sensation in your muscles after lifting weights? After tensing and working muscles, they feel much more relaxed than if you try to relax them from a resting position.

Practice tensing and relaxing your muscles by making a tight fist with your hand. Pretend that you have a wet sponge in the palm of your hand and you're trying to squeeze all the water out of it. Hold the fist for three seconds and then relax your entire hand for three seconds. As you are releasing the fist, focus your attention on the relaxed feeling and the difference between the state of tension and relaxing. As you get used to identifying the difference between tense and relaxed, you will be able to spot muscle tension as it forms and release it before negative consequences result.

Now that you have the idea of this process of progressive muscle relaxation, you can practice with other muscle groups. The order in which you go through muscle relaxation is not particularly important, so you can try it different ways to see what works best for you. Sit in a chair and work on the following muscle groups, tensing for three counts and relaxing for three counts. Pause between each set to recognize the relaxed feeling.

1. *Face.* Scrunch all of your facial muscles together as if you just tasted something sour and you're puckering up from it. Pretend you are trying to pull all your muscles into a point at your nose. Hold all of these muscles tense for three seconds and then release for three seconds.
2. *Shoulders.* Shrug your shoulders up toward your ears; feel the relaxation as you release.
3. *Neck.* Look down and relax as you come back to center.
4. *Chest.* Flex your chest muscles in as if trying to tighten the muscles under your armpits.
5. *Upper Back.* Roll your upper back to make your chest concave. Feel the tension in your upper back and then release.
6. *Biceps.* Hold your arms up to the sides and flex your biceps. Be careful not to flex other muscles, since you are focusing just on the biceps.
7. *Triceps.* Pull your arms in to your sides and push them back as if trying to push the backs of your arms into a wall.
8. *Wrists.* Flex your wrists back so that your hands are perpendicular to the floor.
9. *Hands.* Make a tight fist.
10. *Stomach.* Squeeze your stomach in toward the back of the chair, as if your stomach were a sponge you're trying to squeeze out.

11. *Lower Back.* Collapse in from the lower back, making your stomach concave.

12. *Buttocks.* Squeeze your buttocks together. You should rise a bit off your seat.

13. *Quadriceps.* Sitting with your thighs on a chair and lower legs perpendicular to the ground, lift your legs, from your thighs, about one inch off the chair.

14. *Hamstrings.* Do the same flexion as above, but straighten the legs out in front of you and lift.

15. *Calves.* With your legs out in front of you as above, point or flex your toes to feel your calves tighten.

16. *Ankles.* Return your feet to the floor and lift your toes while keeping your heels on the floor.

17. *Toes.* Curl your toes together in a ball.

Practicing progressive muscle relaxation regularly has a cumulative effect. The best way to beat tension is before it starts. It's like taking all your vitamins and minerals and getting plenty of sleep on a regular basis to ward off sickness. Don't wait until you have a major performance, practice muscle relaxation regularly to build up your immunity and resistance to speaking jitters.

The Power of Strategic Exercise

Exercise is a great way to beat symptoms of anxiety. Picture the last time you had a very intense, invigorating workout. You were probably dripping with sweat, muscles trembling, and totally exhausted. How did you feel? On edge? Most likely you did not, because, simply put, fear is incompatible with exercise. In fact, exercise gets your body used to feelings like a pounding heart and sweating, so when they happen while you're on the speaking platform, they don't feel like such a big deal.

Regular exercise can decrease general unease, making you less susceptible to attacks of fear when speaking opportunities present themselves. The best form of exercise to reduce stress and anxiety is a combination of cardiovascular exercise, such as running, brisk walking, or elliptical machines, and strength training, such as weight machines or free weights.

Adding 30 to 40 minutes of cardiovascular exercise three times per week, and 30 minutes of strength training three times per week, can make a tremendous difference in your ability to cope with stressors such as public speaking.

You can also choose exercise strategically based on speaking performances. The rule of thumb is that it is great to exercise before a talk, but not right before. One of the side effects of exercise is increased energy. While you may want to get rid of your energy when you're nervous, you do in fact need the energy. It's the nervous energy that you should burn off with activity. Exercising a couple of hours before a talk can help you get out some of the nervous jitters and habituate to symptoms of anxiety. In fact, many symptoms of anxiety are the same ones induced by exercise (out of breath, sweating, racing heart, and so on). When you purposefully bring forth these symptoms, your body habituates to them and becomes used to them. This makes it less of a big deal when they return as you anticipate speaking. In fact, the physiological responses may actually be lessened after you have habituated to them through exercise.

Resistance training, such as weight lifting, is also wonderful because it works like progressive muscle relaxation. After exercising your muscles, they feel more relaxed, and you experience reduced tension.

Exercise also boosts self-confidence, which can make you feel more comfortable speaking with and in front of others. Exercise can help you get or stay physically fit, which can enhance your body image and self-esteem. Most people find an increase in self-confidence when they exercise, not necessarily because they're in better shape physically, but because they're pleased that they take care of themselves and because of the beneficial effect exercise has on mood.

Be sure, of course, to refuel and rehydrate after exercising so that you have energy (dehydration is a major cause of exhaustion) and do not become light-headed before or during your speech. Lack of hydration is a major cause of fatigue and distraction.

Unless you're dragging and you need to pump yourself up, do not engage in rigorous exercise right before a speaking engagement. Instead, do some lighter exercise, such as walking, stretching, or yoga. Lifting light weights to decrease muscle tension prior to a speaking engagement can also be helpful.

What to Do When You Feel Awful Before Speaking

You know this feeling: You're going to have to speak in public soon, and you're miserable about it. You may feel a sense of dread. You probably feel nervous and worried. You may feel depressed and hopeless because it's so difficult to speak in public. This bad feeling may kick in a couple of minutes before you need to speak, as it did for one of our clients, Yao, when he needed to speak up in meetings. Or it may kick in a week ahead, as it did for Jennifer, as she worried about her upcoming interview.

At times it is possible to just decide to be in a better mood, but typically it's not as simple as saying to yourself, "Don't be anxious." If it were this simple, you would not be reading this book, right? Instead, the best approaches to change your mood are the methods of changing your thoughts, behavior, and biology that we have discussed so far and will present in future chapters. What follows are a couple of quick tips for improving your mood during the time you practice an upcoming presentation or while you get ready to go to a social event.

Improving Your Mood

In general, two of the best ways to improve your mood (whether it is anxious, depressed, or any negative emotion) are to increase the activities that bring you joy and to add activities that make you feel like you're accomplishing something.

Activities that bring you joy can be as simple as preparing your favorite meal, going for a walk in the park, or spending time with a close friend or family member. If you can predict a bad mood coming on (or if it has already started), make a point of doing several enjoyable activities each day.

Activities that give you a sense of accomplishment can range from getting your grocery shopping done, paying your bills, washing your car, getting a new outfit, or giving your dog a bath. Some activities will serve the purpose of enjoyment and accomplishment, such as shopping, if you like to shop. Other activities create an improved mood after you've completed them because you're glad they're done.

If you find it helpful to talk with others when you're in a bad mood, that's great, but be careful not to use the time to dwell on whatever is causing your mood. Take a few minutes to get your problems off your chest and then get engaged in something else. While in a negative mood, you are susceptible to misinterpreting information and might well conclude that you'll do poorly with your presentation or communication. For the same reason, do not work through your presentation when you're in a bad place emotionally. Of course, you don't need to be in a fantastic mood, but try not to prepare while you're in a horrible mood because you'll develop a negative association with your presentation. Do some of the pleasant and productive activities first to give your mood a boost.

Distraction Can Be Useful, or Not

Distraction can be a useful way to break the cycle of ruminating about your worries, fears, or frustration, and it can help improve your mood. The activities we just discussed can be thought of as ways to distract yourself and immerse yourself in other things.

As with the concept of "strategic exercise," we call this "strategic distraction," because not all distraction is useful to alleviate or lessen anxiety. In fact, distraction can be harmful if you find yourself using it as an overcompensating behavior. That is, if you never allow yourself to face your fears head on and truly experience the anxiety, you'll never learn whether the consequences you fear actually come about. Many people mistakenly engage in distraction as soon as a negative mood comes on and thus never learn how to manage the negative mood. It's necessary to completely confront your anxiety at *the right time*.

If you're stressed out, sleep deprived with a newborn baby at home, in the process of moving to a new house, and under a tight deadline at work, it may not be the right time to volunteer for a major speaking engagement. If you don't have a choice, get a copresenter to divide up the work, keep your presentation focused and brief, clear other things that are on your plate a few days before your presentation, and be sure to take care of the things you can control, like eating well, exercising, and resting before your presentation. Give yourself a reward after your talk (like your favorite lunch or iced mocha) and a few minutes to relax and relish the accomplishment of having done something difficult during a stressful period in your life.

Axing the Anticipatory Anxiety

Anticipatory anxiety before you have to speak in public is likely to put you in a pretty negative mood. By the time you have to talk, you're probably already worked up and miserable. The anticipation often lasts much longer than the speaking engagement itself. Many people describe an upward spiral of apprehension as a speaking situation gets closer.

Research has shown that people who are nervous about giving presentations tend to more readily recall negative descriptions about themselves before giving a speech. This negative recall only occurred when participants were about to give a speech, indicating that you too will likely become more nervous before a talk, and that your thinking patterns will be distorted, thereby increasing anticipatory anxiety.

The anxiety of anticipation can be one of the last forms of anxiety to get over. It can be difficult to get rid of, especially if you have thoughts such as, Last time I managed to squeak by, but this time is sure to be a disaster. The key to overcoming this type of negative thought is a numbers game. If you put yourself into 100 speaking situations and have 95 great experiences, you can tell yourself: "Ninety-five percent of the time it went okay, so this is likely to go okay as well."

Another extremely useful strategy is to embrace the fear as soon as it comes on. If you embrace it sooner rather than later, it will decrease naturally. Think about it: If you spend a week before a talk fighting off your anxiety, you'll be exhausted, fed up, frustrated, and *very* anxious by the time you have to speak. If, on the other hand, you immediately say to yourself, "Okay, here comes the rush of nervousness about giving that talk. I'm going to use it to energize me to help me prepare well and give a great talk," then the distress will be fighting a losing battle.

Often, anticipatory anxiety diminishes over time as you work through all of the other exercises we have recommended. It typically stops days and hours before a speaking engagement. The sudden rush of anxiety before speaking may stick around longer, but it will decrease in frequency and intensity as well.

The relaxation exercises described earlier in this chapter and the preparation exercises described in the last chapter will also help you take a proactive approach to anticipating a speaking engagement. In addition, in the next chapter we'll walk you step by step through the stages of preparation before a talk. When you put all of these ideas into action, there will be little room for anticipatory anxiety. When it does arise, recognize that it's normal and that it will decrease over time as you gain more experience.

Put the Postmortems to Death

The harsh and critical thinking patterns after we speak make us feel bad, depressed, and hopeless about having to speak again. Larina and her colleagues call these self-bashing sessions "postmortems." There is evidence that people who are socially anxious engage in extensive processing once speaking events are over. These destructive mental sessions perpetuate anticipatory anxiety. If you interpreted your last public speaking situation as horrible, then you will be more nervous the next time you have a similar situation coming up.

Some people think that this type of critical thinking after they talk will help them realize what they did wrong so that they won't do it again next time. *This is not true.* There is absolutely nothing useful about these sessions in which we slam ourselves after speaking. To build confidence, we all need to be our own best advocates rather than our harshest critics.

When you're anxious and revved up, your thought processes are likely to be unproductive. While still in the midst of anxiety (which you may or may not be by the end of your communication), your mind thinks with emotion rather than reason. Because you feel horrible, you're likely to decide that you were horrible. But this is often faulty reasoning, and it produces inaccurate interpretations.

One client told Larina that she was getting great at putting herself into speaking situations. Her anxiety, however, had not diminished, so Larina asked her what she said to herself *after* her public speaking experience. It turned out that this woman was worrying about her performance a great deal after she gave it. She would go over the things she said and think of better things she could have said. At one time or another we have all told ourselves, "I should have said . . ." This replay is not helpful, and it was responsible for the woman's ongoing anxiety.

As another example, let's say you have a conversation with a neighbor or a colleague at work and become nervous during it, but you try not use any overcompensating behaviors that might decrease your anxiety. Instead, you ride out the wave of fear and get through the situation. This is great because you confronted your fear, got through it, and realized that you can do it. Afterward, to avoid replaying the conversation over and over in your mind, you decide to engage in strategic distraction. This is a helpful strategy because it replaces the postmortem critical evaluation, which is not necessary or useful. As a result, you'll be less apprehensive before your next speaking experience.

The bottom line is: Stop the self-defeating postmortems. How do you do this? The first step is to recognize when you're doing it. This may seem simple, but it's not, because these thinking patterns may be habitual. So, first, spot the behavior and tell yourself, "Oh, here's a postmortem that isn't productive."

Second, turn your attention to something else. You can focus on what you did nicely in your conversation or presentation. You will be tempted to conclude that everything was bad about what you said or how you said it. Instead, write down all of the things you think went well during the experience. Then use this list the next time you have a speaking opportunity to remind yourself that you're capable and to boost your confidence.

Alternatively, if you're unable to focus on all the good things right away (What, there are no good things!), simply turn your attention to something else so that you don't begin beating yourself up. Engage in a sport or exercise, go to a movie, go out to dinner with friends, play with your child—whatever it takes to get you to break the cycle of postmortem thinking. And congratulate yourself for having done the thing that made you nervous.

We've gone through some things to do (and not do) before a talk to help you relax. Now we'll explore some preparation strategies in greater detail. In the next chapter you'll learn not only how to get rid of the confidence-draining thoughts that we often have before a speaking engagement but also how to take strategic actions that will help make your public speaking successful and stress-free.

7

What to Do and Not to Do Before a Talk

HARRISON ADMITS THAT in his early years as a business presenter he often waited until the last minute to get prepared for his talks. He was an A student and a quick study. He retained his topic material well and was able to draw on facts and statistics when he needed them. But he realized that during extensive Q&A sessions he didn't have the breadth of knowledge a true subject-matter expert should have, nor was he able to elaborate much beyond brief answers and explanations to an audience's queries. He always had a mild case of anxiety that a particularly well-informed audience member could "blow his cover" and point out flaws and holes in his knowledge on the topic of his talk. He knew he needed to step up his level of preparation.

One day during that time he was having coffee with a news anchor friend of his when the discussion turned to former *Nightline* news anchor Ted Koppel, one of Harrison's favorite journalists. His friend mentioned Koppel's legendary capacity to research and retain massive amounts of information that would be at his disposal whenever he interviewed decision makers, heads of state, and other movers and shakers during his illustrious career. Koppel is known in the news business as a master of preparation.

Harrison decided to emulate the smartest man in journalism. He started preparing methodically and diligently for each event, audience, and speaking occasion far in advance of the scheduled date of the talk. When he had only little notice prior to a talk, he would start preparation as quickly as possible to get a thorough understanding of the issue or topic at hand, as well as of the type of audience, to be well informed and give his listeners the most relevant information he could.

Larina has also noticed this pattern in herself and her clients: Too little preparation is likely to result in anxiety. If you aren't well prepared, it's likely you'll be more anxious. The exception, of course, is a presentation that you've given many times, or a subject area that is your primary area of expertise. Larina, for example, knows topics related to anxiety like the back of her hand, so she needs less time to prepare for a presentation on one of these topics. When we have a *new* topic for presentation, we plan for extra preparation

Before we get into the details of preparation, we'd like to issue a word of caution. We have discussed (and will discuss in greater detail in the next chapter) the way in which nervous speakers have a tendency to overcompensate for their anxiety. A common mistake that particularly nervous speakers make is to overrehearse and overprepare. As a result, they appear stiff and unnatural, and increased anxiety results. In this chapter, we discuss the benefits of comprehensive preparation *up to a point.*

Remember that, optimally, performance increases as preparation increases only up to a point, and then it starts to deteriorate. If you're so busy memorizing inconsequential details that you lose sight of the point of your talk, your talk will suffer. If you stay up all night preparing, you'll be bleary-eyed and lack energy for your presentation the next day. If you're a total perfectionist about your preparation, you'll create impossible standards for yourself and end up more anxious. As we've discussed, both underpreparation and overpreparation can increase anxiety and decrease performance.

There are also times when little or no preparation is possible, and we will discuss this in Chapter 12. You'll also learn more about spontaneous speaking situations in later chapters. In this chapter, however, we discuss how to prepare when you know you have a presentation coming up. Our goal is to help you find the right amount of preparation to give you maximum confidence and the knowledge you need to excel in your speaking.

When Less Isn't More

Generally, the more time you have to prepare for your presentation situation, formal or informal, business or social, the better off you are. In this chapter you will get valuable information on what to do and what to avoid doing during the week prior to your talk, as well as during the last couple of hours and minutes before you're "on stage," to make sure you present yourself and your message effectively. You may have more time than the amount we're discussing here, or you may have less; either way, you will still be able to apply the various components of preparation to your situation.

The Week Before

Whether the task of giving a speech, presentation, or informal talk just happened upon you or you've known about it for a while and you've procrastinated until now, it's time to get busy.

Researching the Topic Is Vital for Your Speaking Success

At the beginning of your week, get a good overview of your topic. Find the key information available in books, magazines, newspaper, and online articles and draw out the items that are recent, relevant, and interesting to your prospective listeners.

Investigate whether the information you find is the best data available, or whether you will need to subscribe to several publications online that give you a broader selection and more details. Helpful research sites include questia.com, forbes.com, hoovers.com, or any other database or publication that hosts information on your topic.

A quick search on Google can give you an idea of what's out there on your topic. Be careful, though: A search on a fairly general term like "investing for retirement," for example, will generate over 48 million results. That's a lot of needles to sift through to find the one most appropriate for your talk. The more specific your search terms are, the more relevant the search results will be.

Read and "own" the material. When you present information to a live audience, it is helpful to have relevant information at your fingertips, or better, in the back of your mind, ready for instant recall. Limit your knowledge database to key information, because overloading your memory bank can result in remembering nothing. And you don't want to share all the information you've gathered; you just want to give your audience the most relevant parts. The rest is backup intelligence for you to have ready at a moment's notice for Q&A sessions or discussions that spring from a potential lively interaction with your audience. A good rule of thumb is to give the audience 40 percent of what you know and to keep 60 percent in your "back pocket" to present when it is useful. In other words, don't fire your ammunition all at once. Some of it may come in extremely handy after your talk too.

When you research during your "crunch week," don't hesitate to dive into the details. It's easy for people to get superficial information on just about anything, but to be considered an expert and assert your credibility when you talk, you must go deeper. And always consider the source. It pays to be a *healthy* doubter (but an excessive doubter is an anxious one). So much has been written about just about anything that, when researching, you must apply a critical perspective in digging up information. Is it recent or out of date? Is the source prejudiced? Is it credible? Where do they get their information? Has the information been verified by a credible third party? Are studies, surveys, and statistics available? And the $1 million question: Will you bet your reputation on the information you are going to present?

As you spend a large part of your week looking up everything you can get your hands on that has to do with the nature of your talk, don't forget to pay attention to the news. Gather the necessary intelligence from as many different sources as you can, but absolutely include the latest information available from the news media.

Harrison likes to get his news online first thing every morning from a variety of sources. Google.com has a "News" feature that posts the latest world, business, entertainment, technology, science, and health news from over 4,500 news sources all over the world. He feels that it is the most efficient way to get updated on various new developments on just about any issue in the media and on the public's mind. Due to Google's vast search capacity, you can just type in the topic for which you'd like to see the latest news coverage, and Google will pull it up immediately from a number of online news outlets.

Some Key Questions to Ask Yourself

1. What material and evidence do I have at my disposal to talk about this topic?
2. Where can I find the additional information I need?
3. What are the main points of my topic I need to get across?
4. What main parts can I divide my topic into?
5. What information is crucial to my message and what is unnecessary or simply "nice to know" material?

Questions to Make Your Talk More Personal

1. What is particularly important, fascinating, and compelling about my material, for me personally?
2. When gathering the information, what came as the biggest surprise to me, if anything?
3. What drives me to share this information with my audience?
4. Are there members of my audience whom I perceive as more important than others and who need to receive this information?
5. Who are my allies in the audience from whom I can draw confidence if necessary?

The Audience: The Only Reason You're Talking

If there were no audience, you would have no reason to give a talk in the first place. They are your most important element to consider during this week prior to your talk.

And with this critically important focus firmly in mind, one of the first questions ask to yourself is: "Why am I giving a talk, speech, or presentation to this particular audience in the first place?"

Is your goal to entertain your listeners and provide comic relief? Are you informing them of important changes or developments? Are you giving people instructions on how to do something better or differently? Or is your objective to change their minds on an issue that is important to you? Are you looking to persuade them to agree with your point of view?

Right from the start, it's important to keep in mind that you will be addressing an audience of thinking, feeling people. Not a wall of faces. That's why you'll never hear us recommend that you picture your listeners naked or in their first-grade pictures. We actually want you to focus on your audience, not blur them out with silly tricks.

Almost everything else you do to prepare for your speaking moment will revolve around your audience—the target of your message. Now it's time to find out what the composition and makeup of your audience is. Or as Jerry Seinfeld likes to ask: "Who are these people?"

To get an appropriately detailed answer, you'll have to do some digging. You'll need to find out more than the basics such as job descriptions, gender, age, and other demographic information. You should research your audience's wants, needs, and motivations. Find their emotional "hot buttons." Learn about their attitudes, values, beliefs, fears, problems, and hopes. If you can prepare to address some or all of those issues in your talk, openly or below the radar, targeted at their subconscious, you are on the right track to connect with your listeners' hearts and minds.

You'll want to start by focusing initially on the things you have in common with your audience. Instead of preparing to speak to a bunch of strangers or people with a different point of view than yours, train your awareness on the universal experiences you share with them. It will be easier for you to relate, mentally reducing the "distance" you may be experiencing toward them. During this week, decide consciously that you will share interesting, relevant, and important information with your listeners. This will also help you create in advance a positive mind-set for your talk.

Spotlight on the Audience

In preparing for your talk, you and the audience are an idea that is "joined at the hip." During this week, you'll contemplate how much or how little time you have left to prepare, what information and materials you need to gather and from where, and how you're going to sift through it all while editing it for clarity and structuring it for a logical flow. The most important questions to ask yourself, however, are: What exactly is my objective in giving this talk to this particular audience in the first place? What need of mine am I meeting in talking to these people a week from now? And how can I match my need with the needs of my audience?

Let's look at the example of Michael, a start-up entrepreneur who is seeking funding for his new business idea:

> *Michael has five minutes to make his pitch. The group of venture capitalists and angel investors he is about to address have no time to waste and are now waiting blank-faced for this young entrepreneur to present his idea. Michael knows he has to get to the point quickly and focus his talk squarely on the key issues this particular audience cares about most. They want to know: What's the idea, why should they consider it, how much will it cost to fund, how big is the return on investment, and how soon will it happen?*
>
> *Start-up investors are a notoriously critical audience and demand that a presenter do his homework and quickly deliver specific answers to their specific questions.*

While this is an extreme example of how focused a speaker must be on the specific needs of the audience, an effective speaker's overall objective will look like this: You are communicating specific information to a specific audience to inspire a desired reaction or result within that audience for your mutual benefit. Notice we said "mutual" benefit. That's yours and theirs—hence the importance of your deliberate focus on the audience and what they'll need and want from you. By focusing on this type of information, you will save time and more efficiently perceive, select, and evaluate your content for the talk you're about to give.

Too many inexperienced speakers and presenters start the preparation process by asking themselves what they should talk about and what information to include in their talk. While that's not entirely wrong, it is equivalent to putting the proverbial cart before the horse. Because before you can ask "What?" you have to ask "Who?" The "who" will clearly determine the "what."

Knowing this will save you hours of valuable research time that may otherwise be wasted on gathering way too much information you may think you need to include. There is no shortage of information. In fact, we're all up to our eyeballs in information. But information that is relevant and important to a particular group of people, without all of the clutter, is rare indeed. Marketing departments the world over spend billions of dollars annually to figure out how to target audiences better by providing them with the most relevant information that will trigger a buying impulse. You have to do the same. Only you typically have to do it on a shoestring budget.

Preparing with Your Listeners in Mind

Now that we agree that the most important component about a speech or talk is the audience, we start preparing with a clear image of our listeners in mind.

That's why your objectives should not be based on your interests alone, but also on the interests of your audience.

By the time you finish speaking, your audience should have gained valuable knowledge, important insights, delightful entertainment, or deep understanding of an issue of concern. The audience must perceive the considerable value of your speech. And the value your audience should perceive will determine the specific content and the objectives of your talk.

Remember too that an audience is never an empty container to be filled with your content. Most likely your audience already has certain biases, knowledge, and information related to what you are going to talk about. The question is: How much? Your job is to add to this knowledge and to create additional meaning and insights.

As you prepare for your speaking event, learn what prior knowledge, attitudes, and types of evidence your audience has, and what additional data they need to accept your message and do what you want them to do.

Choose your words and terminology based on the specific profile of your audience. Avoid jargon that they do not know and that would be irrelevant to them. Use jargon only if it matches the audience's specialized vocabulary. Simple English always does the job and ensures that everyone—not only those who are "clued in"—has the opportunity to understand your message.

In your preparations, choose a speaking style appropriate for your listeners, the occasion, and the specific context of your talk. Remember, your audience determines content format and style. Ask yourself the following questions as they relate to your audience:

1. To whom am I giving this talk?
2. What are their cultural, socioeconomic, and educational backgrounds?
3. What does the audience expect of me?
4. What prior knowledge does my audience have about the topic?
5. What past experiences does my audience have regarding my topic?
6. Which information is new, interesting, and important for my audience?
7. What is the audience's attitude toward me?
8. What is the audience's attitude toward the topic?
9. What do they hope to get out of my talk?
10. Was it the voluntary decision of each audience member to attend this talk or were some or all of them required to attend?
11. Will important decision makers be in the audience, and will I have to impress them?

It takes some time to get answers to all of these questions, so start researching immediately. The information you gather will determine the direction, content, and level of customization of your talk.

You can gather intelligence on your audience by consulting some of the following resources:

1. Industry periodicals
2. Google or other major search engines like yahoo.com, altavista.com, and dogpile.com
3. Newspapers
4. Supervisors and management
5. Peers and colleagues
6. Magazines
7. Trade books
8. Competitors
9. Consultants
10. Human resources departments

These are just some of the sources that can help you piece together a profile of your target audience. The more sources related to your audience that you consult, the likelier it will be that your final audience profile is accurate. With the special interests of your audience in your mind's eye, start working on the structural and stylistic design of your talk.

Construction and Organization of Research Material

Effective speaking makes it easy for your audience to follow your train of thought. As we discussed in Chapter 4, the structure of your talk represents the mental path that will guide your audience. They will be much more willing to follow you if your organization is clear, interesting, inspiring, and, ideally, exciting at various parts of your talk.

An effectively structured talk divides the content into its thematic components and provides the audience with the unambiguous meaning of your message. A solid structure simplifies complex content and guides the audience effortlessly to your conclusion, while giving you opportunities to emphasize certain aspects of your talk along the way. The following information is designed to give you the summarized version of what to do as you structure and organize your data for presentation.

Standard Structuring

A well-structured talk is always divided into an introduction, a body, and a conclusion. If this sounds a bit too stifling or is too reminiscent of public speaking and speech class from the "oppressive" days of high school and college, think of it this way:

- The introduction is the beginning of your talk, and you can't help but begin somehow, right?
- It's the same with the conclusion. You know you *will* end your talk at some point, so you'll want to make sure the ending makes sense and reminds the audience of all the good points you made in the body of your talk.
- The body, sandwiched between the beginning and the ending, is where you drive home your message and lay it all out for your listeners. It's where you flesh out your ideas, points, and assertions and back them up with as much material as necessary to prove your claims or statements so that no one can trip you up by saying your research is flawed or flat-out wrong.

Each of these individual parts has a specific function. The following nutshell version of what to consider when you put your talk together during this week of preparation can be adapted and expanded depending on your topic, purpose, intention, and audience.

- *Introduction.* Welcome the group, state the topic or the issue, highlight the problem or question, capture their attention, create curiosity, give them a great reason as to why they are there, and let them know what to expect.
- *Body.* Illustrate your key points, make your case, argue your position, provide solid reasons for why they should believe what you want them to believe, explain your point of view, and present your perspective.

- *Conclusion.* Summarize, conclude, and reiterate your message. The conclusion is especially important because the audience will most likely remember it the best, since it was the last part of your talk and will be most vivid in their minds. Trial lawyers call it the "law of recency."

How to Time the Writing of Your Talk

Often, the time it takes to prepare depends on the length of your talk or on the complexity of your message and content. It further depends on whether your talk will be based on a detailed manuscript or whether you'll speak from bullet points only, that is, from a PowerPoint presentation.

For less structured talks and presentations you'll need less time to prepare. One week or less for preparation and practice may suffice if you speak from notes, you have a solid objective, and you're an expert in the area of your talk. It should also give you enough time to research and collect the necessary information for your talk, rehearse it in front of a test audience that is willing to give honest feedback, and tape your talk with a video camera to catch distracting nonverbal or vocal habits that need to be eliminated prior to your speech.

Talks based on a more detailed script generally take longer to prepare unless you're extremely experienced in developing and delivering formal and informal talks. The reason is that when we write out our talks, we automatically revert to the written word. Yet, a written speech is not ideal to use verbatim, because it's smoother to read than to actually hear. We have more time to think when we write compared to when we speak. This means that during the writing process we keep thinking of new aspects and angles to our topic, causing us to get lost in unnecessary details. Typically, only veteran speakers are able to write the way they speak, allowing them to work word-for-word from their prepared manuscript. We'll talk more about this in the next section.

Your Manuscript

Do you want to write your talk out word for word, or do you just want to use memory joggers such as index cards, notes, or bulleted lists? The option you choose depends somewhat on your comfort level with the material you're presenting. Of course, as discussed above, you should never read a written manuscript, as this practice tends to decrease your connection with the audience and can increase your discomfort, self-focus, and anxiety. Your reasons for writing out a manuscript word for word should primarily be to understand and dissect your material and message, to match your words to the audience for the most impact, and to provide you with the essence of your talk, from which you will consciously stray only when you see a clear benefit in doing so.

One of Harrison's clients was preparing for a major presentation to a panel of city council members, including the city's mayor. At stake was a $200 million land development contract, for which his client needed final approval from the city. To complicate the situation, the town council had twice before rejected this person's bid based on seemingly insurmountable obstacles on which neither side could see a compromise in order to move forward with the project.

When the client sought out Harrison's services, he knew the major message he wanted to convey but was unsure how he should put it in words and how to ultimately deliver those words to his audience in order to persuade them. Harrison worked with him over the course of two days, coaxing and shaping the speech from his client by helping him write out word for word what the points of the message should be. They eliminated jargon from the speech and trimmed as much unnecessary detail, lower priority points. and personal feelings as possible, unless they presented an important strategic benefit.

Within a few hours of hard thinking and rigorous writing and editing of the upcoming talk, Harrison's client ended up with a final product that was a concise, well conceived, and ultralean speech that he could use as a script for his high-stakes presentation. Once the content of that speech was created, the client was able to focus on style and delivery of the speech, receiving coaching from Harrison on using effective nonverbal communication techniques such as posture, eye contact, gestures, choreography, and vocal tonality. (We'll go into these techniques in detail in the next chapter.)

To reiterate, you never want to write out your talk so that you can read it to the audience verbatim, or even partially verbatim. The reason you might want to write your message out before you present it is to literally look at it, to find phrases, words, stray thoughts, and details that may be unnecessary to your overall objective and that might reduce the impact of your speech.

Using a Manuscript

If you're writing out your talk, be sure you pay attention to the following:

- Write for the ear. Your talk should be immediately comprehensible to your listeners without having to translate complex language.
- The language and delivery style should be appropriate for the particular situation and audience. I can reread a complex train of thought or written statement, but I cannot relisten to something a speaker said when I may not have grasped the meaning.
- Your manuscript should help you during your speech. Design it in such a way that it has a logical flow and structure that will help guide your train of thought during the presentation. Many speakers like to use PowerPoint slides to orient themselves to the various bullet points of each slide and to make the flow of the talks natural and logical.

Memory Joggers and Notes

A memory jogger, like a mnemonic device, can be extremely helpful when trying to remember specific information during a talk. Mnemonics are memorizing techniques that allow us to easily recall information by the use of acronyms, acrostics, or the mental connection of strong images to the information that needs to be remembered. If a speaker talking on the topic of identity theft prevention wanted to remember the key points of Credit Report, Awareness, Loss Prevention, and Law Enforcement, she might form the acronym CALL 911, by combining the first letters of each point she wants to make during her speech.

Another powerful mnemonic device is the association of mental images to words we want to remember. An example is the speaker who wants to remember the names of his audience members so that he can establish rapport on a deeper level. An idea would be to attach a mental picture to each name in order to easily recall the name when needed. Bill, the fellow in the second row with the red hair, could become Fire Marshal Bill because of his fiery mane. Sylvia, the lady a little farther back in the room, could be imagined wearing a big round Olympic silver medal around her neck. The trick is to make the picture associations bold, simple, and colorful, as well as relevant to the name of the person or thing you need to remember so that it can be recalled instantly. Memory joggers can also be key information and cues in the form of simple notes on anything from a sheet of paper, a number of three-by-five index cards, or even a napkin you scribbled on at Starbucks.

Regardless of which memory jogger you choose, its importance is that it helps you to conduct your talk effectively. If you are using notes, a quick glance will help you move your talk along effortlessly. For this purpose make sure you:

- Underline key words.
- Write clearly and legibly.
- Write slightly larger than you normally would so that you can still read your notes from three feet away. Picture them as the miniature version of the cue cards that talk show hosts use to stay on track with their scripts.
- Use symbols when a picture says more than a thousand words.
- Use different colors to indicate different points.

Talks that are given with the aid of memory joggers are usually less structured. The advantages of this type of speaking are immediacy and the flexibility you have in incorporating examples, audience feedback, and appropriate analogies. Memory joggers also allow you to fit in last-minute news that can add relevance to your topic. Speaking freely like this, however, requires you to be confident and in command of your topic, to have a good vocabulary, and to be at least somewhat comfortable with your audience.

Practice and Rehearsal

Here are some tips that will help you make the most out of your preparation and rehearsal time as you work on your manuscript.

1. If you decided on using a manuscript and wrote out your talk word for word, it's time to edit and cut out superfluous language. Add or delete as you see fit. Start shaping the final talk.

2. As you're reading through your notes or manuscript, underline or highlight key words. By making these key words stand out, you create a path through your talk.

3. Check the relevance of your key words, and here too add or delete.

4. Next to your key words you can add direction comments for yourself such as "dramatic pause," "longer eye contact," "make eye contact with specific members of the audience," and "raise or lower voice."

5. Don't include too many key words in your notes, otherwise it's like highlighting too many passages on a page; they don't stand out.

6. When you know exactly what your key message is and you have the basic script and the words down and committed to memory, you want to work on the delivery and rehearse your talk in front of an honest test audience that's willing to give you straightforward feedback. You'll want them to answer questions like: "Do I appear credible?" "Do I project energy?" "Do you believe me based on my nonverbal language?" "What distracts you from my message?" "Am I convincing?" "Do I appear to believe my own message?"

Handouts and Other Audience Materials

During this week you also want to make sure you have prepared, copied, and bound or stapled any materials you want your audience to have as part of your talk. Don't delay this task until the last minute, as many presenters do—you'll increase the chances of forgetting something, missing or mixing up pages.

The Night Before Your Talk

When Harrison was in school, back home in his native Germany, he "tested" all of the tried-and-true preparation techniques that have made their way into every schoolkid's arsenal of studying techniques—from sleeping on the research material stuffed under his pillow to falling asleep while listening to a tape of his own voice recording of the material. After all, a cassette tape on autoreverse would replay the recording all night long and slowly but steadily enter the subconscious mind of the learner, wouldn't it? Well, unfortunately for millions of high school students, there is no scientific evidence that this actually makes a difference and no reliable data, based on widely varying results in Harrison's early years of "sleep-and-learn research," that would support such practices as useful learning aids.

So what are some helpful ways to spend the night before an oral presentation, an important interview, or a high-stakes talk to a roomful of listeners?

The following advice will help get you ready for your audience the next morning:

1. *Get as much sleep as you need in order to be fully rested.* For some people that's eight hours, for others six hours is enough to feel refreshed the next morning. Only you can know what that number is. Listen to your body.
2. *Arrange on your bed or closet the clothes you'll wear for your presentation.* As it applies to your gender and preference, pick the shoes, belt, socks, shirt, dress, skirt, suit, tie, jewelry, watch, and anything else you're going to wear and lay it all out as you picture yourself presenting and speaking to your audience.
3. *Create a mental motion picture.* Movies are announced with 30-second trailers to give the public an idea of what they can expect when they go to the theater. They're designed to get

people excited about a movie and to create the impulse to go see it. To get yourself excited about your next-day performance, create your own little mental trailer as you run through the highlights of your speech, picturing the best-case scenario of yourself interacting with the audience. Imagine their body posture at the edge of their seats, trying to capture every word you're saying. Visualize their eyes steadily focused on your face so as to not let a single word escape their awareness. Picture their relieved and delighted expressions as you expose the lighter side of a serious issue, giving everyone a chance to breathe a sigh of relief and to relax with big smiles and genuine laughter.

Athletes run through their program several times just before the actual event, as well as at various stages of preparation. They call it "positive visualization," and every time they visualize their process and actions, they successfully complete each move. They are conditioning their nerve and motor functions with the power of positive mental imaging. As many times as you like, you can run a similar success sequence in your mind as you visualize all of the positive interpersonal moments between your audience and yourself during your talk, conditioning your mental and physical faculties to peak performance for the actual event.

4. *Do not eat a heavy meal* that will weigh you down, cause physical discomfort, or create physiological processes in your system that will make themselves known to you when you least need them, like in the middle of your speech the next day. For this reason, don't drink any alcohol the night before your talk and avoid exotic spices that normally aren't part of your diet.

5. *Go through your preparation materials once, but not right before bed.* As far as "owning" the information and material you're going to present, waiting until the night before to commit the results of your research to memory is less than ideal, as you can imagine. And as we discussed earlier, literally sleeping on it won't do much for mastering your topic either. So if you're still struggling with the data you need to

internalize prior to your talk, simply read over the information again and ask yourself questions such as: "Why is this important again?" "Why will they need to know this?" "Who cares about this?" "What is particularly important about this piece of information for my talk?" By "confronting" the material as opposed to just reading it, you are anchoring the information more securely in your mental archives so that when you're in the moment during your talk, the "need" for the information will trigger the answers you've stored for the audience.

A Couple of Hours Before Your Talk

Whether it's time for breakfast, time for lunch, or even time for dinner, keep your food intake to a minimum a couple of hours before your speech. Speaking for a purpose requires all of your mental and physical faculties to operate at optimum performance. Don't sabotage the processes that take place by burdening your system with anything other than what you need for energy and proper hydration. Eat a light, healthy meal consisting mostly of protein and carbohydrates. Limit fats and fiber right before a talk. This means limiting your liquid intake drastically at this point, aside from small sips of water to keep your mouth hydrated and your throat from getting dry due to preperformance jitters.

Whether you're speaking at a familiar venue, such as your organization's conference room, or an auditorium in a city thousands of miles away from home, you want to make sure you've actually seen the place before the talk. Especially if you're using presentation technology, you want to make sure that all of the outlets, cables, light switches, and writing surfaces are where they're supposed to be and available for you when you need them.

Visualize the positive outcome of your talk again as you think over the highlights of your speech. Think about your message and what it will mean to your audience. Think about the difference the information you present will make for people, either in their day, their work processes, or their lives. Think again about the opening words of your talk. You've prepared your opening statement during the week's preparation period and now you're about to present it to your audience. Look forward to it. Think of it as a present you've carefully selected and packaged to give to your listeners at just the right moment. Think of the reaction you want from them.

If you have a chance to exercise before your talk, do it, even if it means just doing some crunches on the floor or push-ups against the wall. Of course, it could also be a full-fledged workout in the gym. The exercise will release endorphins, the hormones that make you feel good, get your heart rate up, and give you the energy you need to project as you speak later on. You'll come across as a much more dynamic person if you do this. Plus, you'll feel good about yourself, which has never hurt any speaker's purpose. If you're prone to becoming anxious, exercise an hour or more before the talk, because you won't need the extra adrenaline for your performance itself and it will help to release it ahead of time. Then, immediately before the talk, engage in light, relaxing activities, such as stretching.

Avoid any major distractions this close to your talk. Anything that will take your focus off your talk should be delayed until later if possible. Major decisions, difficult conversations, and creative input into a different project should be avoided until the important task at hand has been accomplished. You will need all of your resources to achieve your talk's objective.

A Few Minutes Before Your Talk

You've made it to Presentation Day. Your talk is just minutes away. The audience is in the venue; they are exchanging "Hellos" and "Nice to see yous," shaking hands, joking around, and otherwise making casual small talk. One by one they're getting comfortable in their chairs, arranging their notepads, and pulling out pencils and pens to take notes with, anticipating what you will share with them and what you'll be like as a speaker. Remember, they are there with positive expectations—they do not expect you to fail; they want you to do well. In psychology, a positive expectancy affects how we view things. If we expect something to be good, we attach a positive bias and view it as good. This will help you—the audience is on your side!

Recognize whether you need to pump yourself up or calm yourself down—if you have adrenaline pumping through you and feel jittery. Consider the nature of your talk (high energy, or more calming and relaxing) and your natural response to the anxiety. Energize yourself up by doing some jumping jacks or push-ups or by listening to energetic music. Quiet yourself by taking slow, deep breaths and saying a soothing trigger word to yourself that captures how you want to feel, such as "poised" or "smooth."

What to Do During the Final Minutes Before Your Talk

Your preparation and rehearsal are about to be put to the test. The following steps will help you center yourself and get ready for the moment of truth as you prepare to face your audience.

1. Find a quiet place where you can focus on important aspects of your speech.
2. Loosen your jaw by opening and closing your mouth wide as if you were yawning.
3. Take several deep breaths and let the air expand your abdomen; feel the energy starting to surge through your body.
4. Catch a last glance of yourself in a (preferably full-length) mirror and make sure nothing is out of place, such as a turned-up collar, a crooked tie, a pant leg tucked in a sock, a stain from breakfast or lunch, or any other physical distraction.
5. Mentally run through the first two minutes of your talk by turning up the energy and speaking the introduction either out loud or in your mind.
6. If you have the chance to introduce yourself to some or all of the audience members, mingle with them for a few minutes and give a sincere, friendly handshake. Smile, look them in the eye, and tell them you're looking forward to speaking to them in the next few minutes and that you're glad they're here.
7. Rearrange your notes in the right order and put them in a strategically appropriate place where you can easily access them when you need a memory jogger. If a podium is available, you can put them on the surface and place them so a

quick glance can give you the information you need to make your next point. If you don't have a podium, place your notes on a table or desk surface close to you, where you only have to take a few steps to get to them.

8. Focus on increasing your energy level, because you want to capture the audience's attention right away and take their minds off wherever they were the moment before you started your talk. Pump yourself up by visualizing your success with the audience. See them clapping, cheering, and rising to give you a standing ovation if you have positive news to share. If you're presenting bad news, realize that your audience needs your compassion and empathy. Focus on your personal involvement and the elements of your talk that truly mean the most to you.

9. Take small, quick sips of water and make sure your mouth is moist and refreshed, as the first few minutes of your talk are the most likely to give you "dry mouth" and "pelt tongue" due to the heightened anxiety you will might be feeling at the beginning.

10. Before stepping "on stage," focus your final thoughts on your objective, the one thing you want your audience to get out of your talk.

11. Expect that you may have a sudden surge of anxiety when you step out in front of everyone, but know that it will quickly subside. Anxiety rises and falls like a wave. Ride it out, and you'll be a great, confident speaker.

It is important that you make effective use of your time prior to any important communication situation, and the higher the stakes, the more the knowledge you've gained in this chapter will benefit you in your communication efforts. Now that you have a good idea what steps to take during various phases of your preparation period, in the next chapter we'll show how you can gain influence over your thoughts and behaviors in order to work with your anxiety.

PART III

TOOLBOX FOR THE NERVOUS SPEAKER

8

Change Your Thoughts and Behaviors

NOW THAT YOU have a solid understanding of how anxiety works, how your public speaking anxiety manifests itself, some of the situations where it's common to see speaking anxiety come up, and some great strategies for preparing yourself to best overcome anxiety, it is time to get to the important question: "How do I stop these dreadful thoughts?"

Great news! You *really* can change. It is completely possible for you to get up in front of people and speak with poise, confidence, and assurance. It will take a bit of work and practice to change your thought processes and habits, but we're here to help you know exactly what you need to do. So if you're ready, you are on the path to changing the way you speak in front of others. In fact, you've already come a long way at this point in the book. You may even have experienced some reduction in anxiety as a result of identifying it appropriately; and, hopefully, you are already starting to change your attitude toward anxiety and public speaking.

In this chapter we'll take you through some specific approaches to help you change the fearful thoughts and the behaviors that are sure to hold you back from being a confident, spectacular speaker.

A New Approach

The approach to overcoming speaking anxiety may be quite different from ideas you've heard before. It is also different because it *works*. If you're reading this, there's a good chance that much of what you have heard in the past has not worked. This is not your fault. You simply have not learned the right tools to beat the anxiety for good. As we've mentioned in previous chapters, the material you learn in this book is likely to be most effective when you go through it with a cognitive-behavioral therapist or a public speaking coach who's versed in these principles.

The approach we present to you has been validated by empirical research with people who are likely to have much more significant social anxiety and speaking phobias than you. If it works for people with severe speaking anxiety, it can work for you! Clinical research and treatment at world class centers for the treatment of anxiety, such as the Center for Treatment and Study of Anxiety at the University of Pennsylvania, under the leadership of internationally renowned anxiety expert Dr. Edna B. Foa, have shown this cognitive-behavioral approach to be extremely effective.

The main tenet of our approach is this: *Confront and embrace your anxiety!*

Sound crazy? It may, but it truly works. Have you ever heard that dogs can smell fear? Well, anxiety can smell fear too. Is it best to run away from an angry dog? Is it a good idea to get worked up and attack the dog? No, of course it's not a good idea to get into a fight with a dog that can tear you to shreds. You do not want to respond out of fear because that can exacerbate the dog's ferocious behavior. The same works with anxiety: If you try to run away from it or beat it down, it will fight back.

Confronting the anxiety and accepting it is like approaching the angry dog and giving it a bone. The dog might just become your new best friend. No dog is inherently evil, mean, or bad, and anxiety is not either. Like your fiercely loyal dog who wants to defend you, anxiety is around to protect you. When you join together with the anxiety, you use it to your advantage and it works for you rather than against you.

We will introduce many methods for changing how you deal with the fear of speaking. The ones that work best for you will depend on your particular situation and the way nervousness comes up for you. Have patience, because change typically does not occur overnight but rather as a result of repeatedly trying these new skills and behaviors. You *can* teach an old dog new tricks, but it takes repetition and consistency. Let's have a look first at the thoughts that make you nervous about speaking up and then at the behaviors that reinforce your speaking anxiety.

Change Those Anxiety-Increasing Thoughts

As you are probably aware, changing the way you think is not the easiest thing in the world to do. But you can do it if you practice these simple steps:

1. Learn what anxious thoughts come up for you.
2. Challenge these thoughts.
3. Come up with alternative explanations.

The First Step: What Was I Thinking?

The first step in the process of putting an end to anxious thinking is to recognize it. Have you ever noticed that you become even more anxious after a certain thought runs through your mind? You may not notice this happening because thoughts can be so quick and fleeting; however, in most cases of speaking anxiety, some thought has either triggered or increased the nervousness. A certain thought is usually prevalent in many of your speaking situations. Recognizing these thoughts can be like asking a fish to recognize water—they are such a part of your existence that you may not even notice them. Other times these thoughts cause so much distress that you are keenly aware of them.

Larina often says that beating anxiety is like playing a friendly game of soccer. You give it your all to win (and show the anxiety who's boss), but the game is a sport, and it's fun—you are not trying to beat down the other team. Then once you've shown that you can win, you all go out for drinks together (you join the anxiety and allow it to help you). To win the game of soccer, you would do well to first know the opposing team's moves, strengths, and capabilities. Once your opponent's moves are predictable, you can plan the proper moves in response. Therefore, this first step of uncovering the anxious thoughts is very important. Without this knowledge, you won't be aware what thoughts come up for you, and you won't be able to take the next steps.

Complete the What Was I Thinking? worksheet to start recognizing your thoughts. The best time to complete this form is when you just had an anxiety-provoking situation, or as soon as possible afterward. This is because your memory will be the most accurate if you write these things down right away. Try to record your thoughts as quotes, writing them just as they went through your mind, word for word.

Step 2: Challenge the Idea

When you complete the What Was I Thinking? form, you'll see how many opportunities you can have to challenge the thoughts that fuel the anxiety. To really gain a broad understanding of how your thoughts make you nervous, try to fill out this form for about 10 different situations.

When you know what your thoughts are, you can start to do something about them. The key is to learn to challenge these thoughts in a compelling way. Many self-help books tell you to stop thinking negative thoughts or to simply think more positively. Unfortunately, it's not that simple. In fact, trying not to have a thought or thinking simplistic positive thoughts or affirmations can do more harm than good. Trying to suppress a thought typically results in the thought coming up more.

Thinking positive thoughts or saying affirmations can be helpful, but they are often disappointing because they are not compelling processes. It does no good to tell you why you might want to think and believe the positive thought. Your mind may go on the defensive. If you have the negative thought, which verbalized would be, "The sky is always gray and dull," an opposing positive thought would be, "The sky is blue and beautiful." Your mind actually starts to defend its

WHAT WAS I THINKING?

Situation where anxiety came up for me:_____

_____

_____

_____

_____

Who else was present?_____

_____

What was I thinking as I anticipated the situation?_____

_____

_____

_____

_____

What thought went through my mind as I entered that situation?

_____

_____

_____

What was I thinking as I was in the situation?_____

_____

_____

_____

What did I fear was the worst thing that could happen?

_____

_____

_____

What went through my mind after the situation?_____

_____

_____

_____

WHAT WAS I THINKING?
(Completed Example)

Situation where anxiety came up for me:
I was going into a meeting where I would have to present new
information to the design team, including one of the top
executives of marketing.

Who else was present?
Six people on my design team, two from sales, and two senior executives.

What was I thinking as I was anticipating the situation?
"I don't think this is going to go well because I feel horrible right now.
My stomach hurts, my heart is racing and I'm starting to sweat."

What thought went through my mind as I entered that situation?
"This could be very embarrassing and I have no idea how I'm going
to face all of these people after this. I'm really starting to get sweaty
now, what if the pen falls right out of my hand because it is
so slippery?"

What was I thinking when I was in the situation?
"All these people staring at me . . . how long until this will be over?"

What did I fear was the worst thing that could happen?
"I was thinking that I could stumble through the whole presentation,
make a total fool of myself, and eventually lose my job because
I cannot present any of my ideas."

What went through my mind after the situation?
"I guess I got through that and I am still standing, but I should have
talked more slowly. I think people looked really bored and they
probably saw how anxious I was so they were uncomfortable. I really
could have described the part about the potential clients more
clearly . . . " Why didn't I think of a better answer for Sam's question?

original position because the new position is too extreme and is not convincing. To change your thinking is a complicated process. You need to present your mind with a compelling argument to work hard to make those changes.

The way to present a compelling argument is to present both sides and see which side is more convincing. Think of yourself as a high-powered attorney (easy if you are one) and anticipate what the other side would say. Look over the evidence for both sides and see which one makes the most sense.

Say, for example, your thought is: "I will not be able to speak well when I get up there." Let's look at the evidence for and against this assertion:

Evidence in favor of the thought:

- I've had two situations in which I was given feedback that my voice was hard to understand when I'm speaking.
- When I get nervous, I find that it is often more difficult to speak loudly.
- I might stammer more or say "um" more when public speaking.

Evidence against the thought:

- I have received a lot of positive feedback after my talks.
- Most people have said they can hear me fine.
- My boss has asked me to do more talks, so my voice must not be atrocious.

The Final Step: You Be the Judge

Now that you have the evidence for both sides, you can figure out which is most compelling and then come up with some other ways of thinking that may be more accurate. Using the example from above, a new thought could be: "I may speak quietly at first, but most likely I will be able to speak."

Do you see how this is different from the typical approaches that simply tell you to think a more positive thought? You do not want to dismiss your fears and come up with some overly simplistic, artificially "positive" thought. Instead, you want to look at the validity in the thought and see where some of the cognitive errors may be coming into play. Complete our What's the Verdict? worksheet to weigh and evaluate the evidence.

End the Distorted Thinking

Remember our discussion about the anxiety-increasing cognitive distortions? Let's now go through them one by one to look at how to beat them.

1. *All or none thinking.* Oh no, my heart just skipped a beat. That means my talk will be horrible!
   Instead, think: My adrenaline is kicking in. I am ready to go! The likelihood that my racing heart will result in a horrible talk is low because many times before I've had a racing heart and spoke just fine.

2. *Fortune-telling.* If I get up there, everyone will lose all respect for me, and I will never be promoted in my job.
   Instead, think: I don't know what will happen when I get up there, but I'm going to use my speaking skills to do my best. Eighty percent of the time in the past I have done okay, so the odds are in my favor. It's highly unlikely that five minutes of speaking will undo five years of hard work and a great professional relationship.

3. *Catastrophizing.* People are going to fall asleep or burst out laughing and won't want to talk to me anymore.
   Instead, think: No one has ever fallen asleep or burst out laughing when I have spoken, so that's pretty unlikely. Even if someone fell asleep, it would be more embarrassing for them than for me.

4. *Emotional reasoning.* Because I'm so anxious and feel sick to my stomach, I'll speak poorly.
   Instead, think: I have heard many people speak and was surprised to hear them say they felt awful inside, because they spoke so well.

WHAT'S THE VERDICT?
Evaluating Your Thoughts Worksheet

Thought:_____

_____

_____

_____

_____

_____

Evidence for Thought:_____

_____

_____

_____

_____

_____

Evidence against Thought:_____

_____

_____

_____

_____

_____

New Thought or Explanation:_____

_____

_____

_____

_____

_____

_____

WHAT'S THE VERDICT?
Evaluating Your Thoughts Worksheet
(Completed Example)

Thought: The audience members look bored, restless, tired, and annoyed. I must be dreadfully boring.

Evidence for Thought:
1. Someone just yawned, and someone else is falling asleep!
2. One lady keeps moving around in her seat; my talk is making her restless.
3. A couple of people won't make eye contact with me; maybe they're embarrassed for me.

Evidence against Thought:
1. Maybe those people have had a long day or didn't sleep well last night.
2. Those people who are tired may have a young baby at home.
3. People may not be making eye contact because they are not great at eye contact.

New Thought or Explanation:
The way people are responding may be based on their own experiences rather than on the way they feel about my talking. Maybe they would do the same thing while an incredible speaker was talking as well. It probably doesn't have much to do with my performance.

5. *Minimization.* If I forget that point, there is no way I can recover.
   Instead, think: If I forget that point and pause for a minute, I can deal with that. Sometimes it looks thoughtful and adds emphasis when people pause.
6. *Tunnel vision.* That one man in the middle of the audience is really glaring at me. I must sound like an idiot.
   Instead, think: That man does not look friendly, but look at the nodding, smiling people around him. Maybe he's in a bad mood today.
7. *Probability overestimation.* I will definitely pass out if I have to go up on that stage.
   Instead, think: Since I have never passed out in my entire life, I probably won't now.

When you catch yourself making one of these "cognitive errors," you can work to change them by using some of the tools we discuss throughout this chapter.

Food Doesn't Taste Good When You Have Stomach Flu

The distortion described above, emotional reasoning, is extremely common with public speaking anxiety. People conclude that because they felt anxious, their talk did not go well. Do you think this might possibly be a biased way of determining how well you did? Of course it is.

This is like going to a five-star restaurant while you have the stomach flu. Someone asks you how the food was, and you say, "Oh, it was horrible. I felt sick the whole time. I could never go back there." It is not an accurate way of making decisions, since the food tasted awful because you felt sick, and it probably would not have tasted awful otherwise.

In our experiences helping people overcome the fear of public speaking, we often ask others to rate people's speaking performances in conversations and while giving talks. Invariably, the people with speaking anxiety rate their performances as significantly worse than others rate them. Do not make the stomach flu mistake and judge your performance on how things felt—look for other ways to measure performance, such as the ways we're providing you throughout this chapter.

What You Expect Is What Happens

Another strategy for changing your thoughts and feelings is: Change what you expect to happen. Have you ever heard the term "self-fulfilling prophecy"? This is the idea that what you expect to happen is often what does happen. Why do you think this is? There are a number of factors, but often the fulfillment rests on the fact that our thoughts strongly influence our behaviors. Can you think of a time when you told yourself you would definitely fail at something and it did turn out poorly? This is the self-fulfilling prophecy at work.

It can also be true that what others expect from you is what turns out to happen. This is called the "expectancy bias." There are studies that show some teachers were led to believe that a group of kids of "average" intelligence were "gifted" and that another group of kids of "average" intelligence were "average." The investigators tracked the children's progress and test scores, and guess what ended up happening? Even though in reality there was no difference in the kids' abilities, the group the teachers thought were gifted performed significantly better.

When others expect something of you, and likewise, when you expect something from yourself, that something is often what ends up happening.

When you expect yourself to do well, you're likely to act in ways that result in doing well. When others expect you to do well, they are likely to treat you in ways that will make you do well. When you act confidently and perform well initially, observers may see all of your behavior as positive. This is called the "halo bias." When they think someone is good at something, they see other things in a more positive light, as if you have a halo following you around.

How can you use all of this to your advantage? Two ways: First, change what you expect of your own performance, and second, change how others see you. There are many strategies to achieve these ends, but since we are now talking about how you think, let's explore some ways of thinking differently.

You may be wondering: How am I supposed to think I'll be great when I really *don't think I'll be great?* The good thing about this strategy is that you do not need to believe it 100 percent. What you need to do is pick out the aspects at which you think you'll do well and concentrate on those. If you think you'll do everything wrong, then take a step back and review some of the cognitive errors, such as all or none thinking, because it's highly unlikely that you would do everything wrong.

Let's say that I think I will be very good at making eye contact with and smiling at the audience. For a positive expectancy, I can picture myself standing comfortably before the audience, making eye contact, and having audience members make eye contact with me. I can picture smiling appropriately during the speech and noticing audience members nodding or smiling back at me.

Another way to frame your expectancies positively is by the language you use with yourself. Your mind will remember the emotionally laden words. If you say to yourself, "Don't mess up," your mind will remember "mess up." This is a negative expectancy and will likely be self-fulfilling. Instead, come up with one or two words that exemplify the way you want to feel as you're talking. These words can be different for different situations. With a casual conversation, you may say to yourself "friendly." With a talk with an intimidating person, you can say "poised" or "relaxed."

Gain Perspective

It is common to lose perspective when you become nervous about speaking in public. We begin to think we'll make an irreparable negative impression that will have a devastating impact on our careers and social lives. Most of the time this is simply not true.

Gain perspective by asking yourself these questions before and after you speak up:

- How do I *know* (objectively speaking) that it will be/was absolutely horrible?
- What is the *worst* thing that can happen? How likely is that to happen? And after the speaking engagement: *Did* it happen?

- If a disastrous outcome *did* actually happen, how can I recover from it? Am I doomed *forever* or is there something I can do to save face?
- Are there any potential *positive* outcomes that can occur if I speak less than perfectly?

When you answer these questions, you'll probably gain a new perspective and think differently about the thing you once feared.

Change Your Attention and Change Your Life

Your attention plays a highly important role in how anxious you feel. The more you focus on yourself, the more you will be self-conscious. The more self-conscious you are, the more the cycle of anxiety will spin out of control. The way to transform this process is to switch your focus to something external. It is hard to change your focus, and doing so may take lots of practice. The key is to practice in situations that do not make you anxious, because changing focus will be more difficult to implement in fearful situations.

This is a critical point in overcoming speaking anxiety. Work on focusing externally rather than getting caught up in your worries, on uncomfortable physical feelings, and on all the things that you think are going wrong. Use your five senses to focus externally: Notice the smells in the air, the sights around you, the sounds, the feel of the air or ground under your feet, the appearance of people. The key to this process is to do it *nonjudgmentally*. Don't make interpretations about the things you observe—simply observe them.

Practice Exercises

1. *For five days in a row* have at least two conversations per day with someone with whom you're comfortable, such as a parent, spouse, child, or close friend. In the first conversation, keep your attention 100 percent on yourself. Try to say things very carefully and be aware of what is going on internally, such as

your thoughts and physical sensations. Notice what happens. For your second conversation, keep your attention 100 percent externally focused. Try to become immersed in the conversation and to focus on what the other person is saying. Notice any difference? In which conversation did you feel more relaxed and comfortable?

2. *For the next five days* practice the external attention conversation with someone with whom you are comfortable. Try to make your focus 100 percent external and hone your abilities to focus on what the person is saying, how he or she looks, how he or she sounds, and so on.

3. *Practice anytime.* You can also practice focusing externally in nonspeaking activities. Mindfulness skills in which you remain completely focused on what you're doing in the present will help you learn to gain control over your attention. For example, if you're going for a walk, keep yourself grounded in the moment (and not caught up in your own thoughts) by feeling the breeze, smelling the cut grass, and listening to the sounds around you. Practice at least one mindfulness-type activity per day in which you are externally focused and completely present in the moment.

4. *Start tackling more challenging situations.* Now begin practicing the external attention talks in progressively more difficult situations. Make a list of 10 situations in their order of difficulty. For instance, if you have 10 people at work with whom you can talk, rank them in order of who you are most comfortable with, who is easiest to talk to, and who you know best. Have conversations first with the people who are easier for you and move up to the more difficult ones.

5. *Practice positive visualization and mental rehearsal.* Think of exactly how you want to look and feel as you're speaking in public. Create a five-minute visual narrative of yourself in your feared situation. In your mind's eye, you are calm, at ease, and confident. You are delivering your speech well and are engaged in conversation—in short, you appear however you want to

appear to your audience. Go through this image in your mind twice every day. Note how you feel after you've practiced this image. Once you become skilled at eliciting this image, use it strategically before your talking engagements. As you practice, make the image shorter and shorter so that with time you have reduced the essence of the scene into a two-second image.

Change Those Anxiety-Increasing Actions

The action most correlated with anxiety is *avoidance*. Whenever you avoid something intimidating, you not only miss out on learning that you *can* do it, but you also increase your anxiety about attempting to do it the next time. Over time, the more you avoid something, the more anxious you become about it, and the less likely it is that you'll do it.

Avoidance comes in all shapes and sizes. It's often tricky and subtle, so we need to be on the lookout everywhere so that we can eliminate it. What speaking situations do you avoid? Use the Finding Your Avoidance worksheet to identify avoided situations. Once you learn what you avoid, you can start facing those fears, which we discuss in the next step.

Stop Avoiding, Start Doing

What do you think we will say about avoiding speaking situations? If you're thinking we'll tell you to *stop avoiding*, you're absolutely right. Avoidance is the number one factor that maintains speaking anxiety. Once you can see exactly what types of things you've been avoiding, it's time to start doing them. Remember this: *Stop avoiding, start doing!*

The key is not only to do the things on this list, but to do them without the overcompensating behaviors, with your new way of thinking, and with your attention focused externally. Write down the avoided situation you will practice: to explore how anxious you thought it would make you, to record the behavior that you will practice, and to note how anxious you actually felt in the situation. Rank your activities in order of difficulty and then begin with the ones that feel a little easier. Take a few

FINDING YOUR AVOIDANCE

Avoided Situation	Check Here If You Avoided
1. Going to a party	☐
2. Speaking up at a meeting	☐
3. Talking with strangers	☐
4. Speaking about yourself	☐
5. Being the center of attention	☐
6. Introducing yourself to a stranger	☐
7. Calling a stranger on the telephone	☐
8. Giving a presentation	☐
9. Answering a question	☐
10. Participating in a small group	☐
11. Talking to an authority figure	☐
12. Having a conversation with someone intimidating	☐
13. Volunteering to give a talk or training	☐
14. Appropriately disagreeing with someone	☐
15. Talking in front of a large group	☐
16. Introducing yourself or someone else	☐
17. Talking for as long as you could/should have	☐
18. Saying something spontaneously	☐
19. Asking a question	☐
20. Returning a phone call	☐
21. Expressing your opinions	☐
22. Disagreeing with someone	☐
23. Leaving telephone messages	☐

minutes to plan situations and behaviors to practice (in order of difficulty), and to see that anticipatory anxiety is often higher than actual anxiety. Realizing that anticipatory anxiety may be futile can help dissipate it or make it less intense before a speaking situation.

Nix the Nervous Behaviors

Do you notice yourself doing little things when you're nervous that seem to be like nervous habits? These might include pacing around, shifting your weight, playing with something in your hands, giggling, jiggling change in your pocket, or saying "um" or "you know" a lot.

Nervous behaviors are different from overcompensating behaviors in that they are manifestations of anxiety, whereas overcompensating behaviors are things you do to try to hide your anxiety from others or make yourself feel less anxious.

In general, nervous behaviors tend to increase anxiety and make your anxiety more obvious to others. They can also be distracting for the audience, ultimately making your listeners appear less engaged and you more nervous, so it is a good idea to stop doing them.

Proceed with caution, however. Why? Do you remember our discussion about the importance of where you focus your attention? We want you to practice focusing your attention externally. What do you think happens if you're saying to yourself, "Okay, do not pace and do not say 'um' and do not giggle . . . "? Your attention will shift internally, and you're likely to feel more anxious.

Therefore, getting rid of nervous behaviors is an advanced skill to practice *after* you've mastered the art of controlling how you focus your attention. The time to start eliminating nervous behaviors is when you can easily shift your attention back to external after you think about what you'll try not to do. Practice the above attention exercises several times before working on eliminating the nervous behaviors. Also keep in mind that many nervous behaviors disappear on their own as you gain practice, change your focus of attention, beat negative thoughts, and feel less anxious. This is why it's better to work on the other strategies first before focusing on nervous behaviors.

Overcome Overcompensating Behaviors

As you now know, the problem with overcompensating behaviors is twofold: that you'll think you won't speak well without these behaviors and that these behaviors often make you more anxious and thus come across poorly to others. Even though they are designed to make you feel less anxious, overcompensating behaviors often work in the opposite way. The more you focus on trying to do these behaviors, the more you will be focusing on yourself. This makes your focus internal and can cause you to become self-conscious and therefore more nervous and uncomfortable.

These types of behaviors can actually impair your speaking performance. Picture yourself having a conversation with someone else. You're trying to be careful about saying only interesting things and not saying stupid or silly things. So you carefully go over what you're going to say in your mind before you say it. How does this look to the other person? It probably looks a bit unnatural, forced, or awkward. The person you're talking to is likely to think that you are not really into the conversation, which in fact is the case because you are into your own thoughts.

Still not sure if this is true for you or if you're ready to let go of these behaviors? Try these practice exercises to find out.

Practice Exercises

1. Have conversations with people in which you practice using and not using your favorite overcompensating behaviors. Have two conversations with the same person, using the behavior in one conversation and not using it in the other. For instance, if you're nervous about appearing too self-centered, and as a result you often try not to talk about yourself much, in one conversation be very careful about how you're coming across by not talking about yourself. In the next conversation, offer a few points about yourself and see which conversation goes better. Try this type of thing several times to learn how helpful these behaviors truly are.

2. Practice giving presentations without the typical overcompensating behaviors you would normally use.

3. If you use the common behavior of trying to write out what you will say in meetings, try to make at least two completely spontaneous comments in every meeting. Do not think about what you'll say at all; just open your mouth and start speaking.

4. If you use the common behavior of making sure you look as perfect as possible before all eyes are on you, practice speaking without looking perfect. Mess up your hair a bit, wear an unironed shirt, go without full makeup, or whatever idea makes you nervous. Then go out and talk to five people. Observe how the conversations go. Do they go fine? People probably don't even notice these aspects of your appearance, and this shows you how unimportant overcompensating behaviors actually are. Do the conversations go worse? If so, it could be because you're acting with less confidence and comfort, and this demonstrates that how you act is more important than how you look.

Put Down That Drink

Okay, we're not telling you that you can never enjoy your favorite gin and tonic or glass of merlot. What we *are* telling you is to stop drinking in situations where you normally do *because* you think a drink or two or three will help you be more comfortable and speak better.

For many people, alcohol actually serves as an overcompensating behavior. You may think that you're more sociable, more friendly, and less inhibited when you have a few drinks in your system, and in fact this may be true. Why? It's likely because you may become less focused on yourself when you've had some drinks. Have you ever had a few drinks in a situation where you normally would have been embarrassed or insecure but had the thought: I don't really care? This attitude *can* reduce anxiety.

There is evidence that some alcohol consumption actually intensifies a current emotion. So if you're feeling nervous, alcohol can increase nervousness. Plus, alcohol can interfere with our ability to control our emotions and can cause us to act in a manner that is unlikely to be helpful.

Even if you're someone who finds that a drink or two can be comforting, if you feel you need a couple of drinks to get to that point, it can become a problem. You probably can't bring a martini into the boardroom, and you can't take a swig from a flask before answering questions in a conversation (well, you could, but that might not be the impression you want to make), so let's help you relax without the alcohol.

Another problem with relying on alcohol is that often you may think you're speaking better after having had a few drinks, but in reality you're speaking less effectively. We have all seen people who get annoyingly loud, boisterous, or inappropriate when they drink. Why should you take this risk?

And of course there are all of the health and social problems that come with using alcohol to deal with nervousness about speaking. Bottom line: Using alcohol is not an effective way to help you improve your speaking. Think about this scenario: Mary goes out to happy hour with some colleagues at work. She is nervous about what she will say to them, how she'll come across, and that she may not have answers to questions people ask her. Mary arrives at the bar at 6:00 p.m. She sees her colleagues and thinks, Okay, I need to get a drink right away. She says hello to a few people and gets up to the bar at 6:15 p.m. She orders a drink and finishes it by 6:35. She gets a second drink and finishes it around 7:00 p.m. At this point she's feeling a little calmer and thinks, Good thing I had those two chardonnays. I feel much better now.

Why does Mary feel better at 7:00 p.m? Is it because of the chardonnays? Actually, it may have nothing to do with the wine. Remember the principle of habituation? It is the idea that anxiety naturally diminishes when you keep yourself in a situation. It's quite possible that Mary's anxiety would have been reduced an equal amount in an hour by virtue of her being in the situation for one hour. She may have simply habituated to the anxiety and overcome the anticipatory and initial anxiety of a new situation.

If this is true, it's a shame that she could not have found out that she could have handled the situation just fine without the drinks. From the scenario above, Mary walks away thinking that she can be fine with work associates *if* she has a couple of drinks first. What if she walked away thinking, I really can speak well with colleagues. I may be a bit nervous at first, but that goes away, and then I'm pretty comfortable.

Believe it or not, we also recommend that you put down your glass of water during your talk, because holding a glass of water or drinking water can be an overcompensating behavior. Dry mouth is a common symptom of anxiety. It does not mean that you're thirsty, and drinking a lot of water will not cure it. Professional speaking expert Lilly Walters recommends that those who experience dry mouth picture in their minds a juicy lemon and then lightly bite the inside of their cheek or press their tongue to the top of their mouth. If you can suck on hard candy or chew gum, that can help stimulate saliva production as well.

Practice Exercises

1. Try going to a party, a happy hour, or a social event where you normally would consume alcohol to feel calmer and instead have a soda or other nonalcoholic drink. Do not do this just once, because it will feel strange and different the first time; instead do it 10 times before coming to a conclusion.
2. Give a toast at a gathering or wedding without first drinking alcohol.
3. Try making yourself the center of attention by telling a story to a group of people without first drinking alcohol.
4. Minimize your water intake during a talk and try some of the strategies above instead.

Putting the Thoughts and Behaviors Together

Can you see how your thoughts and actions influence one another? At this point you should see how the big culprits of speaking anxiety (distorted thinking, self-focused attention, avoidance, and overcompensating behaviors) have been maintaining your fear. You've learned some strategies to change these things—now it's up to you to use them!

In the next chapter you'll begin to learn how to use your body, face, and voice to improve your confidence and speaking abilities even more.

9

Using Your Body, Face, and Voice

OUR BODY, FACE, and voice comprise a whopping 93 percent of all of our communication efforts, according to an oft-cited study conducted in the early 1970s at the University of California at Los Angeles. You'll learn more about the study and the social scientist who conducted it later in this chapter. Suffice it to say for now that in order to become a confident speaker, learning the language of the face, the body, and the voice is critical to your development as a compelling conversationalist and a persuasive presenter. Rest assured also that your audiences will be vocally or silently grateful if you're not one of those boring dullards who relies on the content and the words of their message alone to get the point across. You've been an audience before, a bored or puzzled one likely, so no doubt you understand what we mean.

The chapter you're about to read will give you the insights you need to compel audiences with all of your communication channels. Your body, face, and voice are your keys to being a charismatic speaker. And when you're charismatic, people are more prone to like you, buy from you, or help you out. Before beginning this chapter, test your natural charisma quotient. Go to www.TheConfidentSpeaker.com and take our free quiz: "What's Your Charisma Quotient?" Then, as you read through this chapter, think about how the points you learn can help you become even more charismatic.

Your Body Language Speaks Volumes

What is commonly referred to as "body language" includes our gestures, facial expressions, and other visuals that people perceive as they watch and listen to us. Too often speakers focus only on their gestures, neglecting other important aspects of the nonverbal communications they project.

Aside from the way we use our hands and facial expressions, our audiences draw important conclusions about us by how energetic we appear, our posture and stance, our movement, the quality and ensemble of our clothes, the presence or lack of jewelry, how healthy and fit we seem, and our grooming, among many other signals.

For the occasional speaker this may seem like an overwhelming list of issues to consider, especially without the input of a qualified coach. The truth, however, is that we often need to make only minor adjustments to communicate with more impact and credibility.

Harrison had a client whose business was financial consulting for a Big Five firm. Upon meeting the client for the first time, Harrison noticed his oversized shirts. The client tried to cover up his self-perceived flaw of a few extra pounds with shirts that were two sizes too big. The result was exactly what he was trying to avoid. On camera and to his audience, he came across as being bigger than he actually was. Harrison suggested he get a couple of shirts that fit him well and come back wearing them for his second day of coaching. The client immediately saw the difference in the playback of the tape and was astounded by how "svelte" he appeared.

How can we know when we send unintended nonverbal signals? Like Harrison's client, we often need to seek input from others who know what to look for. Whom we ask can make all the difference, however.

Tape Yourself

The camera doesn't lie, and the use of video for feedback and critique is imperative when we coach clients. Considering the ubiquity of the camcorder, it is surprising how few of our clients have ever seen themselves on videotape before.

Taping your performance is the next best thing to personal coaching. While on video, we see ourselves from the second perspective, that of the audience. Try to be objective and look at everything from your hair, to your dress, to your posture, to your gestures and the way you move. Take note of everything that stands out for you. Divide your list into positives and negatives.

The next step is to turn off the sound and just focus on your body language, facial expressions, and movements. Does what you see appear fluid and in control and positioned toward the (imagined) audience, or do you see lots of distracting motion such as swaying, fidgeting, unnecessary gesturing? Do you see no movement at all? Also look for your overall energy. Do you appear dynamic and enthusiastic, or does your face say, "I'd rather be sailing"?

When we look at footage of ourselves, we may have difficulty judging our own behavior objectively. To get the most from your taped rehearsal performance, assemble a team of advisors who commit to giving you their honest feedback regardless of your relationship with them. It's often easier for someone not too close to you to give objective feedback on your nonverbal communication. Try to go beyond your inner circle of family and friends and recruit others whose opinions you respect. This could include your boss, a colleague, someone from your church, or members of other organizations to which you belong. Unless you're working with a qualified communications coach, be sure to get more than one person's feedback.

Myths About Eye Contact

Angela was nervous. She had a hard time looking into the eyes of her audience. As a young start-up entrepreneur looking for funding, she was several minutes into her presentation to a small group of venture capital investors when she remembered what her high school public speaking coach kept preaching about eye contact. Whenever she felt nervous and at risk of losing her train of thought, all she had to do was to focus on her material and find a spot on the wall just above the heads of her audience. That way they'd still feel as though she was looking at them, without her having to look directly into their eyes. And if the group was smaller and this strategy was too obvious to the audience, she was to focus on a spot right between the eyes of the person she was directing her talk to at the time, thereby avoiding the "dreaded" direct gaze of the critical observer.

The problem with the first strategy, Angela found, was that every once in a while some of the people to whom she was talking would turn around to the back of the room, wondering what the heck she was looking at. "Did someone enter the room?" their puzzled expressions seemed to ask. "What's on the back wall that's so interesting?"

If you've ever tried tricks like these from well-meaning "public speaking experts," you're not alone. For many novice speakers, eye contact is one of the most intimidating aspects of the public speaking and interpersonal communication process. And it is undoubtedly the most critical as far as building rapport and conveying your emotions and attitude toward the audience is concerned.

What is it about meeting someone's gaze that many speakers find so threatening? When others look at us for an extended amount of time, even just a few seconds, our sympathetic nervous system gets a jolt, causing us to respond by either returning the gaze or glancing away. One social researcher suggests that the reason we avert our gaze from someone else's is because the retina in our eyes is an outgrowth of the forebrain, and that "peering into someone else's eyes is not unlike seeing into the brain itself." Indeed, in our experience many reluctant speakers report that they "feel" that the audience can *see* how nervous they are.

Nevertheless, when you make effective eye contact as you communicate your message to an audience, you signal your attention to them.

Not only does this let your listeners know that you're speaking directly to them, but it also shows that you're seeking a connection with them.

Another reason for the importance of eye contact is that you can both give and receive feedback. By paying attention to the physiological reactions of your listeners—facial expressions, head movements, body positioning, and so on—you can draw conclusions about the effect you are having on them at any point, thus allowing you to modify your approach as necessary.

The Myths and the Reality

Tricks such as looking at a point above the audience's head on the back wall and focusing on the area between their eyes are representative of the safety and avoidance behaviors we want you to stop doing. We consider them myths. You will achieve a more favorable outcome and feel less anxious when you abandon them.

Here are five myths that belong in the public speaking and interpersonal communications "Hall of Lame" because they encourage bad habits that are anything but helpful in building a connection with people or getting your message across in a talk.

Maintain Eye Contact for Three to Five Seconds
Rules like these only serve to keep you out of the moment when you're speaking to others. In other words, you are so busy counting seconds that you don't pay attention to the true connection you're creating with your audience. In order to be fully present, mentally and physically, connect with as many audience members as you can by looking them in the eyes and mentally asking them for a response.

When you converse with someone, you would usually speak in a way that inspires feedback. You would be doing things such as nodding, narrowing or widening your eyes, smiling, frowning, and making vocal sounds of understanding like "Uh-huh" or "Hmm." Naturally, you don't count to five when you do this, because you can sense when it's time to look away and then look at the person again. The length of time you'd look into someone's eyes depends on the response you want. If you look at an audience member and ask, half rhetorically, "Wouldn't you wish for a better future for your kids?" chances are the person you're looking at will nod to signal agreement. You'll see others nodding too, because they will feel addressed by you as well.

How long will it take? Who knows, a second, maybe two. Or it could be you won't get a response at all because the person doesn't have any kids, and perhaps will look away. Don't dwell on it; move to someone else as you present your next thought. And if you don't ask a question but instead give an explanation or instruction of sorts, how long will you look at an individual audience member? Until you either perceive a physiological response or you complete a thought or point you're making. Harrison makes a point of establishing meaningful eye contact with every audience member if the group is of a manageable size and he can see the eyes of his listeners. That way everyone is included and remains engaged. The only truth to this myth is to not frantically scan back and forth as you look at the audience.

Picture the Audience Naked

This is another one of those safety behaviors that take you out of the moment and prevent you from being fully present. This advice sprung from the idea that the audience will seem less threatening when you "see" them naked. It doesn't work. Neither does picturing them in the first grade. Instead, try to perceive as much from the real audience as you can. Notice their clothing, their eyes, their hairstyles, and their body positioning. The more you deal with what you perceive to be present, the better your connection with your listeners will be.

Focus on Friendly Faces and Speak to Them

The good news is that there is always a friendly face. The bad news is that most of the audience may look less friendly and might appear neutral or even wear a frown. What are you going to do about them? Ignore them? Pay less attention to them? They need you just as much as the happy faces that make you feel safe, so don't leave them hanging.

Just because audience members have blank or neutral facial expressions does not make them unfriendly. Often when we concentrate, we take on an almost frowning expression that people perceive as angry or upset. Catch yourself sometime when you're thinking, focusing on something, or watching TV. Are you smiling? Probably not—and neither is your audience. A reason could be that they're captivated by your talk.

Maintain Constant Eye Contact

There are those who subscribe to the motto, "There's never too much of a good thing," and eye contact is good, right? Few things that are taken to an extreme have a positive outcome. Give people a break, literally, when speaking to them. Break eye contact to give your listener an emotional moment to breathe, because eye contact arouses emotions, and to overdo it means you are exhausting your communication partners.

Take your cues from other people by closely observing and noticing how they make eye contact. If they tend to look at you with brief glances and keep looking away while talking, match your gaze rhythm to theirs. Similarly, if they look at you while speaking but take little breaks by looking up or down at certain intervals, do likewise. By matching the eye contact habits of your counterparts, you are creating an atmosphere of synergy, which can never be a bad thing in communication. You'll also avoid making other people feel uncomfortable with a steady gaze that could be seen as domineering or confrontational.

Those Who Avoid Looking You in the Eye Can't Be Trusted

Sometimes this may hold true, but just as often it doesn't. This piece of advice must be taught in the world's Armchair Psychology 101 courses, because it is widely accepted as common sense. That's probably why so many people get duped by the con artists of the world who have also taken this "course" and have no trouble looking someone in the eye while telling a big fat lie. As we mentioned above, eye contact behavior can vary from person to person and should always be considered within the context of the situation.

Your Voice: Liability or Asset?

Now that you have a better grasp on what is real and what is myth in the art of speaking confidently, we'll have a closer look at one part of your communication that is as real and as personal to you as it gets—your voice. Many people have strong feelings about their instrument and the sounds it emits. If you're one of them, we say "Good for you." Because as you'll learn in this section, a natural and pleasant voice can lift your message into hearts and minds with ease, whereas a whiny and nasally voice can get an audience to shut off their mental receptors before the first bathroom break.

If you belong to the latter group of the vocally challenged, don't despair. Just read on and learn how you can improve your horn to the point where the audience focuses on your message and not the sound carrying it.

> When Ted walked into the lobby of our offices to discuss presentation coaching, we were surprised. After speaking on the phone with him several times over the last week, we expected to meet someone much younger. His appearance and body language were those of a 40-year-old man, but his voice sounded like that of an 18-year-old. On the phone, we hadn't discussed any kind of voice coaching, and as we talked about his options for presentations training, we asked him if he'd ever gotten any feedback about his voice. He nodded and said that over the phone he occasionally he gets mistaken for a woman, while at other times people ask him if they could speak to a manager at his office, thinking that he's an intern or recent graduate due to the higher pitch and nasal tone of his voice. He told us that the gender confusion bothers him less than being mistaken for a "kid." Upon learning that Ted was in the business of selling commercial real estate, his challenge became quite clear.

The sound of someone's voice creates a distinct first impression, particularly at an initial meeting in person and over the telephone. We make snap judgments about someone's character after hearing him or her speak, often labeling the person with a nasal voice as difficult, whiny, and with an attitude. People who have a monotonous voice with little or no inflection are perceived to lack enthusiasm, while a soft and thin voice is often thought to be a sure sign of those who are insecure or immature. Likewise, people who tend to speak fast and have a louder than average voice can be seen as pushy, aggressive, or manipulative.

While these characterizations may be unfair and not at all based in reality, they may be your audience's and clients' perceptions of you, and it might determine how your interaction will unfold.

In the example above, Ted had a problem with his perceived credibility due to his higher-pitched, younger-sounding voice. In a business where credibility is initially established over the telephone, especially where multi-million-dollar projects are transacted, a strong, warm, and confident voice is a definite asset.

Besides being a component in our perceived credibility, the effects of our vocal tonality often determine how likable we come across to others. We may like the head of marketing whose voice is deep and and reassuring, while the senior VP of human resources grates on our nerves with "pipes" that sound high-pitched, whiny, and nasal. How would you feel about attending a 90-minute training and development session with this VP as the presenter? Chances are you'd tune out early to avoid what you perceive to be an assault on your ears. That of course can be bad for you, as you may be missing out on important information, and bad for the presenter, as a tuned-out audience is as effective as a room full of empty chairs in accomplishing one's objective.

Your voice is either an asset or a liability in the way you come across to others. Realizing this is the first step in improving your impact on your public.

You Are What You Sound Like

Why is it that we place so much value on the sound and quality of someone's voice? Can we truly make assumptions about someone's character and personality based on vocal tonality?

Research says yes. A professor of psychology at UCLA, Dr. Albert Mehrabian, conducted a series of communication exercises in 1972 and found that we draw 38 percent of the meaning from another human's communication from vocal tonality. The study further concluded that nonverbal communication is responsible for a whopping 55 percent of the meaning of the message. That leaves just 7 percent of the meaning to the words.

You've heard the saying, "It's not *what* you say, it's *how* you say it"? Try this experiment: Tape yourself saying the phrase in quotes below in the most neutral way possible. Don't cheat here, as you need to listen to the playback in order to get the full effect. If you can't tape it, ask some friends to listen to you and have them give you feedback as to the *meaning* they take from the different ways you say the phrase.

"I knew you'd be here."

Now that you've said this in a neutral and unemotional way, infuse different meanings into the same words. Say the same phrase alternately sounding angry, joyous, surprised, hurt, scared, sad, sarcastic, triumphant, disgusted, tired, accusing, and seductive.

You've just given the same little five-word sentence 12 different meanings. As you can hear, the sound of your voice carries all of the meaning.

We often communicate carelessly, thinking that our words should do the talking, but the fact is that most people make judgments about us on a subconscious rather than a conscious level. These judgments are far less subject to rational analysis than conscious thought, and thus much more powerful and persuasive in directing others' gut feelings about us. So, if you want your audience to get the "right" message, make sure you make your voice match your words.

Mastering Voice Projection, Inflection, and Delivery

If the sound of your vocal instrument is less than compelling, there are several ways you can improve the situation.

The key to all of this is *variety*. In the age of 800 cable channels, 24-hour news programming, and downloadable audio content from a million sources, variety is not only the spice of life, it's also a necessity in keeping your audience's stimuli-bombarded minds from wandering and to emphasize your main points. Make sure you vary your rate of speaking (from fast to slow), your volume (from loud to a whisper), and make liberal use of pauses to lend emphasis and salience to a thought and of inflection to give meaning to your words. The drama in your talk derives from the vocal contrast that you give it.

Here are the main points for giving your voice full power:

1. *Pronounce and enunciate.* Your diction should be distinct. Don't swallow syllables and endings; articulate the consonants and enunciate the vowels. Lazy speech is learned, and it can be unlearned. Listen to newscasters, the good ones like Tom Brokaw, Brian Williams, and Ted Koppel. Buy audio books narrated by Charlton Heston and James Earl Jones and tune into BBC once in a while—not to acquire a faux British accent, but to listen to the origins of the English language and see how proper diction is practiced.

2. *Modulate and inflect.* Monotonous speakers are the pits. They come. They bore. They achieve nothing but annoy the audience. A monotonous teacher can make a student's favorite class seem like sleep deprivation torture. To avoid the label "Tedious Bore," vary the pitch from a benign word to one you want to burn into the minds of your audience. Inflection creates interest in what you have to say. It's the tonal ups and downs you infuse into your sentence that give it meaning and make your listeners' ears perk up. Inflection can turn a question into a statement and vice versa. This is the music that carries the words of your talk into the hearts and minds of your audience.

   For a demonstration of the effective use of modulation and inflection, tune in to any Sunday morning televangelist. Billy Graham was the "Altmeister" of this form of speaking, but the apprentices that followed in his footsteps are just as effective in capturing the attention of millions. Look for the broadcasts of Joel Osteen, T. D. Jakes, and the older programs of Billy Graham and listen to how they give weight to their words with their voices. Emulate them and create your own speech, or get your hands on some poetry to read aloud. Rehearse in the shower or in the car on your way to work. If monotony in speaking is your affliction, you'll soon start noticing improvement.

3. *Project.* If people can't hear you, they can't respond—emotionally or behaviorally. To project effectively, you must propel your words to your listeners. This doesn't mean shouting. Just make sure you have enough air in your lungs. Then tighten your abdominal muscles to give your words velocity as you utter them. Good posture is critical here, as your airways need to be unobstructed to allow for good propulsion.

   Try this for a quick demo: Point your chin toward your sternum, form an O with your lips, and make a sound. Remember the sound. Now tilt your head all the way back and do the same thing. Remember that sound too. Now keep your head erect and make the O sound. Notice the difference? Your sound is clearer and deeper. As you increase your volume, your pitch will get higher, but if you keep your airways flowing without obstruction, your pitch won't sound too high but rather clear and rich. So remember: Keep your head from tilting up or down, and your voice will sound its most natural and compelling.

4. *Vary pace and rhythm.* If you keep one speed during your talk, it's a bit like driving in second gear wherever you go in your car—it's bound to be too slow or too fast at one point or another. When speaking conversationally, it pays to match your speaking rate to that of your counterpart, as it establishes rapport more quickly. When you speak to a group of people or a larger audience, make sure you vary the pace of speaking depending on the level of complexity of your talk and the emphasis you want to create as you speak.

   Most people speak at a rate of 150 words per minute but listen at a rate of 800 words per minute. If you speak too slowly, minds will wander; if you speak too quickly, your audience will get exhausted and tune out, not to mention miss half of what you're saying. Emphasis can be achieved with a rhythmic delivery that changes pace according to the different parts your message.

5. *Pause.* This is the "queen" of the speech, and arguably the most underused and underrated component of the spoken word. Some speakers mistake their delivery for an AK–47, firing their words at the audience in relentless fashion. A large part of meaning is created in the pause. A moment of deliberate silence, even in mid-sentence, to let poignant words sink in, promotes understanding and clarity. It lets your message reverberate in the minds of your listeners, giving them a moment to process what you just said. It also creates a bit of drama, because who knows what's coming next? Watch their faces as they anticipate your next dose of wisdom. It takes a bit of courage, but the pause is the tool of the master. It increases exponentially your impact on your audience.

Your voice is a powerful instrument. It brings your words to life and adds meaning where ambiguity would otherwise reign. If people compliment you on your voice, consider yourself lucky, because you obviously please the ear. Now all you have to do is heed the advice above to deliberately train your pipes to create maximum vocal impact with your message every time you speak in public.

If you're unhappy with your voice, and children run when you offer to read to them, there's hope. Unless your problem is pathological in nature, in which case you should seek the services of a trained therapist, there is much you can do to improve the sound that comes from your chest. Practice what we've taught here and your credibility will soar, and audiences will stay tuned in to what you have to say, instead of mentally changing channels.

What Your Face Can't Hide

Let's revisit our client example of Martin, the man who dreaded questions during a speech.

Martin stood in front of the assembled crowd. He was about to give a talk to a sympathetic and anticipating audience of prospective clients who where looking to choose the "right" architectural firm for a large construction project. Martin was one of the architectural firm's key designers, and he needed to convince his audience that they were in good hands with his firm and that he understood the job and the needs of the client better than anyone else they invited to bid so far. Yet when he started to speak, thanking the audience for the opportunity to present to them and telling them that he was excited to share his firm's vision with them, his face betrayed him. There was no sign of joy, nor was there even a hint of excitement or any other positive emotion on his face. His words were in sharp contrast to the emotions he felt and portrayed. Martin felt as if his facial muscles were frozen in place. Unable to muster a smile during his introduction, or even a neutral relaxed facial expression, he looked tense, uncomfortable, and anxious.

Like Martin, many of us mirror in our faces what we're feeling inside. When people say, "He wears his heart on his sleeve," they mean that they can clearly see in someone's face how that person is feeling. For the most part, it's very difficult for us to conceal our moods from others. Every emotion is reflected in the expressions our faces make. In times of severe stress, such as when we're subjecting ourselves to the critical appraisal of an audience, the eyes may quickly dart from focal point to focal point, while the corners of the mouth draw downward, brows furrow, and the muscles of the chin or lips start twitching. It doesn't take much for others to correctly guess at the status of our inner lives with faces that can't hide the truth.

Should You Adopt a Poker Face?

When you're at the dealership shopping for a new car and your eyes turn the size of saucers at the sight of the latest model BMW, and your mouth hangs wide open in a moment of detached bliss and admiration, you'll be no match for a veteran sales pro when it comes to negotiating the price on your dream ride. The salespeople at the dealership are trained to watch your face as you browse the showroom, and they can easily tell when you have emotionally already decided on a particular car. Now they just have to make it financially feasible for you.

Similarly, at the office your boss has just given you an unexpected assignment that will put you even further behind with your workload than you already are. You try to smile and tell her that it shouldn't be a problem to have it all done by Monday morning. After all, your annual review is coming up, and you want to show that you can handle what's thrown at you. But as you're about to turn on your heel to walk out of her office, she asks, "Is everything okay?"

"Oh yeah," you say in mock surprise, "I'm fine."

But something in your expression lets her sense that you're distraught and emotionally at odds with your semicheerful smile.

So what we often do is to try to mask our emotions by putting on a "poker face." We think that nobody will know what we're really feeling if we just keep a straight face and appear as neutral as possible, or at least try to portray an emotion we feel is appropriate for the situation. To fool others completely, we even manage to fake a decent smile here and there, provided the situation is not too stressful or threatening.

The problem with this is that as we're constantly training ourselves to mask our emotions, we eventually project nothing but dull and blank expressions, even when we're trying to connect with our audiences as communicators. We become accustomed to hiding our true feelings, and when we need to show empathy, enthusiasm, and passion, we can't get them past our trained-on facial masks.

In his book *Emotional Intelligence*, author Daniel Goleman writes about the importance of recognizing the feelings of others and reacting to them with empathy. He asserts that we should be able to feel what someone else is feeling and respond empathetically to establish an emotional connection. We cannot accomplish this important connection with our audience with a protective poker face. While a neutral facial expression can be helpful in situations when showing our emotions may have negative personal consequences, the key in connecting with our audience lies not in hiding our emotions but rather in channeling, directing, and matching them to the emotions we want to create in our listeners.

To Smile or Not to Smile

A study conducted during the 1984 presidential campaign tells of the late ABC News anchor Peter Jennings's tendency to smile more when he spoke on the air of incumbent president Ronald Reagan than when he spoke of his challenger, Walter Mondale. The study showed that viewers who watched ABC News during that year proportionally voted in higher numbers for Reagan than those viewers who watched other news programs. Just a coincidence, or is there more to it? Can a smile influence the decisions of millions of people to vote for one candidate versus another in a presidential election?

The business world certainly thinks so. During the latter part of the 1990s, U.S. supermarket chain Safeway Corp. mandated that its employees smile at each customer they made eye contact with. Their marketing brass concluded that this would make customers feel more welcome and that they would thus spend more time and money in the stores. Eventually, this mandatory smile policy appeared to produce some undesirable side effects, as female store clerks reported unwelcome sexual advances by male customers who seemed to mistake the beaming smiles as come-ons by the clerks. At least 12 female Safeway workers reportedly filed grievances with their employer.

The fact is, however, that from Finland to the Fijis, the smile is a universally recognized form of communication that can put people at ease and warm them up to you. The genuine smile is an expression of a pleasant emotional reaction. We also use smiling deliberately to create and enhance social rapport with others. In awkward interpersonal situations, a smile can ease tension and add meaning to an otherwise ambiguous message. The key to making this most effective rapport builder work for you, however, is to make sure your smile is sincere and not perfunctory.

We see the fake version every day, from people who try to sell us something we don't need, coworkers who congratulate us on the promotion they deep-down-inside feel they deserved more than we did, and the romantic interest who doesn't want to hurt our feelings and puts on a show to conceal his or her true emotions. Rarely, though, are we actually fooled by the insincere smiler. We intuitively know that we're being given a performance and not the real thing. But how do we know? What is it about someone's smile that gives him or her away as being phony as opposed to being genuine?

Researchers have found that during a real or genuine smile, we activate a number of facial muscles. We contract the *orbicular muscles* of the lower eyelids instead of just the *zygomaticus major* muscle, which is the principal muscle in the lower face, and, according to one researcher, likely the only active muscle in the lower face.

Can you rehearse and "fake" a genuine smile? You most certainly can, as a small and very exclusive group of professionals have proven time and time again. They dazzle us with "genuine" smiles on command and make us believe the emotion. They are called Oscar-winning actors. There is of course more to it, as many of these masters of their trade are actually able to summon the emotions that lie at the foundation of the genuine smile. In other words, they actually "feel" the joy before they project it with the entire face, including the eyes. We've all seen the ones whose performances we don't "buy." It's because we sense that the emotion is disingenuous and not actually felt. The nonverbal cues don't match the words the actors are saying.

So how do you avoid the fate of being labeled as insincere, phony, or awkward when you speak to others even when you're smiling?

The answer is simple and challenging at once. You have to feel the emotion. If you can't, don't force the smile. If, however, you can instantaneously find something, the smallest thing, in the corners of your mind, that can make you smile, use it. But be careful that it doesn't take you out of the moment with your audience. Relate it to what you're talking about. Most topics can be connected to universal experiences we share with other members of the audience. It could be the birth of your child, the purchase of your dream home, thoughts of a loved one, chasing your puppy around the house, making money, closing a big contract, accomplishing an important goal, or simply the joy and gratitude of being able to share your message with this particular audience. With a genuine thought of joy going through your mind in less than a nanosecond, which is less than a billionth of a second, you have a source from which a genuine smile can radiate brightly.

Now there is a school of thought that says you can actually *feel* a certain way by *acting* a certain way first. The thinking here is that emotions follow behavior. An oft-cited social experiment refers to a "feedback smile" and states that the simple physiological act of smiling, even if you initially don't feel like it, can produce a faint feeling of happiness. Social scientists Stephen Davis and Joe Palladino assert that "feedback from facial expression [e.g., smiling or frowning] affects emotional expression and behavior."

One famous study had a number of participants watch cartoons while holding pencils between their teeth, producing physiological smiles. Another group was not allowed to smile. As a result, the group who created the artificial smiles with the pencils actually rated the cartoons funnier than the group instructed to keep their faces neutral. In other words, the feedback the first group's nervous systems received from the physiological action of smiling caused their moods to lighten and affected their emotional expressions and ultimately their behavior.

What Davis and Palladino found in their studies is also one of the bedrock principles of a popular movement called Neurolinguistic Programming, or NLP for short. NLP literature often refers to one's physiology as an underused resource that can be tapped for improvement of emotional states. In order to illustrate the effects body language has on one's emotional state, NLP practitioners frequently instruct their followers to try experiments such as pointing the chin toward the chest, slouching forward while slumping the shoulders, and shifting one's weight to one hip.

Can you easily think of any positive thoughts in this altered physiology? NLP says no. And what about the opposite approach? When you are emotionally and physically "down" and you alter your physiology so that you are standing up straight, with your head held high, your chest expanded with air, and your body weight fully centered on both hips and legs, do you feel an elevation in your mood? Is it easier to think positive thoughts and harder to think negative ones? Try it and see for yourself. If it works for you, it will be an easy way to help you shift from a bad mood into a more positive emotional state, thus helping you project a genuine smile that helps create critical rapport with your audiences. And there is one truth that requires no social experiment, and that is: When you smile at people, they usually smile back.

Choreography Is Not Just for Show Business

As Michael hears the words of the person introducing him, his knees start shaking and his palms turn noticeably clammy. I can do this, he thinks, wiping his hands across his pant legs under the table. As the welcoming applause starts and the master of ceremonies looks over at Michael with a nod and a smile, he gets up and slowly walks over to the podium, careful not to look at anyone for fear he might trip on the way to the stage. After adjusting the microphone on the podium, he grips the sides of the lectern with both hands, determined to hang on for dear life until his speech is over.

And so he does, mostly at the expense of the audience and the impact of his own message. People in speaking situations often think that simply standing in one spot—behind a lectern, for instance—as they unload a barrage of content on a stationary audience, is what's expected and accepted as standard.

What these speakers and presenters neglect to consider is the powerful impact purposeful movement and audience-centered nonverbal communication has. While the content of one's talk has to be well-researched, organized, and targeted to the audience, it is the ability to effectively convey the message nonverbally that will determine whether they will accept, retain, and act on the message.

It Starts with Your Walk

It actually starts with the visual signals people get from you the moment they see you, but the moment you get up from your chair to step into the spotlight, your audience will look for further clues as to your personality, temperament, credibility, and confidence. They'll notice if you slowly and sluggishly, perhaps reluctantly, rise up from your chair, or if you spring up with energy and stride confidently to meet them, ready to address the issues of the day.

Choreography describes the most effective predetermined and rehearsed series of steps and movement a performer presents to an audience. And while this term mostly refers to the world of entertainment and show business, its usefulness for those of us who are constantly presenting our *self* to others, either on a public stage or in interpersonal situations, should be noted and explored.

By "stage" we don't necessarily mean the kind that is elevated four feet above the audience and with a podium at its center; nor are we particularly referring to the kind of stage that has lights and cameras waiting for the performer's presentation. A "stage," as we use the term, is the general area you will use to communicate your ideas to your listeners and viewers. It could be the front of a boardroom, a seat at a conference room table, the area in front of the jury section in a courtroom, or the center of the living room at a dinner party.

Whatever your personal stage may be, you can plan and rehearse the most compelling entry and movement before your actual presentation. Practice getting up from a seated position and walking to your stage. Vary your pace, your step, and your overall movement. Observe the swing of your arms, the position of your head, and, most important, your posture.

Improve what you don't like until your choreography matches the impression you want your public to have of you as you step up to speak.

Find the ideal walk that demonstrates your confidence, fluidity, and eagerness to share yourself with your audience. Don't rush, do breathe deeply through your nose, and, if appropriate, acknowledge members of your audience as you make your way to the front of the group. If you've ever watched the Academy Awards and seen Oscar winners head to the stage, you'll notice that they greet other audience members and smile as they make their way to the microphone. Perhaps they close the button on a jacket and acknowledge applause with a wave. A similar ritual takes place with the U.S. president just before he gives the State of the Union address. As he makes his way into the Capitol, a well-rehearsed process takes place where he greets senators and shakes the hands of congressmen and -women and other guests on his walk to the podium.

You may not enjoy audiences as engaged or enthusiastic as those encountered at an Academy Awards ceremony or at a State of the Union address, but your audience will be watching your every move just the same.

Lights, Camera, Action

You're on, and the audience is anxiously awaiting your first word. The positive nonverbal impression you just created as you made your way to the front of the audience must now be reinforced.

You'll take a deep breath, again through your nose, before you say anything. Inhale and exhale at least once before speaking. Allow the audience to take you in visually before you address them audibly. This gives you a moment to center yourself with both feet firmly grounded. It also allows you to adjust your posture and collect your thoughts, giving your introductory sentence the necessary weight and attention it deserves.

As you stand ready to speak, notice your body weight evenly balanced on your legs and feet, firm but not stiff, flexible but not loose. You feel totally in control of the slightest change in your body position by consciously feeling the ground below your feet. As you move about the stage, you vary the distance between your feet, noticing how this influences your overall balance and body position. If your feet are too close together, you'll have less control over your movements and balance and send a signal of insecurity and reluctance to take charge of your territory. If, on the other hand, your feet are too far apart, you stand the risk of looking too aggressive; this will also limit your mobility unless you correct your position first by bringing your feet back together. Both positions look awkward and send the wrong signal to your audience.

By adopting a neutral stance, with both feet parallel to each other and approximately hip-width apart, you are in the best position to move around the stage as you interact with your audience and share your ideas.

Are You an Anchor or an Actor?

News anchors don't move around; they stand or sit in one spot throughout their presentations. Due to the nature of their objective and job description—to give you an unbiased account of the events and news of the day—there is no need or room for them to convey their personal emotions and unique perspectives on the issues. It is therefore sufficient for them just to deliver the information verbally, supported only by their vocal tonality.

If you tried to sell your audience on an idea, rouse them for a worthy cause, or convince them of the importance of a change in behavior, you would fail terribly in achieving your objective if you were to adopt the stationary style of the network news anchor. You most likely wouldn't be able to hold the attention of your audience very well either, which is why news programs are kept typically short and interspersed with audiovisual images, video and film clips, and several commercials.

Rarely is this talking-head presentation style appropriate in a business, professional, or social environment. It is appropriate only when the information can be conveyed in a brief and succinct communication session and does not require emotional involvement or action by an audience.

As we mentioned above, a more energetic and mobile nonverbal style is needed when you need to establish an emotional connection with your audience. This can be achieved only by using all of your communication channels, including the nonverbal channels of gestures, physical proximity to the audience, body positioning, and head movement.

The best actors in the business are able to convey authentic emotions with their interpretations of the physical lives of the characters they play. This skill draws their audiences into the stories and allows the audiences to suspend their disbelief. Like the actor, you too have to be aware of your stage and the way you use the space you're in. Your audience is watching closely. Make sure they stay tuned in.

The information in this chapter most likely confirmed what you already knew: Communicating with confidence requires the use of all of your senses and communication channels. You now know better than ever the important role your face, your body, and your vocal tonality play in connecting with others and getting your message across with maximum impact.

In the next chapter you'll learn how to boost even further the power of all your communication efforts by employing important techniques that will increase your confidence and spellbind your audience, just as the master orators you admire do.

10

Techniques to Increase Confidence

Courage is not the absence of fear, but rather the judgment that something else is more important than fear.

—AMBROSE REDMOON

If You Could Bottle It, You'd Be a Billionaire

We know when we're in its presence, because we can feel it. Without it, we're at the whim of those who have it, collecting their leftovers. It is undoubtedly a major key to social and professional success. What is "it"? It's called "confidence." If you could bottle it, you'd be a billionaire, because everyone would want some.

Confidence is power. When we feel confident, we feel in control. Confidence is sexy. When we exude confidence, others are attracted to us, regardless of gender. Confidence is credibility. When we believe in ourselves, others believe in what we have to say.

Confidence can also be elusive, because it is virtually impossible to be confident at all times. We all have bad days, and we all experience moments when we're more aware of our shortcomings than our strengths. During these periods of doubt, our personal balance statement seems to be all liabilities and no assets. It's okay to feel that way, as long as you don't make it a habit to routinely focus on the negative, failing to recognize what is positive in you and your life. The best communicators are those who maintain a healthy balance between humility and confidence. They keep their egos in check, yet they are able to convey their ideas with conviction and make an impact on their audiences.

In this chapter we'll show you how to deliberately increase your confidence level. This knowledge will benefit you in many situations, both public and personal. Maybe you need to inspire others to follow your leadership. Maybe you want to create rapport with a single person. Or perhaps you must accomplish a particular critical objective where retreat and failure are unacceptable outcomes.

Confidence at will? Is it possible? A fair question, especially since confidence typically eludes us when we need it the most, such as when we're about to speak to an audience of peers or superiors. Yet, the techniques that we're about to present to you are as simple as they are powerful. All you have to do is to adopt and practice them.

Physical Fitness, Appearance, and Appropriate Dress

Our bodies and nonverbal signals are powerful symbols. Others attribute meaning to these symbols, as we do ourselves. The human body is never neutral in meaning to us; neither are its accessories, like clothing and jewelry. We assign labels of thin, athletic, chubby, or fat to others and ourselves. For clothing, we say it looks cheap or expensive, sloppy or well-tailored, sophisticated or casual. The meaning we create from these symbols and this type of nonverbal communication and the information we extract and interpret from the perceptions of others shape our attitudes and direct our behavior toward them.

For instance, we act differently toward someone with unkempt hair, an unshaven face, dirty fingernails, and an overall slovenly appearance than we would toward someone who is well-groomed and wears expensive-looking clothing and shoes. People hold their own biases. Some will feel less comfortable around those who have an "expensive" or wealthy look.

Biases are real. Similarly, we reward people with bodies that match the beauty standards of our culture with favorable attention and admiration, as opposed to the indifference and disdain we may show people who are obese or physically "unfit." In the book *Blink*, Malcolm Gladwell points out research that says people associate height with power, especially among men. In America the average male CEO is three inches taller than the average man.

Does this mean we might as well not show our faces to an audience if we don't match the beauty ideal of the culture we live in? Does it mean the perceiving public will automatically dismiss us if we are less than perfect? The answer is no; far from it. But knowing what meaning is created by appearance, and that we're always communicating nonverbally whether we want to or not, allows us to at least influence the communication we send out in our favor, as opposed to letting it happen randomly. In other words, if I know that the color white makes me look pale and sickly, I won't choose to wear a white shirt that will create this impression in the minds of my audience. Similarly, if my body type is endomorphic, and I look stocky and rotund in pin-striped suits, I avoid the pattern and choose a more flattering garment.

The important thing to remember is that our objective is not to change deeply ingrained cultural perceptions. Our goal, when we put ourselves on that proverbial stage, is to influence people to like us, believe us, trust us, or follow us. Confidence is the foundation to accomplishing this.

Let's look at the ways we can inspire confidence in ourselves by actively influencing the meaning others perceive from the way we present ourselves.

Know the Dress Code

If you've ever shown up for a party where you understood the proper attire to be formal, and you were the only one in a tuxedo or an evening gown, you know how uncomfortable that can be.

Whether you're giving the keynote at the annual National Cement Contractors Association meeting or you're presenting your department's budget to the executive board on a casual Friday, educate yourself about the proper dress code for the purpose of your talk. Ask a meeting planner or others who will be in attendance and whose self-presentation you trust. Appropriate dress removes one potential source of negative influence on the outcome of your presentation.

Be Confident in Your Appearance

If there's something you dislike about your appearance and it's possible to change it, focus on doing so. There's almost always room for improvement when it comes to how we care for our bodies. Start an exercise program, eat more healthfully, get more rest, and drink lots of water. Not only will your appearance improve, but your energy level and your positive feelings will increase too. Feeling healthy, energetic, and in control is a great way to increase your confidence in your appearance and yourself.

Work with What You Have

You most likely do not have time to drop 10 pounds before your impending event. There are also many things we may dislike about our bodies, such as height or body type, that we don't have the power to change. There's no reason to be discouraged about this. People come in all shapes and sizes, and as long as you make the best of your assets and limit the influence of your liabilities, you're on the right track.

Buy clothes that flatter your body shape, hair, and skin color. Enhance your appearance, but be sure to keep it within reason and stay authentic. Audiences see right through desperate attempts at masking one's perceived flaws. There's the short fellow who, in order to appear taller, wears obvious platform soles as though it were 1977. Or the lady wears a too-tight suit because she wants to believe she's a size 12 instead of a 14. Know that good posture makes you look confident *and* thinner and taller. Accept, for the moment, what you're working with and present it in the best light. Then work on improving what you don't like for next time.

Overcome Body Anxiety

It's also important to understand that your conceptions of your body do not accurately reflect reality. The possibly disparaging labels that you attach to yourself or your appearance are not fact; instead, they are based on a long history of self-conception, which is frequently motivated by the viewpoints of others.

Even when you don't have the power to change your appearance, you do have the power to change the way you view yourself. Realize that far from being infallible, your self-perceptions are largely arbitrary. By attempting to view yourself in a more positive light, despite your shortcomings, you will increase your confidence.

Practice, Practice, Practice: Rehearsing Like an Actor

As we discussed in Chapter 9, actors face many of the same challenges as public speakers. There's the need to perform successfully, particularly when the stakes are high and the pressure is on, whether it's at an important audition or a stressful board meeting. There's the need to dramatically and compellingly present a persona, whether it's a fictional character in a film or one's trustworthy character during a negotiation. And there's a constant need for improvisation, creative leadership, and quick-thinking.

It takes practice to develop these skills. It also requires a sense of yourself, your reactions, and your own abilities. Those who are most successful at public speaking have become that way through a commitment to practicing and perfecting their presentation skills. That's where rehearsing like an actor comes into play. You can enact various scenarios, run through different scenes, and understand your own talents and reflexes. You'll also get a sense of your own emotional and physical freedom and perceived limitations.

Of course, when rehearsing like an actor, you wouldn't want to just memorize your "lines" or practice delivering the same speech over and over again. The result would be a dry, robotic delivery, which would feel automatic and unconvincing to your audience. Furthermore, if any interruption or unforeseen event were to arise, you'd be rattled with anxiety once again, because you wouldn't have rehearsed your reaction to this particular situation.

You can never be fully prepared for every disruptive event that might occur. Likewise, you can never have perfectly fitting comments prepared to address every objection or interruption. But if you practice the skills of public discourse—if you rehearse the scene from many different angles and perspectives—you can be well-prepared for most situations. What types of actions should you rehearse? You should practice the skill of observing the nonverbal reactions of others, listening carefully to what they say, and responding appropriately. Hone this skill through repeated rehearsal, and you can increase your confidence in your ability to react to others.

This idea takes its inspiration from a school of acting instruction known as the *Meisner technique*, favored by actors such as Robert Duvall, Tom Cruise, Diane Keaton, and Jeff Goldblum. The Meisner technique is based on the following fundamental ideas, which are relevant to us in our attempts to become more confident through rehearsal.

1. *Developing strong improvisational skills.* Students are encouraged to practice scenarios with other actors, enacting imaginary roles convincingly without a script. Spontaneity is stressed, as is "staying in the moment."

2. *Gaining understanding and sensitivity to one's emotions.* The key is to be intimately aware of the self: how to engage oneself emotionally, and how to draw on this emotion.

3. *Using these skills to bring a script to life.* After developing the ability to accurately understand and respond to another's emotions, and the self-knowledge to delve into one's own emotions, the student is ready to work with a scripted text.

4. *Preparing and rehearsing extensively.* Relying on improvisation doesn't mean just "winging it." Instead, hours of rehearsal develop the skill of responding authentically to another person on stage, creating the skills and confidence that make improvisation possible.

This last point is especially important. You may have watched actors performing in improvisational situations, such as talk shows or live events. Their timing is perfect, their off-the-cuff remarks are actually funny, and their delivery feels authentic and unscripted. They also seem confident and at ease. Undoubtedly, this is partly due to a natural personality bent, something not easily obtained and often the result of one's upbringing, cultural environment, and many other influences that shape a personality. However, a great deal of it is due to practice and preparation, something that is easily within your grasp.

If you've watched the Oscars in the last 15 years, there's a good chance that you saw Billy Crystal, eight-time Oscar host and major contributor to the Academy Awards legend. His one-liners and offhand jokes might seem entirely spontaneous and unrehearsed, but this perception is far from the truth. In fact, countless hours of prep time go into writing jokes before the show. Most of them are never used, but the preparation is essential to his confidence and ease during the event. As Crystal said in an interview with the *Milwaukee Journal Sentinel*, "It's almost like creating a football playbook with options. We bank thousands of jokes—and then, hopefully, you don't need any of them. The best ones are the ones that just arise spontaneously."

Mastering the Art of Storytelling

Story-telling is the original form of teaching.

—E. Martin Pederson

When you've mastered the art of narrating real or imagined events in such a way that the audience is spellbound and captivated, hanging on to your every word, you know you've come closer to becoming a powerful and compelling speaker. This experience of taking the imagination of the audience for a ride to wherever you want them to end up is one of the most powerful confidence-building methods known in professional speaking.

Tell a good story and they'll listen. The better you are at telling the story, the more intense the feedback from the audience. And the more enthusiastically your audience reacts to your storytelling skills, the more confident you will feel the next time you tell the story.

Most people have plenty of practice telling stories. In fact, if you have a child, you've undoubtedly been asked the perennial question: "Will you tell me a story?"

Yet, while children may be more likely to ask for them, they aren't the only ones who love hearing stories. As humans, stories are one of the most essential ways we communicate. By tapping into the basic events of our daily lives and our natural form of communication, storytelling has a powerful, persuasive effect. In "The Use of Storytelling in Department of the Navy," Deputy Chief Information Officer Alex Bennet writes:

> Conveying information in a story provides a rich context, remaining in the conscious memory longer and creating more memory traces than information not in context. Therefore a story is more likely to be acted upon than normal means of communications. Storytelling, whether in a personal or organizational setting, connects people, develops creativity, and increases confidence.

In other words, information that's provided in the relaxed and non-threatening context of a story will have a bigger impact on listeners, remaining in their memories longer. So the information is more likely to have an influence on their ways of thinking, and by extension, their actions. E. Martin Pederson agrees: "A relaxed, happy relationship between storyteller and listener is established, drawing them together and building mutual confidence."

Obviously, this is powerful stuff. But how can you tap into this influential and powerful technique? What does it take to master the art of storytelling? And how can you use it to build your confidence?

Becoming a great storyteller is another skill that requires practice and dedication. One of the best ways to become an accomplished storyteller is to seek out the stories of others. Read all types of stories and consider the way they're put together. Look for personal anecdotes in relevant communication and your personal life. You can even ask people to tell you their own personal stories. By absorbing all kinds of stories, you'll find it easier to identify the compelling narratives in your own life and experiences. You'll also develop an intuition for how to construct powerful tales.

When choosing a story, it should fit the context. It should make sense to your listeners and be relevant to their needs and experiences. It should be a story that matters to you, something that affects you in some heartfelt way. And, needless to say, it should be deeply tied to the goals of your presentation or speech. Screenwriting coach Robert McKee offers a great example of just such a story:

> Consider the CEO of a biotech start-up that has discovered a chemical compound to prevent heart attacks. He could make a pitch to investors by offering up market projections, the business plan, and upbeat, hypothetical scenarios. Or he could captivate them by telling the story of his father, who died of a heart attack, and of the CEO's subsequent struggle against various antagonists — nature, the FDA, potential rivals — to bring to market the effective, low-cost test that might have prevented his father's death.

Another important issue to consider when choosing your story is simplicity. Your story is your tool for illustrating your point in a way that could never be achieved by charts and graphs or by pontificating and lecturing. The meaning of your story should be immediately clear so that nothing detracts from its power.

So you've chosen your story. How do you go about telling it?

You should be very familiar with the story, but don't do anything so dull as to memorize it word for word. As the headline of this section implies, storytelling is an art. If the story matters to you — and if it matters to your listeners — this energy alone will drive the story forward. It's much more powerful to have memorized the general points of the story, including the beginning, climax, and resolution, and let the story happen in your own words.

But this doesn't mean you don't need to practice. Rehearse telling the story over and over again in your own words. Rather than getting comfortable with a certain phrasing, try to tell the story in different words each time. That way you'll get comfortable with the story itself, and the words won't matter. This is just another method of practicing spontaneity. If you rehearse in front of people, ask them what parts of the story drew them in and which felt like filler. Ask if they were curious for you to expand on any of the parts. If you rehearse the telling of the story rather than the exact words, you'll be better able to let the story happen authentically and naturally. You'll be more confident in your ability to get the point across even if you miss a line or two halfway through.

Cultivating a Quick Sense of Humor

We all love to laugh. Laughter is a great tool for defusing tension, as well as for making listeners more relaxed, receptive, and trusting. This makes humor a very successful way of connecting with an audience. And what is more confidence-inspiring than an audience full of smiles and the feeling of rapport that shared laughter creates?

On the other hand, you've probably had the unfortunate experience of being in the room with a speaker who believes that the way to entertain his audience is to deliver a series of tired jokes, all of which feel stilted and artificial. This speaker may get some polite laughs from the audience, but he's not truly connecting with them.

The best way to make your audience laugh is to develop your sense of humor. There are several ways you can do this.

One of the best ways is to watch and learn from your favorite comedians, speakers, and actors. Observe the people who make you laugh and ask yourself what makes them funny. Watch their timing, listen to their use of language, and notice their nonverbal communication. This is not so you can imitate them, but so you can learn from them. What gets a laugh from the audience? What are the components of a funny joke, beyond just the words involved?

Stretch your sense of humor by seeking out funny things: humorous articles or books, amusing television shows or movies. Enjoy the laughs, absorb the technique, and learn from it. By learning to see the unusual angles of a situation, you will train your sense of humor, allowing yourself to see the funny and absurd. All of this will help you become more confident to make a witty observation or deliver a clever one-liner when the moment calls for it.

This should be one of the easiest parts of preparing to present with confidence. After all, who could complain about having to watch more funny films or read more funny articles? The best part is, once you've learned the skill of making your audience laugh, you'll find it easier to approach your audience confidently. You'll have the assurance that you can help deflect any tense situation with humor. And there are few things more encouraging than the warm, positive vibes you get from a relaxed and amused group of listeners.

Drawing Your Map: Enforcing Tight Organization

If confidence has an enemy, it's uncertainty.

Uncertainty is the polar opposite of confidence. It derails our efforts, miring us in self-doubt and chaos, when we should be forging ahead. To defeat uncertainty, we must first evaluate where uncertainty comes from.

Much of the uncertainty in our lives stems from disorganization, both mental and physical. Mental disorganization leads to ambiguity and confusion about what our message and our goals are. Physical disorganization leads to difficulty in achieving goals because we get distracted by the problems of dealing with daily interruptions and inconveniences. The good news is that by achieving organization, you can help minimize uncertainty and do a great deal to boost your confidence.

Mental Organization

The first step in mental organization is preparing your speech. Spend some time beforehand planning carefully so that you can deliver your message in the most organized, logical manner. Remember that audiences can easily get lost (and frustrated, distracted, and bored) throughout the course of a speech, so they need frequent summaries and reminders about where you've been and where you're heading. Build these signposts into your structure. Spend some time outlining this structure. You should know ahead of time exactly what points you intend to cover, in which order you'll hit them, and how they relate to one another. By knowing the structure of your speech and sticking to it, you'll eliminate the uncertainty of fumbling for your next talking point. Narrow your options, and your mind will be clear and focused while on stage, secure in the knowledge that you know exactly what you need to say next.

Along with knowing the structure of your speech, you should also have a clear outline for timing. This is another area where lots of practice will come in handy. Know how long you should spend on each point in order to give yourself proper pacing and an appropriate mental picture of passing time.

If it helps, as you prepare, mentally visualize your presentation as a road trip. Each point you need to make is a stop along the way. You should have a clear route mapped out, a perfectly planned course from point A to point B to point C. You should also have a researched estimate on how long each portion of the journey will take.

Imagine how much more confident you are as a driver in a strange place when you have this information ahead of time. The alternative is equivalent to driving through a strange city without knowing exactly where you're going or how to get there, and checking the map while driving. Many of us have done this before too, and it isn't pleasant.

Physical Organization

We can never plan for every unforeseen conflict or last-minute emergency. Sometimes negative events occur that are outside the sphere of human control. But there are also lots of problems we *can* control. Instead of wasting energy worrying about all those unavoidable possibilities, focus on accounting for the problems that you *can* control. . . last-minute emergencies such as losing your keys, misplacing your notes, or dealing with equipment malfunctions. You can avoid these kinds of problems and minimize confidence-killing stress and anxiety by being organized.

You've already taken the time to make sure your talking points are mentally organized. Your notes should be organized too. If you're using handwritten notes, write them neatly and legibly; or better yet, type them. Keep in mind that you'll probably be reading them from a distance greater than what you may be comfortable with, so the writing or font size should be large enough to read from a few feet away. You can't be confident in your presentation if you're squinting down at your notes.

You should also ensure that your notes are organized in a format you can quickly shuffle through. Note cards are a favorite of many speakers because they're compact and easy to handle. You can fit one major point on each card, then flip to the next one. If you were to write down all your points on one large piece of paper, you might experience some confusion as you looked down at your notes. It could be hard to identify which point was supposed to be mentioned next, making the notes less than helpful.

Of course, hopefully you've rehearsed your presentation well enough so notes won't be entirely necessary. Still, it helps to have a backup plan, should your mind suddenly go blank in mid-sentence. Being prepared on every level is part of what being a confident speaker is all about.

This advice doesn't just apply to your notes. Any other props you need for your talk should be organized well ahead of time. That includes slides, PowerPoint presentations, handout sheets, or any other aids you've chosen to help deliver your message. Prepare these in advance, know your approach for use or distribution, and make sure your props are easy to access on the day of your talk. Have them packed in an organized manner so that you won't need to worry about any of them at the last minute.

Likewise, have your clothing for the day picked out well in advance. As we discussed earlier, personal appearance and presentation have a great influence on how we affect others. Your clothing is an important component of the image and message you present, and it's also a significant factor in your self-conception and your confidence level. So it's important that this aspect of preparation be considered carefully. Start thinking about what you'll wear as soon as possible. If you don't have the clothes you need, give yourself ample time to shop for the appropriate clothing. That way, you'll have time to find something you like and feel comfortable in, and you will also have time to take care of issues such as alterations.

Try on your clothes a few days in advance and view yourself in a full-length mirror to ensure that there are no stains or tears or any other cosmetic issues. Make sure your clothes are clean, pressed, and hung in the closet ready to go well before the day of your event. Getting dressed should be the least stressful part of your day.

Many people make the mistake of assuming that getting dressed will be easy since, after all, they do it every day. Then they find themselves running around the house looking for clean socks or their favorite belt. This is stressful and counterproductive to building confidence. Give yourself plenty of extra time in case you can't find those socks or that belt.

If it's at all possible, you should try to schedule a visit ahead of time to the place where the event will be held. The environment in which you're speaking will have a great effect on how participants or audiences perceive your presentation. The size of the room, the acoustics, the atmosphere, and the temperature will all factor into the total experience. There are two reasons why it's good to know these variables in advance.

First, if there's any problem with the room, you may be able to change it. If it's too small, too large, too hot or cold, you might be able to ask for another area or for a visit from maintenance, thereby eliminating the problem entirely. Even if you can't solve the problem, you can adjust your expectations accordingly and create a plan for dealing with it. You might also catch an even more crucial problem—for example, if the room doesn't have adequate seating, and you expect a large audience. Or perhaps you're planning to use some type of equipment for your presentation, until you discover that there's no convenient electrical outlet. You never know what challenges the venue will provide until you visit it.

The second reason you should try to visit the place is because knowing your environment ahead of time will go a long way toward alleviating your anxiety and building confidence. Hopefully, when you check out the room, there will be no problems, and everything will be fine. But even if this is the case, don't consider your time wasted. You have still familiarized yourself with the setting. To return to the metaphor of the road map, knowing what the room will look like is akin to being aware of the landmarks that will mark your journey. It's also an important aid in visualizing your presentation, a helpful way to mentally prepare for success and build confidence.

Having a mental road map and a working plan means that you will be both physically and mentally organized, successfully managing anxiety and building confidence. With your potential problems already faced and your plan of attack in mind, you should feel ready and confident. What's more, you'll have good reason to feel that way.

How Much Preparation? A Lesson from NASA

In this chapter we've discussed several techniques for building confidence as a speaker. Some of these techniques deal with preparation right before the event; others deal with improving your skills as a speaker so you can feel more confident. It's probably clear to you by now that while confidence is certainly a state of mind, this state of mind can be achieved through proper preparation.

If this seems like too much of an investment, consider the preparation and planning that go into a single NASA mission. We've done some coaching at NASA and have had the opportunity to learn a little more about the process behind the scenes. Most people only see the few hours of the launch broadcast on the news. However, this brief public event is backed with days, weeks, months, and years of planning.

Most people would agree that many endeavors that promise great rewards require effort, study, careful planning, and practice. Learning to face an audience with confidence and to captivate them with the power of your message and personality is no different.

Now that you've learned the skills to increase your confidence as a speaker, in the next chapter we'll show you how to work with an audience.

How to Work with Your Audience

Knowing Your Audience

Whenever you communicate with someone, you have an audience. During a formal speech, an informal talk, a conversation or discussion, even a quick hello to a colleague, a communication loop is established and speakers and listeners switch roles from one moment to the next. One moment you are the audience, the next you are the presenter and speaker.

In this chapter we'll show you how to effectively deal with your audience. We'll also show you the strategies that will make an audience perceive you as interesting, captivating, intriguing, and, most important, worth listening to. In other words, we'll teach you how to *connect* and have *impact*.

Let's first make a few safe assumptions about a typical "audience." Since you are the audience for others when they speak, you should be able to relate to the expectations, feelings, and attitudes of a typical audience.

Audiences hate being bored. They don't like it when someone wastes their precious time. They like to receive information that benefits them. They like to laugh. They like to know the secrets to making money, saving money, finding a better job, feeling good about themselves, feeling they are important and respected, finding the love of their life, living in their dream home, starting their own little (or big) business. . . and so on. In other words, most audiences are exactly like you and me.

So what does this tell us about our own audiences? First of all, when they're listening to people who bill themselves as experts, they want to feel confident that the speakers know what they're talking about. Similarly, if people talk to you about investment opportunities, you would be suspicious if they wore scuffed shoes and worked as grocery clerks. And would you accept nutritional advice from those who are morbidly obese or fitness tips from people who smoke two packs of cigarettes a day? We didn't think so.

What every audience looks for first in a speaker is credibility. We like listening to people who demonstrate that they know their subject matter. And in order to be perceived as credible, our actions and words must be congruent. They must match. By saying one thing yet doing the opposite, we lose credibility.

And what about likability? Don't we prefer to listen to people we perceive as likable? We've all met people who make us think, I'm not sure what it is, I just like the guy. Without cramping your personal style, you will be surprised to find out how easy it is to be perceived as likable. And when people like you, they'll listen to you. They're more willing to accept your ideas and opinions and give you the benefit of the doubt when necessary. By establishing credibility and likability in the minds of your audiences, you will find receptive listeners wherever you go.

You may do this intuitively at times, and may struggle with it on occasion. What follows are the proven methods that will help you in every situation.

How to Establish Credibility and Likability

Aristotle, often considered the father of persuasion and public speaking, wrote in the fourth century B.C. that ethos, or one's character, is the foundation of a person's credibility and his ability to persuade others to a point of view.

We hear "Actions speak louder than words" from the time we are children. This saying also points to the essence of credibility. Similarly, to be perceived as credible, your physiology or nonverbal signals must convey the same message as your spoken words. Have you ever asked people how they're doing and their response was, "Great, thanks," yet their body language and facial expressions didn't match the answer? Did you believe them?

When you say you'll do something but then neglect to follow through, your credibility suffers. We admire and like those who do what they say they'll do. It's that simple.

Many of us make the mistake of saying things we don't mean and promising things we don't intend to do. Other times we have the best intentions and fully plan to follow through with the commitments we made to others, only to later find that we don't have the time, the resources, the skills, or the abilities needed to make good on our promises.

Take the example of Jack, a young manager at a four-star hotel who has just been hired to head the guest services department. Among his new staff is the housekeeping department, where most of the employees are Hispanic and speak Spanish. During his first big meeting with the entire staff, including the housekeeping department, Jack makes a promise in front of everyone to Luz, the bilingual housekeeping manager, that he will start learning Spanish so that he can attend staff meetings and communicate with staff members on the issues that concern them. When Luz translates Jack's public promise to her staff, it draws applause and cheers. The staff feels that their boss appreciates and cares about them enough to learn their language. Jack's popularity soars instantly.

Fast forward three months. Jack has been busy. His new position as the guest services manager requires his presence and full attention at the hotel nearly 10 hours a day; as a result his Spanish language skills never got off the ground. Jack hasn't been able to find the time to devote to learning a new language; he vastly underestimated the discipline required to learn the language. Instead, he manages to utter "*Hola*" every time he runs into housekeepers in the elevator, and the housekeepers return his greeting with a smile. But do you think that any of them forgot his initial promise to learn Spanish in order to communicate with them on a more personal basis? They didn't. In fact, they often ask Luz when Jack is going to run a meeting in Spanish. The question is often followed by sarcastic chuckling, because the housekeepers have written off Jack's public promise as posturing and an attempt to ingratiate himself with them. At this point nobody believes he'll ever follow through on his promise or that he even meant it in the first place.

While Jack may well have fully believed that he would learn basic Spanish to communicate with the Spanish-speaking members of the housekeeping department, he lost valuable credibility by not following through on his promise. Anything he'll promise in the future will likely be regarded with doubt and caution. It's hard to believe people whose words don't match their actions.

Other Ways We Convey Credibility

Reputation

Before attempting to communicate with an audience, you should be keenly aware of your reputation with your listeners. If you're widely known, like Queen Noor of Jordan, rock star cum peace activist Bono of the Irish rock band U2, or former South African president Nelson Mandela, you are guaranteed an interested audience no matter where in the world you go. The powerful reputations and the enormous publicity these people's work and their status in the world carry are enough to draw crowds by the millions to hear them speak and present their ideas. Audiences across the world are already under the influence of the aforementioned speakers' reputations before the speakers have even uttered a word to them, proving that reputation is one way credibility can influence audiences.

The following questions can help you determine the influence your personal and professional reputation will have on the level of credibility bestowed upon you by an audience:

- What does the audience know about my accomplishments, qualifications, and overall background?
- Where do they get their information about me? The grapevine or water cooler? Their colleagues? From blogs on the Internet? The bio page of an online corporate brochure? The business

section of newspapers? Critical magazine articles? Prior speaking engagements? Parties? Adversaries? Competitors? Public legal notices?

- What is my audience's attitude toward me? Are they sympathetic to my cause? Are they open to my ideas or have they made up their minds? Will they be hostile, friendly, or indifferent?
- Is there any information in my background I should clear up with my audience before misunderstandings develop? Are there any incidents in my history that would give hecklers and "grenade rollers" fodder to sabotage my talk in front of others?
- Do I make my arguments well or do they give audience members opportunities to poke holes in my reasoning and ask critical questions I can't answer sufficiently?
- Do audiences typically leave my talks with a positive feeling, or do I offend people occasionally? Do I have a tendency to bore my audiences, or do I have a reputation of giving energizing and invigorating talks?

These are some of the questions you may want to answer before speaking to your intended audience. Your reputation is your most precious asset. Make sure you protect and nurture it.

Association

We can often gain or lose credibility by the associations we choose. Fair or not, many people will measure part of your credibility by the company you keep and the circles you travel in.

Harrison once met a financial consultant with a prominent firm whose services he considered enlisting. They established rapport and were on track to do business with each other. Noticing a beautiful woman crossing the street during one conversation at a local café, the financial advisor let it slip that he dates only "strippers." While that was his personal business, Harrison wondered at this man's lack of judgment in revealing this. At the same time, Harrison was glad to have this information, because he didn't want to associate with someone whose reputation might be compromised, depending on how many people knew about his dating preferences. If others in the local business community saw them together, would they assume that they visited strip clubs together? It was quite possible. Harrison made the decision to protect his reputation and not do business with this person.

Similarly, by associating with those who have stellar reputations in business or the professions, you can raise your credibility when others see you or perceive you to be in their company. It gives the impression that you must be worth their attention if you travel in privileged circles and that you are a good business associate. Be aware of the reputations of those with whom you associate. They can help or hurt you in equal measure.

Appearance

Let's face it: We often judge a book by its cover. Consciously or unconsciously, an audience determines someone's worthiness by measuring certain physiological qualities. All of our communication channels, from the words we use, to our vocal tonality, to our other non-verbal signals give an audience an opportunity to form important impressions about us. And what our audience perceives of us will often determine their openness in listening to our message. Does the way we're dressed say we are conservative or creative? Does wearing an expensive watch mean we're careless with our spending, or does our choice of jewelry and accessories purposely convey status and wealth? Does a gray suit mean we're uptight, or do rolled-up shirtsleeves mean we try to influence audiences with the "plain folks" technique that political candidates frequently employ on campaign stops?

Your haircut too will be under scrutiny from audiences. Is yours giving the message that you are youthful and energetic like John Edwards or conservative and experienced like John Kerry? Democratic New York senator Hillary Rodham Clinton has changed her hair numerous times during her many years in the public spotlight. And whenever she did, it was part of the day's news. What does your hairstyle say about you? What about your walk and your eye contact and gestures when you're in front of an audience? We judge what we see. And from what we see, we draw conclusions, right or wrong, good or bad.

Below are some qualities that immediately make an impression on your audience, whether it's an audience of one or many.

- *Body language.* Do you stand straight and confident, or do you have a tendency to hunch over and slouch? Does your body language reveal your insecurities? Do you turn away from people who intimidate you? Do you "lean in" to important conversations and show your interest and empathy? Does your body actively participate in conversations or withdraw into a "ball-like" shape?
- *Facial expressions.* Do your facial expressions communicate feelings of indifference, sadness, joy? Do you appear startled, confused, or anxious? Are you conveying amusement, anger, or sarcasm?
- *Gestures.* Are you aware of your gestures? Do they visually support your words? Do you often rub your chin or tug on your earlobe? Are you prone to scratching your head or clenching your fists? Do you use gestures to substitute for certain verbal content? Do you feel self-conscious about the placement of your hands when speaking, or do you use them to convey just the right meaning when appropriate? Do you play with items such as pens and paper when you speak, or do your arms rest comfortably by your side until the emotion you want to express calls them into action?
- *Movements.* Do you move with purpose, or are you at the whim of your emotions? Are your movements graceful and smooth, or do they seem edgy and nervous? Do you stand still when conversing, or does your body rock back and forth ever so slightly?
- *Eye contact.* Do you look others in the eyes when speaking to them? Do you blink frequently or look away when someone looks at you? Do you make others feel uncomfortable by "staring them down"? Do your eyes laugh along with your mouth, or do they stay neutral? Do you look at the floor in uncomfortable situations?

- *Skin.* Does your skin and complexion say something about your lifestyle? Do you look tired and exhausted or refreshed and rested? Do you blush easily, or does your complexion hide a sudden rush of emotions? Do you tan for a sporty appearance, or do you protect your skin from the sun? Does your skin reveal health issues?
- *Breathing.* Does your breathing originate from your diaphragm, or do you breathe from your chest? Do you take measured deep breaths, or is your breathing quick and hectic? Is it heavy and loud?
- *Vocal quality.* Does your voice sound shrill and high? Is it smooth and deep? Does it sound masculine or feminine? Does it seem nasal? Do you inflect or is your voice monotone and flat?
- *Accent.* Can people draw conclusions about your upbringing from your accent? What stereotypes are often associated with your accent? Is it easy to understand you? Do you mispronounce the same words repeatedly? Do others get a meaning different from what you intend because of your accent?
- *Dialect.* What stereotypes are associated with your dialect? Is your dialect an asset or a liability? Does it detract from your message?
- *Vocabulary.* Do you have a large repertoire of words that can convey the meaning of your content in more ways than one? Do you use simple language, or do you rely on jargon to get your message across? Do you understand most of what others are saying and the words they're using?
- *Delivery.* Do you make use of pauses when you speak? Do you raise or lower your voice for emphasis? Do you use alliterations? Do distracting filler words such as "um," "you know," "like I said," pepper your speech?
- *Hair.* Does your hair look professional, conservative, youthful, or dated? What does an up-do (for women) say about you? Is your hair long or short? What does your hair length say about you?

- *Jewelry*. Do you wear a lot of jewelry? Is wearing jewelry in the first place appropriate for the situation you're speaking in? Does it reveal your taste? Does it convey perceptions of cheap or expensive, subtle elegance or vulgarity?
- *Clothing*. Is your clothing appropriate for the climate and for the occasion? Is it well-coordinated, and are the colors pleasing or are they loud and ostentatious? Does your clothing look well maintained? Does it look wrinkled? Does it fit your body shape, or is it too small or large? Do you look comfortable in it?
- *Grooming*. Does your look say that you are healthy? Do you appear as someone who practices good hygiene? Do you use makeup appropriately, or are you trying too hard? Do you have noticeable body odor? Do you check your breath for freshness after you eat or drink coffee? Is your perfume or cologne overwhelming? Are your nails manicured or dirty? Do your hands appear dry and callused, or do they look smooth and clean?
- Height. How do you carry yourself? Are you comfortable with your height? Do you hunch over and slump to get on the same level as shorter people, or do you compensate for being short by wearing high heels and thick soles?

Every audio or video signal others can perceive will help them form an impression or pass judgment on you. This often happens on an unconscious level and frequently changes as you begin to interact with people, depending on the new signals you use to replace your audience's initial perceptions. Skilled communicators and speakers make the best of their attributes and work on those they feel are lacking. In order to manage your audience's perceptions of you, you'll want to determine the aspects and impressions you want to convey, and then work on creating your most favorable appearance. More than the words we use, our complete image communicates a powerful message, long before we get a chance to utter a single word. It is entirely in our hands to influence this unspoken message in our favor.

The Secrets to Likability

Likability Through Conversation

There are some sayings that point to the secret of likability, such as "birds of a feather flock together" and "like two peas in a pod"or "being on the same wavelength" and "being in sync." These sayings refer to a kind of harmony and synchronicity. We are living, breathing beings, perpetually responding to the rhythms we perceive around us. Whether it's music, the sound of footsteps, our own heartbeat, the dripping of a water faucet, or something else, rhythm is everywhere. It's the same with people's communication signals. When people speak, we can detect certain rhythms, just as their breathing patterns will have certain rhythms. In fact, their moves and nonverbal sounds all correspond to deeply ingrained senses of rhythm.

In order for you to achieve likability and influence, you must try to tap into their rhythms. Pay close attention to the pace with which people speak, breathe, and move, and use this information to create synchronicity. This is also commonly referred to as the nonverbal aspect of building rapport.

None of this is breaking news, as human beings do this quite naturally throughout their lives, off their conscious radar screens. Visualize a person you get along with fantastically, perhaps your best friend, spouse, or twin sibling. Have you ever finished one another's sentences because you knew exactly what the other person was going to say next? Do you smile at the same things and laugh at the same time? Couples in love often report a feeling of "being like one and the same person." This is in response to the ultimate feeling of harmony and synchronicity.

Have you ever danced with someone and moved in total synchronicity and harmony? Do you remember how good that was? No awkward stumbling, toe-stepping, jerking in different directions. You were moving as one. Synchronicity is the ultimate goal in love, business, politics, interpersonal relationships, sports, and athletics. When we're in sync with our audience, we communicate effortlessly.

In order to successfully create such harmony and synchronicity, however, you first have to be able to extensively observe, read, and interpret the behaviors of others.

Obviously, it would be of no benefit to you (or your audience, for that matter) to tap into the audience's hostile or adversarial attitude. It would serve no purpose to escalate audience irritation into full-blown hostility and emotional barricading. Therefore, whenever you sense emotional barriers or other counterproductive (to your cause and objectives) behavior in your listeners, you have to try to immediately establish rapport, initially by acknowledging their noticeable frustration and dissonance and then by trying at least to neutralize it. Doing these things will enable you to open their minds to your person and message. This advice has nothing to do with mimicking, but rather with tuning in to the general mood of others and meeting them where they are at the moment, while gently bringing them along to where you want them to be emotionally. Observe and perceive what they're feeling and thinking and then strive to match any negative emotions by consciously acknowledging them rather than mirroring them. Ultimately the aim is to lead the audience out of negativity with genuine, reasonable optimism as you gradually align their state of mind with yours.

Audience Behaviors You Can Synchronize

The following list offers a number of nonverbal behaviors we can apply to get in sync with others:

1. Physiological rhythms
2. Walking
3. Speaking rate
4. Speaking volume
5. Speaking pitch
6. Breathing
7. Touching
8. Eye contact
9. Posture
10. Laughing
11. Facial expression
12. Physical distance

For example, let's say you're at a business meeting and your conversation partners are speaking at a rate that is slower or faster than your rate of speaking. Check to see who you are most out of rhythm with. Then adapt your speech rate to that person's and watch what happens.

You are consciously creating synchronicity. As you begin to speak at the same rate as your most out-of-sync meeting counterpart, your breathing will follow the same rate. Note that person's behavior toward you and how it changes. Next, adapt your posture to the other person's. Do this subtly and below the radar. If that person's arms are crossed, start crossing your arms imperceptibly. If the other person's foot is tapping to some internal rhythm, do the same with yours but out of sight. Your conversation partner does not have to actually see you doing this, as you will create harmony and likability simply by consciously adjusting to his or her body language and subtly matching it.

Other ways to create choreography with others include using similar gestures, adopting a matching vocal quality, mirroring their posture, and tapping into the vocabulary they're using, whether it's jargon, which we advise you keep to a minimum, or key words and phrases they seem to repeat.

If someone has a tendency to touch your elbow at times while talking, start doing the same. Try to alternate your points of touch. For instance, if someone touches your elbow briefly when saying something to you, touch his or her wrist or shoulder. The key, as always, is to do this subtly and not to overdo it. It cannot be obvious. Remember, people often touch to underscore a point they're making or to lend strength to a statement. Do likewise and you'll put yourself on the same wavelength with your conversation counterpart.

An important thing to remember is that there is often a clearly noticeable point at which you can tell whether a person likes you and you are in sync with one another. You'll be able to tell when the atmosphere feels comfortable and there's harmony between you in words and nonverbal communication, and it seems that you effortlessly agree on just about everything.

Effective communicators understand that the secret to likability is the ability to actively tune in to others and make them feel as though they are the most important people in the room.

A colleague of Harrison's once had back-to-back meetings with two very brilliant CEOs of large multinational companies. While both leaders were highly educated and accomplished in their respective fields and were considered good communicators, their individual styles were markedly different. When Harrison asked a colleague about his impressions of the two chief executives, the response was, "After meeting with CEO John Smith, I was convinced that he was a brilliant and most interesting person, with a fascinating background."

"And what about CEO Mark Jones?" Harrison asked.

Harrison's colleague looked at him as his face noticeably lit up and said, "It's interesting; Mr. Jones made me feel like I was important to him. He asked questions about my background, my family, and my aspirations. I think I did most of the talking." He enthused, "What a likable guy."

Harrison's colleague reacted to a speaker who was keenly aware of his audience and who tuned in to their needs and motivations. He solicited plenty of feedback, making his audience feel as though they were the most important part of the interaction. The CEO didn't let his status as chief executive or his own accomplished background interfere with the flow of the dialogue and the harmony of the conversation. He observed, read, and interpreted; he completely synchronized his style with his audience of one, making the interaction seem natural and pleasant. Which CEO would you rather do business with?

Now that we're aware of this secret to likability, how do we implement it? How do we go about achieving a harmonious interaction with people we don't know, wouldn't necessarily be best friends with, or even speak to?

Likability with Audiences

Achieving synchronicity when faced with an audience can be a more complicated task. You can, of course, get a sense of the audience's collective personality and respond to that. In reality, you'll usually have many different personalities and will likely get many different signals from your audience members.

Research shows that people with public speaking anxiety often hone in on the people who give them a negative reaction. There is also research that people with social anxiety actually interpret neutral signals from audience members as negative. Are these interpretations helpful? Of course not!

Instead, resonate with the people who appear to be enthusiastic about your talk. Overlook the one or two audience members who look bored or uninterested. You can never please everyone. In a presidential election, the candidate who gets the majority of votes wins. If the majority of people appear interested in your talk, you win!

Also keep in mind that the audience is not a faceless mass devoid of personality. It is a collective group of individuals who are just like you — with families, hobbies, and interests. You can connect with them one on one by tapping into as many universal experiences and situations as possible.

Remember the audience's favorite station is WiiFM, or "What's in it For Me?" Give your audience something of value and they will like you for that, if not for your personality. Knowing and effectively managing the expectations of your audience will go a long way toward your being likable.

One more way to achieve likability with an audience is to avoid overcompensating behaviors — trying too hard to be funny, trying to end your talk quickly (before you say something stupid), or trying to hide your shaking hands by keeping them clenched the whole time.

Not only does the audience notice these behaviors, they also don't do anything for you as you try to achieve likability. They detract from your authenticity. Be genuine and be yourself; audiences like this. When you're trying too hard, you are not being you, and audiences don't like that. Remember that authenticity is the key to likability.

Likability is an important component of the next section as well — persuasion and influence. If an audience doesn't like you, it is possible to persuade them otherwise. If you can persuade them to like you, you will establish common ground that much sooner. Next, you'll learn about powerful influencing techniques that allow you to meet your objectives with all kinds of audiences and persuade them to see things your way.

Persuade Your Audience of Your Way of Thinking

Whether you're selling a product, service, or an idea, or whether you're presenting a case in court, applying for research funds, or getting someone to accept your choice of restaurant, you are trying to persuade someone to adopt your point of view. And in all these cases, your audience will be persuaded only when they feel it's in their interest.

Success in persuading an audience does not depend on your expertise on a technical level, nor on the merits of the product, service, or idea you're trying to sell. Your success depends mainly on your skills in translating your product, service, or idea into benefits for the audience, as perceived from their view of the world. So, your big challenge is to figure out your audience and their unique and often "strange" way of seeing things. Easier said than done, right? Actually, it doesn't have to be "mission impossible" if you follow the powerful steps to audience persuasion.

Five Steps to Persuasion

Before giving any type of talk, be clear with yourself about what the main purpose of your talk is. Are you looking to inform people about something? Are you motivating them to work together toward a common goal? Are you giving an award or recognition? Are you trying to persuade an audience to your point of view? To listen to your proposal, buy your product, or try your service? Maybe you're just trying to get your way, as you and your friends are deciding on which restaurant to go to for dinner or what movie to see.

Lieutenant Colonel Larry Tracy, a fellow speech coach, GuruMaker trainer, and colleague of Harrison's, is the former head of the Pentagon Debriefing Team, which gives daily presentations to the Joint Chiefs of Staff at the Pentagon. In his book *The Shortcut to Persuasive Presentations*, he states that the purpose of *any* presentation, meeting, conversation, or talk is to persuade. He writes, "Even if you are not looking to make a sale, to gain a contract or change audience members' minds, you are still attempting to persuade them to listen to you, and to accept your information."

To help you in your quest to persuade audiences to your way of thinking, we've put together a list of five steps that you can use to reach your goals. Learn them well and you'll be able to confidently sell your ideas, proposals, and, most important, yourself, to any audience you choose.

Step 1. Clarify Your Objective

Speakers and presenters often have trouble with the objective. When asked what their objective is, they frequently mention things like, "to let my audience know about the great benefits of buying supplemental insurance," or to "convince the city council that our project has numerous long-term benefits for the community." These types of objectives are always a bit too complicated, and ultimately are not effective for the speaker as he or she is building a persuasive argument.

A clear objective is as simple as figuring out exactly what you want to happen as a result of your talk, speech, or conversation. Do you want people to sign up for supplemental insurance after your talk? Then every word, phrase, and rhetorical device you'll use should lead them to this ultimate goal. Do you want the city council to give its unanimous approval to your proposal, based upon your final presentation? Then you will know exactly what to use in your talk and what to leave out. Anything that doesn't help the objective should be omitted. When persuading someone, you have to be as clear as possible. There's no room for fillers or fluff, unless of course it's instrumental in driving the audience to your desired point, the place where your collective minds and hearts meet.

Keep your simple but powerful objective at the forefront of your mind as you develop the rest of your talk, and it will help you stay on track and create a lean and concise presentation that will have the desired impact.

Of course, equally important as clarifying your own objective is to know what the audience's objective is. Your audience has their own needs, wants, desires, and fears. To be successful in changing their minds about something or in getting them to accept what you're saying as true, you must learn what, specifically, the audience is thinking about you, your topic, and how what you're presenting will impact their lives. You'll also want to find out what their perceptional filters are, how they perceive you and your ideas, and what potential emotional barriers might stop your message from getting through to them. The next point will go further into the issue of gathering knowledge about your audience.

Step 2. Get to Know Your Audience Well

What do you know about your audience before you talk to them? When you have a captive audience whose minds and hearts you want to win, you'll need to know their hot buttons, problems, and dreams. How can you accomplish this important task?

Google your audience. Any of the major search engines, such as Google, Yahoo, Altavista, or Dogpile.com, can give you information on issues surrounding your audience. Whether their industry segment is going through one round of layoffs after another or they're part of the fastest growing multinational corporation in the world, the Internet will be a great starting point for your particular audience profile research.

Other research should include getting feedback from leaders and peers of the audience. Read trade magazines. Find out what areas your listeners live in. Study the lifestyles of your audience members and you'll have a good idea what moves them, what scares them, and what will get their attention.

By making sure that your objective and that of your audience are equally met by your particular proposal and idea, you're well on your way to getting what you want as you persuade your listeners to see things your way.

Step 3. Show That You're an Expert on Your Topic

Before an audience accepts a new idea, they have to know that the person proposing the idea is indeed an expert and knows what he or she is talking about. They have to be able to trust that the speaker has thought through the issue at length and knows their problems and challenges from every angle, convinced that the new idea will make their lives better. Pharmaceutical companies often have an actor portray a physician in advertisements, complete with white coat and stethoscope. While the actor is not actually the expert, advertising executives know that the perception of expertise is just as crucial in getting audiences to change their minds and accept new ideas as actual expertise is. Credibility, or at least the perception of it, is a key component in persuading an audience.

Step 4. Project Your Enthusiasm

Ralph Waldo Emerson said, "Nothing great was ever achieved without enthusiasm."

Enthusiasm is a Latin word. The prefix *en* means "within," and *thusias* means "god." When you're passionate about something, you literally have a "god within." People who care immensely about a subject treat it with a sense of urgency, be it baseball, finance, the law, public service, or the state of education in the public schools.

Most authorities in their particular fields are intensely enthusiastic about their interests, because their topics of expertise somehow add tremendous value to their lives. When you project your enthusiasm while talking to people about a topic you care deeply about, people gravitate toward your energy as if you knew the meaning of life and could give them the answers they seek. Your positive energy can unite you with people you never expected to meet. For instance, James Carville, ex-president Bill Clinton's former campaign strategist, and his wife, Mary Matalin, a staunch Republican, have violently opposed political views, but they re united by their common passion for politics. If you can summon the enthusiasm for your proposal and project it while you speak, your audience will turn into rapt listeners, eager to hear your message.

Step 5. Rehearse Your Talk Realistically

There's a saying in the theater world: "The best actors forget their lines." This statement does not advocate being unprepared but illustrates that the best performances are given when actors portray authentic feelings, giving their words meaning despite hundreds of rehearsals.

When you deliver contrived statements, you give an audience a reason to resist you. They'll feel irrelevant, or that you're trying to coerce them to buy your pitch as opposed to addressing a group of unique individuals with unique needs. Voicing your ideas in language written for the faceless masses is a sure way to be dismissed as a phony. When rehearsing, even with a scripted program, it's important to endow your words and ideas with as much life as they had when you first discovered them.

The art of rehearsing a persuasive talk realistically in front of an audience that is willing to give honest feedback lies in creating a realistic atmosphere in which you have a dialogue and not a monologue with listeners. The emotion you feel must come across to your practice audience, and their reaction will give you valuable feedback on how you'll be perceived by the real crowd. Ask for merciless feedback and constructive criticism. Grill your audience about what they felt as you spoke at various parts of your talk. Incorporate the feedback into your talk and deliver your talk again and again.

Your ultimate goal is to feel that the rehearsal is as real as the actual event so that the actual talk at the key event will become your best and most finely tuned presentation, with just the right amount of emotion and logic. When you reach this level of preparation, you will, as some Eastern philosophies might suggest, "Become one with your audience."

How to Manage Your Audience's Emotions

It is virtually impossible to persuade people without first assessing and then aligning your behavior to their emotional states. If, for instance, you sense a "heavy" or downtrodden atmosphere within the audience, acknowledge the feeling and match the mood of the room, as opposed to launching into an overly cheerful presentation that will only alienate your audience. You have to gradually lift the audience out of their funk and take them to an emotional place where they will be more open to your message. The trick is to trust that *all* your audience members want to feel good about themselves, hence, there's just one major question you need to ask yourself when interacting with an audience you're trying to build rapport with: "Will my next interaction strengthen or weaken my bond with this audience?"

Rapport is a connection with your listeners. The nature of the connection is a matter of choice. The easiest way to succeed is to make your audience feel good about themselves and their abilities, to maximize their confidence, and to demonstrate that you're trustworthy and likable. After all, what value is a compliment from someone you don't like or respect?

With carefully chosen language and authentic nonverbal communication, your audience can experience—instead of just hear—your thoughts, dreams, and plans for a better future. By seeing your audience as an active partner in this interaction, you will generate excitement within yourself and your listeners, creating an emotionally charged atmosphere that can help transport each member of the audience to your desired conclusion.

What to Do When You Face a Hostile Audience

Fortunately, a hostile audience is not the norm. Speaking effectively in public is challenging enough for most people, and for the untrained speaker the prospect of facing a group of vocal skeptics or outright hostile opponents of one's point of view can be nightmarish.

At some point in your career or personal life, however, you may find yourself representing an opinion or view that is unpopular with your audience and that provokes skeptical or negative reactions.

You may, for instance, square off in a heated debate with a group of parents at a PTA meeting, or announce an unfavorable management decision to a group of employees, or try to sell your proposal to a group of senior executives who have no patience for fumbling presenters who don't appear confident and don't have solid evidence that supports their case. Perhaps you'll even get grilled by the Senate Judiciary Committee because you've been nominated to sit on the Supreme Court.

So how do you manage a potentially contentious situation where an audience is predisposed to disagree with some or all of what you have to say? Will you be able to handle the pressure?

The good news is that in most cases you will sense beforehand that your ideas will meet opposition from some or all of those listening. If you *are* surprised by obvious opposition in your audience, it's likely that you haven't done your homework. But first let's look at how an audience can make their disagreement known to you.

How a Hostile Audience Can Destabilize You

Opposition from your audience can range from subtle nonverbal signals, such as toe-tapping or head-shaking, to blatant disruption and verbal attacks. More obvious signs might be a noticeable fidgeting with papers, an incessant clearing of throats, or the making of outright sarcastic comments.

Any of these things can derail your train of thought and shake your confidence if you are not a solid speaker and presenter.

When an audience has it "in for you," there are a number of strategies you can employ to neutralize their negativity. For starters, it's critical that you're able to anticipate this reaction in your audience.

The Value of Anticipation

Whatever your topic or point of view, remember that there may be others with contrary views. Therefore, learn about these contrary opinions and try to understand where they're coming from. Know your topic from all sides, in depth, and you can anticipate and confidently counter any objections from hecklers in your audience. Anticipating objections and treating skeptical remarks with effective counterargument will not only silence your critics but also elevate your status in the eyes of the rest of the audience, possibly including your detractors themselves.

Seven Secrets to Handling a Hostile Audience

1. *Have an objective.* Having a firm objective for your speech, presentation, or discussion can help you stay on message when the audience is unfriendly. A clearly defined objective is imperative in most formal and informal presentation situations, as it allows you to focus on your points while quickly recognizing when critics are trying to undermine your position. Particularly in an emotionally charged environment where some audience members may become quite vocal in promoting their opposing views, it is easy to doubt the truth and value of your own position. But if you're clear on what you want your audience to know, you will be more confident when the skeptics and "grenade rollers" try to distract you.

2. *Stay calm.* By keeping your own temper in check and responding to hecklers with reasoning and facts instead of emotional outbursts, you are increasing your chances that others in the audience will see you as the more level-headed communicator and may thus be more inclined to give your position fair consideration.

3. *Be positive.* Having a positive and optimistic attitude differentiates the leaders from the followers. You cannot expect to make a winning impression and convert others to your way of thinking with a negative attitude and demeanor. Showing an audience the possibilities of your vision with passion and

enthusiasm will go a long way in convincing them that you're on to something. All great communicators know that genuine optimism and enthusiasm are irresistible and often contagious.

4. *Get prepared.* Preparation is critical when you're facing an audience that is inclined to dismiss or oppose what you have to say. If you know which of your arguments the audience most likely will reject, you'll be in a better position to prepare an effective talk that addresses these issues specifically and with sound evidence. Gather as much information as you can about the attitudes, interests, motivations, and problems of your audience in order to get a clear idea about their disposition to your ideas. The more detailed information you have, the better you'll be able to relate to their unique perspectives and prepare for their opposing views.

5. *Stick to the facts.* Consider the evidence you have collected to bolster your claims. When you're under the stress of personal attacks, resist the pull to reach for proverbial straws when making your arguments. Clearly you are on thin ice with this strategy. Stick to the facts and repeat them often if you have to. But don't give in to the temptation of using questionable data that you couldn't verify and that does not originate from positively reliable sources. Stick to what you can prove beyond reproach when the heat is on as you present your message, otherwise you'll leave yourself wide open for your critics to jump all over your brittle evidence and shaky argument.

6. *Be aware of your body language.* A frequently cited study, conducted by Professor Albert Mehrabian, a researcher at UCLA, found that we get most of our information through nonverbal signals when we're communicating with others. The language your body speaks is more reliable and telling than anything your words say. Therefore, whenever you find yourself speaking to an audience, you should know that the nonverbal signals you're sending give them a much clearer idea of what the true meaning of your message is. That's why, if you yourself have doubts about the credibility of your information or you're not sure if the position you represent will hold up to

expert scrutiny, your words and body language will signal incongruence, which a critically thinking audience will immediately sense and draw conclusions from.

Make frequent eye contact with the audience and let your physical expressions and vocal tone naturally support your message. By focusing on your conviction and the value of your message, and maintaining a mental connection with the audience as you look them in the eyes, you're showing them that you stand by what you say.

7. *Establish common ground.* Think about what you have in common with your audience. The awareness of important commonalities can be a strong bridge that will support your statements to your listeners. We all share certain universal experiences that connect us as human beings in spite of our many cultural, educational, and socioeconomic differences. Particularly in front of an audience that is strongly opposed to your ideas, it's critical that you capitalize on those common human experiences by bringing them up early in your talk. With this strategy, even the most hostile audience can't help but relate to you on at least some level and therefore feel less negatively toward you during your talk.

We hope that the principles of persuasion and influence you've learned in this chapter will boost your confidence and provide you with a solid foundation for your speaking skills. Audiences are made up of complex, thinking, feeling human beings with the same fears, dreams, and desires we all have. The more you're schooled in the art of rapport and influence, the easier it will be for you to tap into the desires and motivations of others and lead them to see the world from your perspective.

In the next chapter we'll teach you everything you need to know about impromptu speaking.

PART IV

USING THE TOOLS IN THE REAL WORLD

12

Impromptu Speaking

Now that you have a solid idea of the general techniques for changing your thinking, behavior, and biological reactions toward speaking, and you know how to feel more confident and work your audience, we will go through the ways to put these skills to work in the real world. In this section of the book, we'll help you apply your knowledge to impromptu speaking situations, performances, presentations, and social situations. Over the next few chapters we'll discuss skills for men and women specifically, how to manage a verbal faux pas, and how to find practice opportunities to polish your speaking abilities. We'll begin by discussing impromptu speaking.

Spontaneous speaking is one of the greatest challenges for most people because there is no time to prepare. Many nervous speakers feel they will do okay if they can practice. When you must speak on the spur of the moment, you're likely to get a sudden rush of anxiety. This can throw you off, and it can be tough to gather your thoughts and come up with something meaningful to say.

Another challenge to spontaneous speaking is being succinct. Sometimes you have a few minutes to prepare for an impromptu speech, and at other times you're called upon to speak right away. Caught up in the anxiety of the moment, you often start rambling and don't get to your point; you then feel embarrassed and continue to ramble. When you have more time to prepare, you're more likely to plan and get to your objective more concisely. Winston Churchill is said to have replied, "Two hours," when asked how long he needed to prepare a two-minute speech. When he was asked how long he needed to prepare a two-hour speech, he said, "I'm ready now."

Overcome Anxiety By Experiencing It

One of the most important principles of anxiety reduction is that of exposure, which means exactly what it sounds like: exposing yourself to a feared situation. To do this in the most effective way, a number of things need to occur:

- *You need to allow yourself to experience the anxiety.* This means *not* doing the overcompensating behaviors that you usually do.
- *You need to repeat the exposure* multiple times *before drawing any conclusion.* Do not give one presentation, decide you're horrible, and not do it again. Remember the expression about getting back on the horse if you fall off?
- *The exposures work best if they are for an extended length of time.* Having a conversation for 10 minutes is better than having one for 2 minutes. This is because of the principle of habituation: Your body naturally habituates to anxiety over time. If you are still in the feared situation when the anxiety subsides, you'll be able to have a more positive experience in that situation. And having developed a more positive association with being in the difficult situation, the next time you enter that speaking situation, you'll feel less nervous.

Now let's apply these principles to specific instances where impromptu speaking is likely to occur.

Speaking Up Confidently at Meetings

Remember Yao, the executive who became nervous while sitting in meetings? He would think things to himself such as: I'm going to have to say some intelligent-sounding things today; I don't have anything to say, and the others here speak so eloquently; I'm going to look like an idiot, and my coworkers will wonder how in the world I got this position.

Meetings are tough because you often don't have time to prepare what you're going to say. Some meetings have very vocal members, and it's hard to get air time, so it's much easier to sit back and say nothing.

What do *you* typically think as you enter a meeting? Is it something along the lines of: I hope I do not need to say anything. Or perhaps: How can I get out of presenting today?

If you're like Yao, you probably think about how you don't know what to say, and then you try to avoid saying anything, especially anything for which you didn't have much time to prepare. As you can imagine, we recommend that you act against these negative thoughts and impulses and get yourself to speak up even though it's difficult. Here are four tips to help you speak up effectively in meetings.

1. *Want to talk.* The reason this is so important is because speaking will feel like it's within your voluntary control *and* desire. This is crucial. It is also very difficult to do. You may be asking yourself: "How can I make myself want to talk when I don't really want to?" Come up with some specific reasons why speaking up at the meeting will benefit you and your career. Give yourself some incentives and rewards for speaking. The key is to enter the meeting thinking: I want to say something today.

2. *Do not evaluate.* At least at first, your primary goal should be to say something at the meeting. If you achieve this goal, give yourself a lot of credit and praise and do *not* evaluate what you said, how you said it, or how people responded. These aspects of speaking will improve over time, as you get more comfortable speaking up. When you evaluate your speaking,

you're less likely to feel comfortable, and your speaking abilities will not improve. It's especially important not to evaluate what you're saying as you're saying it. Yao made his goal to just say something, regardless of whether it was an excellent point or perfectly stated. He found that when he took the pressure off himself to say something eloquent, he spoke much better.

3. *Focus on your coworkers and the discussion.* Have faith that you know the material and that the ideas that come out of your mouth will be sound. Stop focusing on yourself. Getting your attention onto your coworkers will help you feel less self-conscious. If you're sitting there planning everything that you can possibly say, you commit two major errors. First, you focus on yourself and become more anxious. Second, you neglect to pay attention to the topic of discussion and are therefore less likely to say something relevant or pertinent. Focus on the content of the meeting and not on yourself and what you'll say next.

4. *Speak up in a meeting every chance you get.* As we have discussed, practice exercises need to be repeated as much as possible to build confidence and competence. While meetings may feel like impromptu speaking situations, you can often do a little planning ahead of time if you know the agenda or topic. You can come up with a couple of key points you'd like to make. This is helpful because then you won't spend the meeting thinking about what to say; you can relax and keep your focus on the meeting rather than on yourself.

Below, we list possible ways to get practice speaking up in meetings in order to build your confidence and beat your nervousness. Add to the list other examples of practice. You can rank the items in this list in order of least to most difficult, in terms of which situations make you most anxious. Begin with the exercises that bring up less anxiety and work your way up to the more difficult ones.

Practice Exercises

1. Offer to present weekly statistics or reports to the team.
2. Introduce a new member, guest, or client.
3. Ask two to three questions per meeting.
4. Answer two to three questions per meeting.
5. Offer to be the meeting facilitator.
6. Take a class and make three to five comments per class in a smaller class, or one to two comments in a larger class.
7. Volunteer to present a summary of your current work or projects.
8. Make two to three follow-up comments on a point one of your colleagues has made.
9. Offer a new or original viewpoint.
10. Say something to present the opposite side of a situation.
11. Another practice:_____
12. Another practice:_____

Talk Spontaneously to Authority Figures

If you recall, our client Petra was a young woman who became very nervous when she needed to meet with her boss. Her boss was somewhat difficult, but not horrible, and Petra's fears greatly outweighed the real difficulties they had when they met. Anxiety magnifies the danger or risk in situations.

Authority figures who make people nervous range from bosses and supervisors to police officers, judges, doctors, teachers, and professors. Some people also become uncomfortable speaking with those who do not necessarily have authority but who have what they perceive as higher social status than they do.

If you become uncomfortable speaking with people in authority, you may fear speaking to authority figures in general, or you may only become nervous if it's an evaluative situation, or if you have to face an authority figure after doing something wrong or making requests for raises, promotions, or time off.

What follows are key principles to keep in mind in order to stop being afraid around superiors at work or others in authority:

1. *They are people too.* Petra became nervous around her boss because she built her up to be a super power. She saw her boss as different from her, and with an "us versus them" attitude, she assumed that her boss would be critical of her. In reality, Petra's boss thought highly of her and just had a direct, no-nonsense attitude with everyone.

   Often when we're face-to-face with a top CEO or someone else who is quite intimidating, we feel nervous and uncomfortable, almost as if we're not worthy to be speaking to them or that they will think we're not worthy or competent. In our work as communications trainers, we often work with top executives, politicians, actors, business owners, and performers, and it can be intimidating to be around people of their stature—even for us, and we're training them!

   People who are comfortable with speaking up in front of groups or chatting with friends sometimes become unraveled when they have to speak with people in authority. We attribute to these people larger than life personas and forget that they're people who have outside interests and lives just as we have.

   Have you seen the classic movie *The Wizard of Oz?* Remember how Oz was thought to be a big, scary, powerful entity but was in fact an awkward little guy? This doesn't mean that your boss or the authority figures who make you nervous are necessarily like the wizard behind the curtain, but remember the bottom line: You do not know what they're really like. They may be just as nervous as you. They may put on an act of toughness but be teddy bears inside.

2. *Get to know them.* This idea follows suit from the first point. The more you can get to know the individual in a nonevaluative way, the better. With a boss, for example, you do not want your only meetings to be your performance appraisals and the only topics discussed to be evaluative in nature. If you

can develop a comfort level and rapport, you'll be able to speak effectively with your boss in any situations that arise.

Get to know authority figures by asking some questions. With a boss, for instance, if you see photographs in his or her office, make an appropriate comment, such as, "What a beautiful child. Is that your son?" or "I had a golden retriever for 10 years. Aren't they great dogs?" or "Do you like to sail? I've always wanted to learn . . . " Anything that your boss has in his or her office is fair game for a brief discussion because the boss has already chosen to share it by displaying it. Don't get overly inquisitive or personal; just show that you have some common interests.

3. *Dismiss any negativity.* Have you had an experience in which your supervisor was abrupt with you and you thought, She does not like me? Or one where a professor made a face when you said something and you thought: He thinks that I don't speak well?

Keep in mind that negativity coming from an authority figure—or from anyone, for that matter—may have *nothing to do with you.* That person may be thinking about something troubling, reacting to a stressful work situation, responding to bad news as opposed to the messenger, and so on. One client who was an MBA student recently told Larina that his professor always gave him dirty looks. It turned out that the professor squinted and frowned when he looked in the direction of this student because the sun was in his eyes. (The student tended to sit in the same place in the room.)

Also, a good deal of research shows that people who are afraid of critical evaluation interpret ambiguous social cues as negative. That is, people with a speaking phobia are likely to interpret a laugh as being directed toward them or a neutral face as being a critical one. Remember this as you're interpreting people's reactions to your speaking.

Try to tell yourself that negative responses may not actually be negative—it's just how you're interpreting them. Or it may be that the person actually does have a less-than-pleasant expression on his or her face but it has nothing to do with you and what you just said.

4. *Act with confidence even if you don't feel confident.* Most people in authority like to feel that they're talking with people who are their equals, or at least who act as though they are. It's unpleasant to feel that you make people uncomfortable. This is where some acting is called for. Sometimes merely acting with confidence can make you feel more confident. It also can make people respond more positively to you, which in turn will make you feel even more confident. For best results, combine acting with confidence and an optimistic attitude. An optimistic attitude is strongly correlated with a successful outcome.

You may be wondering, How do I act with confidence when I don't feel confident? Spend some time observing people who seem very self-assured. Write down some of their specific behaviors. For instance, they:

- Make solid eye contact
- Use a firm handshake
- Do not rush through material
- Smile appropriately
- Have good posture
- Use appropriate gestures when they speak

5. *Think of your strengths.* Another way to feel less intimidated when you speak spontaneously to authority figures is to remember what you have going for you. Make a list of your strengths relative to those of the person who makes you nervous. For example, if you're speaking with the CEO of your company, your list could include:

- Consistently positive performance reviews
- History of excellent sales and customer service
- A major new account you helped your company land
- Several previous positive interactions with the CEO
- Your loyalty to the company as evidenced by several years of employment

If it's a professor who makes you nervous, compose a mental list all of your good grades and positive remarks in the professor's class. If it's a supervisor, summarize and write down all of your glowing feedback from evaluations. This will help you feel more self-assured and act with more confidence (see point 4 above).

6. *Every day, speak with your boss or whoever makes you nervous.* Of course, you may not need to speak to the authority figure every single day, but the idea is to speak to that person or in front of that person as much as possible. If you do not have much access to this authority figure, select some similar people (other professors, trainers, doctors, supervisors, and so on) and speak to them as much as possible.

Below is a list of ways to gain practice with speaking to authority figures. Add other ideas to the list based on your own experiences or fears. Rank the items in this list from least to most difficult or anxiety-producing. Start with the exercises that bring up less nervousness and then work your way up to the more difficult ones.

Practice Exercises

1. Ask a supervisor, professor, or other authority figure for a private meeting. Request some feedback on your performance. This can be a more difficult task because, in addition to your exercise, you're also getting some feedback.

2. Make it a point to walk by the office of people who intimidate you in order to maximize your chances of running into them. When you do bump into them, say hello and ask them how they're doing.

3. Go out to lunch or other informal social gatherings with the people you are nervous around.

4. Direct questions toward the people who make you nervous during meetings.

5. Purposefully sit next to the people who make you nervous at a meeting or in class.

6. Take advantage of a professor's office hours or stop by your boss's office and talk about a project or an idea you had for improving a process.

7. Teach yourself that you can handle the nervousness in the unlikely event that you actually did give a wrong answer or made a minor mistake. Pick a relatively unimportant meeting or class (not a test, just a regular class) and make a minor mistake or give a wrong answer on purpose. This sounds crazy, but it will help you evaluate whether your fear of disastrous consequences is true. Purposefully do what you fear and then see how bad the outcome really is. Is it truly catastrophic? Can you survive it? Chances are you will learn that the result isn't that bad and that you can handle it.

8. Another practice:_____

9. Another practice:_____

10. Another practice:_____

Give a Great Presentation or Workshop

Leading a workshop is typically not an impromptu speaking engagement, but there are often times when you need to respond to a workshop audience in an impromptu way. Most of our clients worry that people will ask them questions that they're unprepared to answer. Giving a presentation can be so intimidating because all eyes are on you and you're the one in charge of the whole thing.

Let's revisit Jorge, the salesperson who dreaded his sales presentations. Jorge was so nervous about being asked difficult questions that he'd cut his presentations short and race out of the room to be sure people wouldn't grill him. Here are some pointers that helped Jorge; they can also help you when dealing with the fear of impromptu speaking during presentations:

1. *Be yourself.* We know that this is a cliché, but it is valuable regarding this type of situation. Often people feel they have to be certain things to lead a workshop or to get up in front of a group to give a presentation. A great way to connect with your audience is to reveal a bit of who you are. If you don't know the answer to something, say so, not in an apologetic way, but in a way that reflects some of your personality. Then offer to get the answer to the questioner at your earliest convenience.

2. *Make it interactive.* Everyone fears speaking up and boring the pants off their audience. One way to help ensure that you do not do this is to make your presentation or workshop interactive. If you're asked something you don't know the answer to, ask the audience if anyone else knows the answer. If no one does, say you'll find out and respond later that day.

3. *List all your fears ahead of time.* Make this list highly specific. Then go through the items one by one and see if there is a possibility that any of them are based on some of the cognitive distortions or overcompensating behaviors we have discussed. For instance, if you're afraid that you will try to hide your shaking hands but that someone will see them anyway, it should ring a bell (overcompensating behavior!). For any cognitive distortion, go through the process we described of evaluating the evidence for and against it. Plan not to do overcompensating behaviors. If you're afraid of what will happen if you do not do the behaviors, list your fear and test out whether that fear truly sets in.

4. *Practice, practice, practice.* You'll need to get many experiences of confronting your anxiety by giving presentations, or through experiences that simulate your fears about presenting. Make sure you get practice speaking spontaneously and answering questions.

Below we list ways to gain practice with giving workshops or presentations. Add other ideas to the bottom of this list based on your own experiences or concerns. As with the other recommended exercises, start doing these by beginning with the ones that are less intimidating and working your way up to the ones that are more so.

Practice Exercises

1. Create a 10-minute interactive presentation on any topic and present it to some of your friends or family members.
2. Develop a short workshop or training on a topic of interest to your colleagues. Then tell your supervisor that you would like to present it to your coworkers.

3. Practice your leadership skills by making assertive statements every day, by delegating tasks, and so on. You will need to be a strong leader to conduct a workshop.

4. Take a class. It does not necessarily have to be on speaking, but it should have numerous opportunities to speak and give presentations.

5. Practice teaching things you know to others. Have them ask questions and answer their questions.

6. Give a topic to a group of friends or family members and ask them to grill you on it for five minutes, asking as many questions as possible.

7. Another practice:_____

8. Another practice:_____

9. Another practice:_____

Speak Eloquently When Being Interviewed

Being interviewed is one of the rare situations in which you are actually being evaluated. And you typically need to speak spontaneously. If you're being interviewed for a media quote, you'll often get questions ahead of time, so let's discuss being interviewed for a job.

People who are nervous about public speaking often overestimate the likelihood that they will be negatively evaluated. Many people worry that they made it as far as the interview and will then ruin their chances of getting the position because of their poor interviewing skills.

Here are some tips to speaking for a great interview:

1. *What's worrying you?* One of the first important steps is determining what you are truly afraid will happen. Are you worried that you'll blow your chances at the job? Are you afraid of saying something idiotic? Scared you won't have any answers to the questions? Once you pinpoint your worry, you can evaluate how likely it is to occur.

2. *Challenge the fear to a contest.* Once you figure out what you're most afraid of, you can begin to challenge those ideas.

If you're thinking that you'll destroy your chances of getting the job, consider how often that has happened in the past, recognize that the interviewer probably realizes that most people are nervous about interviews, and so on. If you think you'll say something stupid, you can ask yourself, "So what?" Many people won't think that what you said was stupid, and even if they did, would they not offer you the job because of one comment? If you're worried about not having answers to questions, you can prepare some answers to commonly asked questions. Also, ask yourself: "So what if I take a minute to think of answers to the questions?" And tell yourself: "I'll look thoughtful and intelligent if I do." It's often better to take your time and give a great answer than to start rambling aimlessly.

3. *Connect with the interviewer.* Build rapport right away with the interviewer by engaging in some small talk and getting comfortable with him or her before the questions start coming at you. Connection equals comfort.

4. *It's a regular conversation.* Tell yourself that you're having a regular conversation with a coworker or colleague. Do not tell yourself that it's a conversation with your spouse or mother, because you have to project more of a professional tone. Do not think of it like an interrogation or other intimidating conversation; instead think about it as how you've talked about your accomplishments with a boss or work associate. As with a regular conversation, you do not want to dominate. If you find your answers going on and on and notice that the interviewer is getting bored, you need to be brief and engage the interviewer.

5. *Refine your skills.* As with all of these speaking situations, the best way to overcome anxiety and perfect your skills is to gain practice the right way.

Here are some examples of ways to practice so that you become confident in any situation for which you're interviewed. Add other practice exercises that you come up with to the bottom of this list. If some look particularly frightening to you, begin with the easier ones.

Practice Exercises

1. Get a list of interview questions from the Internet. Put them on separate pieces of paper and place them in a hat or a bowl. Begin pulling them out yourself and answering them. Later, ask someone else to pull out questions to ask you.
2. Videotape yourself being interviewed by someone. When you watch the tape, try to view it as an objective observer and rate the quality of the responses that you give. Once you master the content, tape another interview. This time when you watch it, focus on your behaviors, such as body position, eye contact, facial expressions, and so on.
3. Interview someone else. Putting yourself in the interviewer position will help you practice approaching the meeting as a regular conversation with less pressure.
4. Practice describing why you are ideal for the position and getting feedback from others to help build your confidence.
5. List all of the things you think you did well in previous interview situations. If you have not had many previous interview situations, think of other intimidating conversations.
6. Watch segments of televised interviews and news shows but turn off the sound. Observe the nonverbal behavior: facial expressions, gestures, and eye contact and see if you can figure out the intention of the people speaking. Are they trying to create rapport, inform, criticize?
7. Another practice:_____
8. Another practice:_____
9. Another practice:_____

Being Called Upon

What is so frightening about being called upon? For most people, it is the unpredictability and uncertainty surrounding the event. We think: I don't know how to respond to that! Or: I have nothing to say. Or: Everyone is staring at me, and it feels like it's been five minutes of silence.

We introduced Daniella earlier. She is the woman who sat in the back of her large lecture class and hoped she was inconspicuous enough so that the professor would not call on her. She looked down and pretended to be busily engaged in taking copious notes. She didn't know that her behaviors kept her from overcoming her anxiety. If you're like Daniella, here's what you need to do to speak up confidently when called upon:

1. *Do not try to hide.* Have you ever seen people who are obviously trying to not be called on? They look down, slouch, look away, and act as though they're busy. It's obvious. The fact of the matter is that they can still be seen, they look silly, and if someone wants to call on them, they will be called on! Whether or not you know the answer or have something to say, make eye contact, look confident, and let yourself be visible.

2. *You can always say, "I don't know."* Let's face it, there will be times when someone wants you to say something and you simply do not know the answer. Rather than stammer through, trying to mutter something, state a confident, "I'm not sure" or "I will have to look into that and get back to you." If you really have no idea what to say, honesty is the best policy.

3. *Take your best shot.* If you have any idea what the answer might be, go for it. Most people find that it's better to try and fail than not to try at all. Generally, we can pull together an answer somehow, based on what's been said, our past knowledge and background, our intuition, or other ideas. Speak in a way that sounds thoughtful ("Well . . . ") but not tentative ("Uh . . . ").

4. *Follow the flow of the conversation.* When you get caught up with focusing your attention on your own thoughts, fears, feelings, and concerns, you'll probably not even hear the question much less know what else has been said so far. If you're doing a good job of focusing your attention externally, you'll know what's being discussed and will be in a much better position to answer the question.

Below is a list of ways to gain practice with coming up with answers and being called upon. Add some other ideas to the bottom of this list. Put them into order of difficulty and begin practice with the easier ones and work your way up.

Practice Exercises

1. Get together a group of questions, such as from a game like Trivial Pursuit. Ask a group of friends or family members to pick one of the questions and talk about it for three minutes (without telling you the question). After three minutes, have them ask you the question. This will make you follow a brief discussion and answer a question that you may not know the answer to.
2. Practice making eye contact during every discussion, knowing that at any moment you could be called on.
3. Raise your hand. Volunteer to answer questions as much as possible.
4. Tell people to call on you. Let your colleagues and supervisors know that you're trying to perfect your skills at thinking on your feet, so you'd like them to call on you whenever possible.
5. Another practice:_____
6. Another practice:_____
7. Another practice:_____

Answering Questions Following a Speech

We discussed spontaneous questions that can come at you during presentations, and how Jorge overcame his fears of sales presentations. Here we discuss questions after a formal talk, such as a lecture or keynote address. The idea is similar to the one about being called on, but this time you're up in front of a group and are *expected* to be able to answer questions *and* answer them well. People assume that you have expertise in the area covered by your speech and on every topic related to it—even when they are only related peripherally.

Answering questions following a speech can be challenging even for the most seasoned presenters. We previously introduced Martin, a professional speaker who feels very confident with planned presentations but dreads answering questions afterward. Martin's case is quite common. You never know what people will ask you, so it can be intimidating to take follow-up questions.

Here are the principles to answering questions after a speech:

1. *Give the audience some guidelines.* When you give a presentation, you are the leader. You can direct the way things go, including the question/answer portion. When you're ready to take questions, tell the audience that you will now take questions about something specific from your talk. For example, "We have a limited time for questions, and people are usually most interested in learning more about the sales dialogue, so I can take a couple questions on that now."

2. *Answer every question.* Nothing is as insulting to audience members as when someone blows off their questions. You may have seen someone do this: It's pretty clear that the speaker does not know the answer, so he or she quickly moves on to the next question. If you do this, you may alienate your listeners and be perceived as rude. Even if you don't have an answer, acknowledge the question. If you don't have anything to say, respond by saying that it's outside your area of expertise.

3. *Offer to follow up with a questioner individually or as a group.* When you do not have an answer to a question, tell the person that you'll be happy to look into the matter and respond by e-mail or telephone. Or say that you know about a good article that addresses the topic and that you can send it.

4. *Remember, you probably know more about your topic than most of your listeners.* Do not feel as though you have to give a "perfect" answer to every question. Many people in the audience will not know as much about your topic as you do, so even if you feel as though you're answering at a very fundamental level, you may be providing a great deal of value to your audience.

226 ◆ THE CONFIDENT SPEAKER

5. *What are you afraid of?* Think carefully about this: Why are you afraid of answering questions and thinking on your feet? Are you fearful of being embarrassed? Looking unknowledgeable? Stuttering or stammering? Saying something ridiculous? Once you know exactly what you're afraid of, test it out. Using the practice examples below, make a prediction about how likely it is that your fear will occur, and then find out whether it actually happens. Do not rely on your opinion as to whether it happened (because you will likely *feel* that it did even if it didn't), but gather some responses from audience members to assess the outcomes.

6. *Answer as many questions as possible.* The more time you spend doing Q&A, the more practice opportunities you'll have. And as we've discussed throughout this chapter, practice is key for building confidence and improving skills.

Here's a list of ways to gain more experience so that you'll be able to answer questions after a talk. Look at the list and add examples.

Practice Exercises

1. Every time you talk, ask people if they have any questions.

2. Before you accept questions, take a moment to focus yourself. You want to feel poised before you start having questions fired at you. Being poised is having the ability to think on your feet. It is grace under pressure. It's something that comes naturally to certain people and for others takes practice. Pick a word that makes you feel poised (calm, poise, grace . . .) and say it to yourself before the questions come.

3. Put yourself in stressful situations to develop poise. For instance, mediate a conflict at work, raise a controversial topic with some friends, have "the talk" with your preteen daughter, and so on.

4. Ask questions yourself and observe how the speakers respond. Use their good ways of responding as a role model for how you would like to appear.

5. Another practice:_____
6. Another practice:_____
7. Another practice:_____

The Next Step: Performances and Presentations

Now that you know how to speak spontaneously and have many practice exercises to try, it's time to move on. The next chapter is for those who want to improve their skills in large lectures, keynote speeches, major presentations, and performance situations. You may want to read this chapter even if you do not need to give large talks, because you may still find ideas that can help you. Ready to face a big audience? If you said, "Uh . . . no!" then keep reading!

13

Large-Scale Presentations and Workshops

SOME PEOPLE SEEM to have been born with the ability to captivate an audience, which can be intimidating to those of us who don't think we have any natural talent. The truth is that more than likely, even the most gifted speaker has had to work hard to make his presentation engaging and flawless. While some people may be naturally extroverted, funny, or charismatic, the rest of us need to work at it—and we can.

What this means is that with a little effort you can convince your audience that you have a natural talent for presenting, and it will be well worth your time to do so. Not only will you be successful at sharing information and inspiring your audience into action, but the poise you gain from speaking in public will carry over into an extra boost of confidence in your daily interactions. Learning to prepare for speaking to a large audience and leading a workshop are great ways to gain confidence and develop your ability to communicate effectively.

Presenting to a Large Audience

Sarah is approaching the entrance of the auditorium where she is about to speak in front of the largest audience she has ever faced. The murmur and muted chatter she can hear from the assembled crowd seems to drill a hole directly into her stomach. I was fine speaking in front of eight people the other day, she thinks. Why am I freaking out now?

It's not unusual for even a seasoned speaker to find her confidence shaken by a new situation, especially when it's her first experience speaking in front of a large crowd. When the audience is comprised of a sea of faces you have never met before, the anxiety can hit suddenly, seemingly robbing you of every last bit of your poise and self-assurance. Public speaking is humanity's number one fear, but like all fears, it can be faced and conquered, even if it involves large audiences.

The term "large audience" is relative and can mean different things to different people. In our experience, most people refer to audiences of 100 and up as a "large" audience. That's because their speaking opportunities and assignments are often limited to small to medium-sized groups of between 8 to 50 participants, typically consisting of peers, colleagues, or clients. Thus, an audience of 100 or more can seem particularly intimidating and unmanageable.

Now imagine an audience of 500, 1,000, 5,000, 10,000, and up. Is there any way to connect with so many people? How does a speaker make use of the all-important eye contact to establish rapport with so many people? And what about the speaker's voice, gestures, and proximity to the audience in order to get his or her message across?

The simple answer is that you still use all of those attributes to connect with your very large audience; you just have to amplify them.

Think for a moment of the speakers you've heard, perhaps even witnessed in person, who had to address audiences of many hundreds or even thousands. Some of the events where an audience of a very large size is customary include political rallies, Fortune 500 corporate shareholder meetings, large-scale religious events in so-called super churches, self-help seminars à la Anthony Robbins, graduation commencement speeches, and, for particularly prolific speakers, media events that are broadcast to millions.

The only way you can effectively share yourself with an audience of "super-size" proportions is to amplify your presentation and communication tools. Specifically, this means you have to make use of microphones, cameras, large-screen monitors, and a platform or stage where people can see you without obstructions.

With the help of audiovisual technology, you can get as close to the audience as you need to in order to get your message across. With close-ups and camera angles, you are merely inches away from every person in the audience. With the help of wireless microphones, you don't even have to stay in one place, but are free to move about your platform. With the help of microphones you're also able to use the nuances of your vocal tonality for dramatic impact, as there is no need to shout or even speak up. Your voice can easily be heard in the remotest corner of the stadium, if that's your venue.

There is an important middle ground however, and that is the presentation or speech where expensive technology is unavailable, but the crowd is still large enough for the speaker's message to get lost.

In these situations, remember the following:

1. *Exaggerate your gestures.* If your listeners can't see you and the output of your passion and emotion—your gestures and facial expressions—they can't be touched by it. Think of it this way: If we see an old friend across the street, we may say hello with the wave of a hand and a smile. But if he or she were a block away, we'd have to wave our arms and lift our voices for the friend to notice us. It's perhaps a silly analogy, but too often, inexperienced speakers who present to a larger audience literally "disappear" in front of the crowd because they can't be perceived effectively, visually and audibly.

2. *Lift your voice.* Hopefully you'll have use of a microphone, but without one you'll still have to make sure the audience can hear your message. Even the person in the worst seat of the house should be able to hear you clearly. Also, vary the speed

of your talk and adjust your inflections and volume as appropriate. Remember that your voice must now work harder in carrying your message to its target.

3. *Remove any obstructions to the audience's view.* Make sure they can see you well and you can see them. Don't just speak to those in the front row because you can see their eyes well. Focus your attention also on the faces in the back and to the sides of the venue.

4. *Move purposefully and project energy.* Nothing is more tiresome for a large audience, particularly the members in the back of the room, than staring at a focal point in the center way up front. Don't let them tune out just because you chose to stand behind a podium like a statue. Engage them with physical movement and walk toward them to emphasize a point. Walk from one side of the stage to the other to capture their attention. Think of your speech as a well-choreographed performance where every movement has a purpose in getting the message across.

5. *Don't blend in with your surroundings.* Make sure that your outfit can be distinguished from your background. Choose strong colors that support your visual image so that your audience can pick you out from any distracting visuals or background on the stage.

6. *Ask the audience to stand up during Q&A.* Well, not all of them, but the people asking the questions. Since we're assuming in this case that you don't have the use of boom microphones to amplify individual audience members' voices, ask them to stand up when asking questions. This way, you can walk toward them to better hear the questions, while other audience members can hear and see them and understand the questions better than if the questioners remain seated. Repeat the questions before you answer them to be sure that the entire audience hears them.

You now have a better idea of what it takes to engage a larger audience. Remember that it's critical for the audience to see and hear a fellow human being speaking to them, no matter how large or small the size of the group. If technology can bring you closer, great. If that's not an option, you must make yourself larger than life in sight and sound to give the audience the opportunity to perceive the message the way you intended and not get lost in the proverbial crowd.

Next, let's talk about what it takes to go for a presentation home run.

Creating the "Perfect" Presentation

The first component of preparing to speak in front of a crowd is to know your audience. As we discussed in Chapter 11, do your homework and find out who will be in the crowd. Then write your presentation with them in mind. If you're speaking to a particular organization, make sure you know its mission and its stand on issues that apply to your speech. The best way to engage an audience is to speak their language, not just literally, but culturally. If you know what issues are at the forefront of the group's mind, you can capture and hold attention by working relevant anecdotes and examples into your presentation. More important, you can avoid unintentionally alienating your audience.

Now that you know who will be listening, you can start formulating your speech on paper. Before you figure out the body of what you're going to say, however, make sure you have a message. There should be a thesis that you could describe in a short sentence if asked. This point should be simply stated at the beginning and the end of your speech. Audiences have a limited capacity for what they remember, so make sure the gist of what you're trying to say is obvious and repeated appropriately throughout your talk.

Even with a good thesis, it's not enough to just put your thoughts down and present them out loud. A good speech is like a novel, with an opening that grabs the listeners' attention, rising action in the middle that keeps them engaged, and a climactic conclusion that satisfies them. The parts should be woven together with easy-to-follow transitions that lead listeners through your story and get them excited and incited.

Start with an engaging introduction, but avoid gimmicks. The last thing you want to do is fall flat on your face at the beginning of your talk.

If you stumble somewhere in the middle, you can keep going, but it's harder to recover from a failed opening. Try beginning with an anecdote, an inspiring quote that applies to your topic, or a thought-provoking question. This is where a speaker gives a listener a reason to pay attention and keep listening. Grab the attention of your audience and then let them know what they're going to learn by stating your point.

The middle of your speech is for sharing information and illuminating your thesis. Remember, though, that less information can mean more impact. A speech cluttered with facts, figures, and trivial information will bore and confuse your audience. Choose a handful of ways to illustrate the primary message of your talk. Use relevant stories and anecdotes to keep the audience's attention. A good story can amuse and clarify as well as reinforce your message.

The conclusion of your speech should leave the audience inspired and clear about the reason for your speech. This is where you leave your message ringing in their ears. Make your conclusion memorable and strong; tie your speech back to its beginning.

Humor can be an effective tool when giving a speech, but use it with care. Writing jokes into a speech, as we've discussed, can be tricky and more often than not the jokes fall flat. Good humor requires excellent timing and a receptive audience. Because of this, the best jokes are often inserted on the fly while talking. When a good line works, you may find yourself using it time and time again in speeches. This is the most natural and effective way to establish rapport with your audience during your presentations. Let humor grow out of the situation, but be prepared to seize upon the opportunity to point out the humor in complex issues that would benefit from a tension-releasing moment of laughter. Skip the jokes, or both you and your audience may be squirming.

Remember too that the most effective presentation is rarely a lecture. Aim to inspire, even when your goal is simply to instruct. Keep your speech simple and entertaining. Write it, knowing that you want to sway the audience to your way of thinking and not just educate them. At the foundation of every good talk is persuasion and entertainment. While most people can manage to stand in front of a crowd and recite a list of facts, those who court success are the ones who actively strive for results from communicating with an audience. Use personal stories or stories of your clients or friends to engage your audience members' curiosity. For more tips on the use of storytelling, download the free special report "Powerful Storytelling Techniques" from www.TheConfidentSpeaker.com.

Preparing the Compelling Presentation

We've said this throughout the book, but it can't be said enough: The best thing you can do to raise your confidence and speak compellingly to audiences is to practice and then practice some more. Practice in front of a video camera. Practice in front of friends and family. Practice in front of patient colleagues. Practice with a speech and presentations coach. Know by heart the content of your talk so that you can focus on impressing your message upon the audience. Plus, the better you know your speech, the easier it will be to manage your anxiety when the proverbial butterflies start flapping their wings rapidly in your stomach. Practicing and "owning" your material will also allow you to focus on your nonverbal communication to your listeners, and it will help keep you from rushing through your talk, which is a common reaction to presentation nervousness.

A word of caution about practicing, however: There's no need to learn your speech word for word. It may actually be counterproductive. A great speech can so enrapture and captivate an audience that it can seem like it's coming straight from the top of your head. If you labor too hard and overpractice, not only will you get bored, but your audience will later join you in a collective yawn. Therefore, do your level best to *can* the canned speech. And speak from the heart.

A knack for ad-libbing can also make a huge difference in the quality of your presentation. It will help you respond to your audience at the exact moment you need to look good—which of course is always—but particular moments of brilliance are always rewarded with admiration from even the stodgiest of audiences. Don't be afraid to change the pace or detail of information if your listeners appear disinterested, and know when to throw in a pregnant pause. Good ad-libbing, for all but a select few people, generally comes with practice and courage, not necessarily through talent. You may consider taking some drama classes at your local performing arts center or making a fun habit of suggesting and playing ad-libbing games at your next dinner party. Knowing you can project your wit to a delighted audience at a strategically important point in your talk will boost your confidence and ground you in your preparation.

Props relevant to your topic are another way to vary the pace in a presentation and keep your audience focused and interested. Slides, Power-Point presentations, charts and graphs, video- and film clips, as well as hand-outs, are all examples of audiovisual props. Any item that effectively and memorably illustrates a particular point you are making is fair game.

Use props liberally if they help clarify and reinforce your message but be aware of their drawbacks. Handouts can give your audience some-thing to pay attention to other than your speech. So you may want to save those for the end if you're going to use them. Charts and graphs should be made simple and easy to understand or you'll lose your audience's atten-tion rather than gain it. Slides and PowerPoint presentations are great if they punctuate your points, but they shouldn't be what carry your speech. Remember that no one wants to see the slide show from their neighbor's vacation to Maui, and they shouldn't feel that's what they're watching during your presentation.

Be brave and creative in your use of props—try something out of the ordinary. One speaker Larina heard used about six different physical props in his keynote. To illustrate his point about an increase in revenue, he calculated a revenue increase of about three pennies per second. He took a giant glass jar and dropped three pennies per second into it, and the sound of the pennies hitting the glass was powerful and brought his point to life. Authors of *How to Persuade People Who Don't Want to Be Persuaded* Joel Bauer and Mark Levy refer to a physical illustration of a point through the use of props as a type of "transformational mecha-nism." The ideas are more memorable, and new ways of viewing a situa-tion are inspired.

Keep in mind that technology is fallible. You never know when equipment might fail or be difficult to get up and running. Depending on circumstances often outside of your control, technology can be a liability rather than an asset. Rely on yourself and your ability to tell the story rather than on hiding behind the crutch of the ubiquitous PowerPoint slide show. When the power goes out, your audience will still be there, so make sure you're prepared to fly without the instruments and land your objective right where you want it—in the hearts and minds of your listeners. People are smart. They know when you're leaning on technology to impress them instead of making great points and engaging them on an emotional level. While any multimedia can be an important piece of a captivating presentation, you, the speaker, are the most important component. It's also important to mention that knowing that the show will go on even if the technology refuses to cooperate will eliminate a good deal of stress.

Presenting Yourself

Despite all your preparation and practice, chances are you're going to be nervous anyway. Not only is that normal, but it's great to be nervous. A little bit of anxiety will keep you engaged and on your toes and prevent your speech from being stale. Many professional actors say that once the butterflies go away, it's time to get a new job. If your heart is pounding a little bit, get up to the podium and go with it. It is your marching drum before you go into battle. It's the powerful motor that will keep your talk from sputtering and stalling out. It's a sign that your emotions are alive and that you take your message and your audience seriously. And that spirit will spill over to the audience in a noticeable way.

When you get up on stage, don't forget to stand tall. Most of us hunch somewhat, particularly the taller folks among us. Your body language will have a lot to do with how the audience perceives you. If you have notes, glance at them to keep pace if you need to but resist the temptation to read them verbatim. Use gesturing appropriately to support your words and move with purpose if you're comfortable walking about and the microphone will allow the movement. Remember that your nerves fuel your talk. So when you feel the anxiety rushing through your body, try not to suppress the energy but let it fire the emotions and vocal tonality that carry your message. What the audience will see is a dynamic and confident speaker.

While you are presenting, engage your audience. Make eye contact with individuals and smile. Don't just scan the room; look people in the eye as if you were having a conversation exclusively with them. This will keep your audience watching and listening to you.

Pay attention to the audience as a whole. If people stop looking at you and seem distracted, adjust your speech. Vary your pitch. Pause. Whisper and raise your volume to give emphasis to important points of your message. Maybe you're spending too much time belaboring a certain issue and ought to move on or wrap up your talk. Generally speaking, it's best to keep your talk under 45 minutes, if possible. Shorter is always better when trying to keep an audience's attention. The last thing you want to do is give your audience a chance to tune out and miss your most important points.

Concluding a Presentation

You're reaching the home stretch and have almost made it, but remember that your audience is most likely to remember the beginning and the end of your speech. Now is the time to drive your point home. Let your audience know with your pacing that the speech is just about to end and that they should listen up. Don't just fade away; get their attention and reiterate your core message. The law of primacy and recency says that people remember most what is said at the beginning and the end of a talk. The rule of thumb is: For a short presentation, put the key message at the beginning, because people will remember the start best. For a longer talk, place the key message at the end, as people are likely to remember the ending best. Trial lawyers live by this maxim of primacy and recency as they strive to influence their audiences of jurors and judges, and you can make it work for you in your persuasive efforts.

If it's appropriate to the presentation and it helps your audience clarify the issues, include a question-and-answer session. Let your listeners know up front how much time you allow for Q&A, but remain flexible if you need to extend the session, providing it doesn't cut into the time of the speaker following you. You may also tell your audience that you'll be available after the question-and-answer period for conversation so that no questions are left unanswered.

Many speakers feel uncomfortable with the Q&A, not realizing the potential to expand their credibility with such a session. When people ask questions, reinforce your message within the answer and also clear up potential misunderstandings.

If you don't know the answer to a listener's question, be honest and offer to provide the questioner with the answer after doing some research. Avoid evasiveness. And don't use the gimmick that some speech trainers recommend of turning the question around to one that you can answer. Audience members will feel annoyed and manipulated, and your credibility will go down. People will look right through any effort at snowing them. Always be honest and genuine—you will be more likable and credible.

Keep your answers short and to the point, reinforcing your talk's message if appropriate. When you're done, be gracious and thank your questioners for their insightful questions.

In a Q&A worst-case scenario, you may get inflammatory questions posed with hostile vocal tonality. When this happens, the best policy is to stay calm. The rest of the audience will give you the benefit of the doubt if they perceive you to be honest and credible, and they will be as uncomfortable with such an attack as you are. The key is to not go after the questioner. The underdog will have the audience's sympathy, so let the heckler be the bad guy and keep your cool. If possible, offer the hostile questioner the opportunity to address his or her concerns outside of the current forum, allowing you to continue your talk.

Every speech and talk you give presents a great learning experience. Remember that the best presenters practice and rehearse, but the most valuable learning comes from every speaking experience. Whenever you get the chance, have your presentation videotaped to learn from the audience feedback and from your own detached perspective, as well as the perspective of a qualified observer such as a speech and presentations coach. When you review your talk on video, ask yourself whether there were nonverbal communication issues you need to work on, witty comments that got a great reaction, or parts of your presentation that just didn't work. Take note of the positive and negative, and resolve to improve what didn't work the next time you give a talk.

There's no mystery to giving talks to large audiences. Preparation and practice will build your confidence and help you develop into a "natural" speaker. Now that you're ready to give presentations to big crowds, it's time to look at something equally challenging, but nonetheless rewarding—leading a workshop.

Leading a Workshop

A workshop environment can be a fabulous way to teach a new skill, solve a particular problem in a group environment, and build teams. Workshops always have a leader, but frequently the point of the workshop is to pool resources, ideas, and experience. Collectively, the members of your workshop may have more experience than you do as a leader. Often, this means that much of your job will simply consist of facilitating. With plenty of effective preparation, leading a workshop will be a powerful asset to your own speaking experience as well as to the lives of those you impact in a workshop.

Creating a Successful Workshop

First, we'd like to make sure you know what we're talking about when we refer to a "workshop," because people use the term in a number of ways, and not always correctly. Different from a speech, where typically you are the only one speaking, or a seminar where interaction with the audience is customary to varying degrees, a workshop is an occasion in which an audience actively works on what they're learning during an instructor-led session.

In order to create a successful workshop, you'll need to start with the basics, and start early. When possible, get busy planning at least six months before the workshop, especially if you are hosting the event yourself (which we describe in this section) rather than delivering a workshop to an organization. There's nothing more stressful or likely to bust your confidence than trying to pull a workshop together at the eleventh hour. Figure out months in advance who you plan on inviting so that you can start thinking about how to organize the event. Know how many people you expect to attend so that you can start looking at facilities. Consider how long it will take to reach your goals so that you can decide if your workshop will last a day, a weekend, or an entire week. Once you've considered all of these issues, you can start working out the details.

Staffing your workshop can be critical if it's a large event. Once you have established the basic design of the workshop, you can delegate the details to someone else. You will need someone to be an administrator.

This is the person who will send out materials, register attendees, do promotions, and manage details such as meals, seating, and equipment. Having a competent staff will allow you to focus on designing the most effective structure and materials for your workshop.

As you develop the workshop, focus on creating a program that keeps your participants involved instead of just having them listen to you lecture. As you gather information, make sure that the data you are presenting are accurate and current. Define and clearly state the goals of the workshop, and with these goals in mind, decide on activities and methods. Carefully work out a schedule that will be easy to adhere to and adjust. Don't forget to allow time for participants to think, collaborate, share thoughts, express concerns, ask questions, and, no less important, enjoy the process.

Preparing a Successful Workshop

One recipe for a successful workshop is effective preparation. That's because one thing you can count on is that during the entire process—from planning to execution—unexpected issues will come up, potentially derailing your best efforts. In leading a workshop, your job is to facilitate learning and focus on the progress of the participants. This would be difficult if your attention were divided by any number of fires that needed extinguishing. You therefore have to prepare for every eventuality so that you can move quickly to "Plan B" in case of an unforeseen event, and thereby keep the focus on effective learning for the workshop participants.

Since progress and the learning objectives of the participants are the reasons you have the program in the first place, make sure you have a profile of the attendees before you conduct the workshop. There are a number of ways to gather information about your audience; one of them is the inclusion of questions on the registration form; another is by asking the meeting planner specific questions about the attendees; and another is by creating a short survey for attendees to complete beforehand (you can do this online with services such as www.surveymonkey.com). By knowing what the participants expect to get out of your workshop and understanding what their needs are, you will be better able to design your program.

Make sure you clarify your own goals when preparing for your workshop, and keep them at the forefront of your mind as you structure the program for maximum mutual benefit. Having goals and sticking to them as you design your curriculum will ensure that your workshop is properly developed and ultimately runs smoothly so that everyone meets their objectives—both you and the participants. It will also give attendees a clear idea of what they can anticipate and should expect to learn for the time they spend with you.

Presenting a Successful Workshop

It's often a good idea to begin your workshop with an assessment of your attendees and their information needs. If your workshop is about increasing knowledge or team building, a short questionnaire can give you an idea of the base level of knowledge in the group. This will help you speak to and facilitate the discussion without talking down to people or over their heads, and to avoid communicating unnecessary information. Questionnaires and surveys are also recommended at the end of the workshop to get a preliminary idea of what attendees have learned, whether they enjoyed the program, and what, if anything, should be modified.

Once you have a handle on how best to conduct the program with your workshop attendees, it can be beneficial to perform introductions and icebreakers. Love them or hate them, these activities can be essential to getting a team of workshop participants working together. A good ice-breaking exercise can quickly introduce everyone and build camaraderie among participants and the workshop leader. Try to be more creative than just having the people simply introduce themselves. Going around in a circle and having each attendee say something is not very effective, since people are usually too busy trying to figure out something clever to say to listen to the introductions before them. Do you do this too? Because of strong feelings of performance anxiety, people may also focus too much on themselves and their fear of public speaking as they take turns with personal introductions.

Instead of doing standard introductions, you could try having people pair up, share personal information for a couple of minutes, and then introduce each other instead of themselves. Another idea, for an icebreaker perhaps, would be to have each person in the group say his or her name, place of work, and favorite food. The next person repeats this information and adds his or her own. This will quickly get everyone to learn each other's names and to laugh and cheer each other on. It also encourages group members to pay attention to each other instead of focusing on their reluctance to speak during the workshop. There are entire books devoted to icebreakers and introduction exercises for workshop leaders and trainers. Make sure you pick activities that are relevant for the age bracket of your participants, or you could alienate and turn them off early on in your program.

Once everyone knows one another and feels comfortable, it's time to get busy. Most of your agenda will already be set and given to your attendees in the form of a handout or program schedule. You can also give workshop attendees the opportunity to contribute to the agenda. Perhaps there are some slots where the participants can choose how to best utilize their group time. Open up the room for discussion and allow participants to comment on what they would most like to take home from the workshop. Remember that you're leading, not lecturing. Your job is to make sure your listeners are get the workshop they want and need.

Once you've got an agenda, though, make sure everyone understands and is ready to adhere to the timetable. The schedule will mostly be your responsibility, and sticking to individual timed modules will help you keep things moving along without any hang-ups. However, if everyone understands and buys into the objectives of the workshop and its timetable, your job of management will be much easier.

If you're running a larger workshop, creating smaller work groups will play an important role in the success of the workshop. Generally speaking, an average workshop has about 20 people, who can be broken into four teams. Depending on your objectives and those of the participants, you will want to make sure that the grouping you assign makes sense. You may even want to watch the group dynamics during the icebreakers and then decide how to balance the groups afterward. The better the mix of personalities, the more effective the group will be. You can also have participants work in a variety of group settings throughout the workshop, using different-sized groupings for different activities such as idea exchange, brainstorming, and information sharing. Groups of twos and threes can be very effective as well, and they give participants the opportunity to work closely with members of the entire group.

As you direct the groups, remember that an effective workshop will require everyone's participation. Look out for participants who constantly speak up, perhaps inhibiting others from sharing their own opinions, as well as for those who sit in the back and never say a word. You can manage this by having the participants write down their thoughts on a particular issue during an activity or exercise and then asking individuals to share their positions one by one. If you have difficulty keeping everyone involved, you might want to focus specifically, yet gently, on including those participants who traditionally keep silent. Take care not to embarrass anyone, but with a little finesse you can get everyone's input.

Workshop participants will have a hard time focusing on you and your material if they are physically uncomfortable. As you facilitate the workshop don't forget to look out for everyone's comfort. Adjust the temperature in the room if it is too hot or too cold. Make sure there's water available and perhaps coffee as well. If the room is too bright or a window is distracting, pull down the blinds. Be aware of the surroundings and do your best to make your attendees comfortable so that you can keep their attention.

Your job as facilitator will also be to maintain a high level of energy in the group. This can be achieved by introducing several relevant and interesting exercises and activities. Have a good grasp of time, limiting activities to 20 minutes, especially after lunch. Otherwise you may be losing your audience's focus on the objectives of the workshop. When you notice a drop in energy, and if it fits into your curriculum, a short energizing activity or team-building exercise can keep everyone from getting droopy-eyed. You might also announce an unplanned break, encouraging people to get up and take a brisk walk. Simple activities such as asking the participants to arrange themselves according to their birthdays or by the distance they traveled can get everyone moving and thinking again instead of yawning. Whatever you choose to do to keep everyone energized, make sure it's done quickly and that everyone has fun. Of course, don't forget to have fun yourself!

Concluding Your Workshop

Just like a good speech, a workshop should have a great ending. Find a team-building activity that is uplifting, or some other inspiring event. Focus to the very end on your workshop objectives. Your want to make sure your participants will have received what they expected to receive in a way that leaves them inspired rather than exhausted and overworked. Perhaps for continued learning, you can encourage participants to discuss what they're going to do with their newfound knowledge or skills. Creating a contact list for attendees to share with one another is a great idea as well.

Even if your perception is that your workshop is a resounding success and everyone is inspired, don't miss the opportunity to evaluate participant satisfaction at the end. After the program, take time to analyze the post-workshop evaluation forms and any survey that you've asked participants to fill out. The little things make a difference, so if the attendees didn't like the lunch served on Wednesday, be thankful they shared that information and take note of it. The next time you lead a workshop, you'll probably choose a different meal. Of course, you'll want to examine the big issues as well, but with all the planning you did, chances are there will only be small issues, and every workshop you lead will only get better.

Overcoming the fear of presenting and performing comes down to two simple things—preparation and the right kind of practice. Preparation will give you a solid foundation for increasing your confidence for the big day, while effective practice and rehearsal will make every program you lead easier and better. Just don't forget that some anxiety is normal, healthy, and helpful. Every workshop leader who cares about his or her audience has it, and the successful leaders learn to work with it to their benefit.

Now that you've gained some tools for speaking in front of a lot of people, we'll discuss keys to speaking one on one or in small groups in social situations.

14

Social Interactions

Maria had a neighborhood party to attend while her husband was out of town. She worried about what she would eat at the party and whether she would appear rude to the guests. She was concerned about what she would say to people whom she did not know very well.

◆ ◆ ◆

Jon also worried about attending parties and social get-togethers. He typically avoided parties because he would have to make small talk with strangers, which made him highly anxious. Jon felt fine about his presentations and meetings about specific work-related topics, but completely incompetent when it came to small talk and socializing. He never knew what to say and when to say it, and he worried that he'd say something silly or embarrassing or would come across as boring. His greatest concern at work was the holiday office party. He dreaded standing around awkwardly, hoping that someone would speak with him.

246 ◆ THE CONFIDENT SPEAKER

Does this sound familiar? Do you worry about socializing with people you don't know very well? Maria and Jon both experience speaking anxiety that arises specifically in social situations. If you experience a similar form of anxiety, you are likely to:

- Feel uncomfortable in unstructured, casual social settings
- Think that you don't have anything interesting to contribute
- Believe you appear awkward and uncomfortable at parties, lunches, and other social situations
- Worry that you'll say something embarrassing or show signs of your anxiety
- Fear that you could lose face and reduce your social standing
- Become nervous about eating or drinking in front of others
- Feel uncomfortable about your physical appearance or conversational abilities
- Worry about meeting people for the first time and making a bad first impression
- Think that you could offend people with your point of view, and so avoid expressing yourself
- Dread introducing yourself to a group or small gathering of people

This chapter will give you specific tools for overcoming each of these common speaking fears, and more. But even if you do not typically become nervous about speaking up in social situations, you can find some pointers that will help you in other circumstances.

Meeting Someone New and Going to Parties

Fear of meeting someone new and going to parties is common. Parties may be anxiety-provoking situations because they often entail meeting strangers. Other common concerns include not knowing what to talk about and making a negative impression. If the party is a work function, you have the challenge of maintaining your professional work persona while simultaneously showing an informal, conversational side of yourself. At work parties, you might interact with people in a different manner and wonder how much personal information it's appropriate to reveal. Many people who are uncomfortable with parties have had negative experiences at parties where they stood around, uncomfortable and unsure of what to do, or had conversations that they perceived did not go well.

Here are six steps to successful party conversations to increase your comfort and confidence.

1. *Ask yourself: What am I afraid of?* What worries you about socially meeting a new person or going to a party? In order to figure out if your fear actually comes true in these uncertain social situations, it's important to know exactly what that fear is.

   Make a list of the very specific concerns that come to mind so that you can evaluate whether they actually occur. List things that can be observed so that you can see whether they happen. We're not as adept at judging the internal thoughts and opinions of others, so focus on behaviors instead. Rather than saying people will think you're boring, say they will stop talking to you. For instance:
   - I'm afraid that my neighbor will quickly try to get out of talking to me and will make an excuse to leave within two minutes.
   - I'll stand around awkwardly with no one to talk to for at least five minutes.
   - I'll have nothing to say when I introduce myself to someone new.
   - My coworker, who I want to get to know better, will be unwilling to speak with me.
   - No one will sit at the table where I sit down to eat.
   - I'll say something ridiculous that will make everyone around me laugh at me.

2. *Know why you want to talk to new people.* When something feels frightening to us, we try to avoid it. To help us not avoid it, we must properly motivate ourselves to confront our fear. Motivation is strongest when we have very specific, tangible incentives.

Rather than "my neighbors will like me more," say, "I can find one or two people with common interests to get together with a couple of times per month," or "I can get the book club up and running, which I've been wanting to do." For a work party say, "I will get to know my team members more, which will help us to better perform as a team." Jon, from our example at the beginning of this chapter, had been successful in earning the respect and admiration of others in his office, and he wanted to build upon these impressions in social settings. His verbalized goal was: "Show my direct reports that I value and care about them by getting to know them and expressing interest in their lives and work."

3. *Go in with a plan.* Come up with a couple of interesting things to say about yourself when you meet new people. Think of things about your work, family, talents, athletics, and so on that make you unique and show who you are. If you're unsure what sounds interesting to new people, ask yourself what you enjoy hearing about when you meet new people and think of similar ideas about yourself. You will feel as though you have some good things to contribute to conversations.

   The key to effectively doing this strategy is to *not* overplan. You do not want to memorize a 30-second introduction because you'll come off sounding robotic and rehearsed. People like other people who sound natural and genuine, not those who have a perfectly polished introduction. Even if you stutter or forget what you're going to say or say the wrong thing, people will like you if you have enthusiasm and a genuine interest to connect with them.

4. *Remember that others are probably nervous also.* Party anxiety is extremely common. You would be surprised to know how many other people are also uncomfortable. Look around you— with some people, you can observe signs of discomfort, and with others there are no signs, but they are on edge internally. It is a normal part of social interactions to experience a few lulls in conversations. And we've all had that awkward feeling of standing near people who are in conversation unsure if we should jump in or wait for them to finish.

A common misconception with people who experience party anxiety is, What's wrong with *me?* Look around—everyone is having a great time, people are friendly, so why am I uncomfortable and nervous? In fact, this is simply not true. We would place a substantial wager that others are also uncomfortable. Some people may have experienced a feeling of discomfort when they first arrived but are relaxed and enjoying themselves by the time you see them. Or perhaps some of the people around you experienced some nervousness about parties at one point in their lives, but they conquered their nerves and are now relaxed partygoers (as you will soon be also!).

Realize that it's likely that you won't show signs of discomfort to others. Remember that people are at the party to have a good time. If you're in a conversation with them and they realize you are struggling to come up with something to say (which is very unlikely, but remember how useful it is to think through the worst-case scenario), they'll step up and guide the conversation some more. Chances are that they've been in your shoes and want to make the party comfortable and enjoyable for you.

People often don't notice your reactions because they're engrossed in their own thoughts and experiences. If they're having a great time, they're not likely to even notice that you're uncomfortable and will naturally guide and enjoy the conversation.

On a related note, realize that it is *not* your sole responsibility to guide the conversation. Many of Larina's clients experience a huge sense of relief when they learn to let the other person in the conversation have equal responsibility. A conversation is like a volley in a tennis match—the ball goes back and forth. If the player on either side stops swinging, the ball will drop. It is only 50 percent *your* responsibility to make sure the conversation goes well. You don't want to make the other person work too hard, but you also want to be sure he or she isn't making you work too hard. If so, a less than enjoyable conversation may be the other person's fault, not yours. Take some pressure off yourself and let conversations unfold naturally.

5. *Your goal is to get to know people.* Make this your primary goal. This goal accomplishes two tasks: It gets your focus off of yourself, making you less anxious, and it makes others like you more. *People respond very well to those who make them feel interesting by expressing interest in them.* Next time you meet someone new and find yourself thinking, Wow, I really liked him, ask yourself whether that person had expressed interest in you. We're willing to bet that the person did.

   When you get to know others by asking them questions and expressing interest and curiosity, they will like you better. They'll see you as someone who has similar interests and who is not egocentric. You know how horrible it is to talk to people and feel as though they only want to hear themselves talk, right? It seems they're not interested in getting to know you. Avoid this mistake by instead getting to know others, and they will want to get to know you too.

6. *Meet new people and go to every party possible.* As you know by now, the key to learning all the skills we've discussed is to put yourself into situations where you can meet people in order to practice everything you've learned. Remember that your goal is not necessarily to make best friends with everyone. It's unrealistic to think that every conversation will go perfectly well and that you'll hit it off with each person with whom you speak. Instead, make your goal simple: to practice. Your secondary goal, of course, is to disprove the fear that you identified in the first step above. If you're afraid that no one will talk to you for more than two minutes, try it and time it! If people stay in conversations with you for longer than two minutes, then you've learned that your fear was unfounded, and you'll feel more confident the next time. If people end the conversation early, it may be a sign that you were focused on your own concerns and not on them.

Below, we list ways to get practice with uncertain social situations so that you feel more confident over time. Add to the list other ideas based on your own experiences or fears. Then rank the items in order from the least to the most difficult or anxiety-producing. Start with exercises that bring up less nervousness and then work your way up to the more difficult ones.

Practice Exercises

1. Introduce yourself to three new people per week. Good places to find them are fitness clubs, networking groups, your office, your neighborhood, your children's school, your university classes, local cafés, and activities groups. Search the Internet for groups of interest near you, such as book clubs, running groups, art classes, and so on.

2. Attend every party possible, large and small. Let your friends know that you want to meet new people, so you'd love it if they would invite you to any upcoming events.

3. Host a small dinner party or cocktail party at your house with eight of your friends.

4. Host a "meet new people" party. Ask everyone you invite to bring one or two people whom you do not know. Introduce yourself to and have at least a five-minute conversation with each one.

5. Around the holidays, go to every single holiday party and office party and plan to get to know at least three new people at each party.

6. Strike up a conversation with one new person per day in places such as the elevator, the bookstore, the subway, the grocery store, and so on.

7. Put yourself into situations of social uncertainty, such as lunches with people you do not know very well. Do this three times per week.

8. Another practice:_____

9. Another practice:_____

10. Another practice:_____

Participate Confidently in Group Conversations

Group conversations represent many different social situations that are unstructured. People are often not sure about when to talk, how to interrupt overly talkative individuals, and what to say. There is an art and finesse to being a great group conversationalist. There is a fine line between being too quiet, dominating the group, saying boring things, and saying inappropriate things. Here are some guidelines to help you:

1. *The group is like a piece of pizza.* Take a minute and get to know the group chemistry so that you can adapt yourself to the group. Think of the group as having a temperature. A hot group is a high-energy, high humor, loud group, and a cool group is more serious, mellow, and philosophical.

   Getting to know your group is like eating a piece of pizza. If you overestimate the temperature, it will be cold and unappealing, but if you underestimate, it will be hot and burn your tongue. Know the temperature of your group and act accordingly.

2. *Once you know the temperature, take a bite.* Do not wait too long to say something. Take a bite before your pizza gets cold!

   Briefly assess the group and then jump in and say something to show that you're part of the group and have something to contribute. If you do not jump in, you'll miss the right time and regret not having said something. We all know this feeling: I should have said . . . If you can't think of something to say, ask people in the group questions.

   Show that you're interested not only in the group as a whole but in the people within the group. By asking someone a question, you show that you're interested, and that person is likely to respond well. Others in the group are also likely to view your question positively, assuming that since you're interested in one person, you may be interested in them too. Questions show interest, and people like those who are interested in them. For example, ask people if they have any weekend plans, what area of town they live in and how they like it, about their children, or what they thought of a recent game if they're sports fans. As a rule, begin with more general and less personal questions until you get to know the others better.

3. *Focus 100 percent on the group conversation.* A group conversation is one of the worst times to use one of the overcompensating behaviors we discussed in earlier chapters, such as planning what you're going to say. When you do this, you get caught up in your own thinking, become more anxious, and are unable to follow the flow of the conversation. External focus keeps your concentration on the group and not on your anxiety. Immerse yourself in the group and pay attention to what others are saying. Your responses will be more spontaneous, natural, and relevant to the conversation.

4. *Know your role.* In every group, people quickly assume roles. Whether it is the leader, the organizer, the peacemaker, the comedian, or whatever, you're likely to have a role in the group. Learn what your role is, shape what role you want to have, and use your role to your advantage.

5. *Get some practice speaking up in groups.* Below we list ways to gain practice with speaking up in group conversations. Add other ideas to the bottom of this list based on your own experiences or concerns. Begin with the ones that are less nerve-racking and work your way up.

Practice Exercises

1. Go out for drinks or to a café with a group of friends and practice using the skills above. Even if you feel as though you know your friends, use the opportunity to assess the group, because the group's mood is always going to be different in different situations.

2. Use meetings at work to practice group conversation skills. Speak up at a meeting at least three times per week.

3. Take a class or join a recreational group (drawing club, new mom group, book club, golf group, and so on) that requires

group activities, and gain a lot of experience speaking up and learning your natural group role. If your natural group role is not adaptive (for example, people see you as domineering), begin to modify your role.

4. Have lunch with some coworkers and jump in on the group conversation. Try to utilize the proper portion of airtime. For instance, if the group is comprised of three people, your airtime would be 33 percent; if there are five people, 20 percent; and so on.

5. Gain experience with leading a group. This may be a different role and can be more or less anxiety-provoking. If it's more anxiety-provoking, practice the skills described above for leading a workshop.

6. Another practice:_____

7. Another practice:_____

8. Another practice:_____

Introducing Yourself to a Group

Picture this: You enter a new social group or gathering and people are introducing themselves to one another. You think: What do I say about myself? I'm supposed to say something interesting—what's interesting? When people are introducing themselves, do I go first or last? Should I try to impress everyone or be more modest? How do I introduce myself to people who are already conversing?

These thoughts go through our minds when we need to introduce ourselves in a group situation. Whether it's a formal group, such as a work group or a networking event, or an informal group, such as a party, introducing yourself can be difficult.

Here are some principles to remember:

1. *Be modest, but not too modest.* There's a fine line between being modest and being shy. If you're too modest and do not discuss your accomplishments or offer some interesting facts

about yourself, you'll come across as boring and dull. People have a bias to assume that the cause of behaviors is our personalities rather than the situations we are in. Therefore, they might assume that you're uninteresting rather than uncomfortable. Don't let this happen. Instead, say something interesting, but do not list every one of your shining star achievements during the first introduction.

2. *Look at the others.* This point has two meanings. First, pay attention to how other people introduce themselves and model your words after one of them. Second, look clearly at the other people in the group as you introduce yourself. Make eye contact with different people but do not scan the room; rather, hold eye contact with each person for a couple of seconds.

3. *Think of a few interesting facts about yourself.* If you feel that you'll be asked to introduce yourself and say something about yourself, think of a couple of things that would be interesting *to that particular group.*

   What is interesting? Ask some people who know you well what they think would be a good thing to say when you introduce yourself. Ask each person for two or three things and see where the ideas converge. If there's one thing that everyone says about you, that is probably the thing that most people find interesting.

4. *Control your first impression.* Perhaps you've heard the expression, "You never get a second chance to make a first impression." This isn't necessarily true, but first impressions are certainly important. To make the best impression as you talk do these things: smile, feel confident by showing your best appearance, do not have hair covering your face, do speak in a tone of voice that is loud enough for everyone to hear, and use the eye contact described above.

5. *Practice introducing yourself.* Below we list some ways to practice introducing yourself to a group and making a strong first impression. If you can think of any other practice exercises, add them to the bottom of the list.

Practice Exercises

1. Put together a couple of sentences to introduce yourself and practice it. Do *not* overpractice, or you'll sound canned, as if you have been doing it in the mirror. Try to practice as many times as possible in real situations rather than with people you already know.

2. Try to say something interesting about yourself in five different situations a week to gain experience and confidence with speaking about yourself in a not-too-modest way. For example, say something about yourself in a conversation with a coworker, such as, "You know, I was mountain biking the other day . . . " to show your interests and what makes you unique.

3. Do not shy away from talking about yourself. A common avoidance strategy is to ask questions, and while it's great to learn about others, you'll miss out on the opportunity to attract people to you if you never talk about yourself. Three times a week, reveal something that others don't know about you. It doesn't have to be something scandalous or earth-shattering, but something a bit personal that makes you feel as though you're taking a little risk.

4. Introduce yourself to a new person at least once a week. This can be saying hello and introducing yourself to the person sitting next to you on the subway, to someone standing behind you in a checkout line, to a person in your fitness class, to a parent of one of your children's friends . . . to anyone, as long as you introduce yourself.

5. Another practice:_____

6. Another practice:_____

7. Another practice:_____

Disagreeing or Expressing a Controversial Viewpoint

A final social speaking fear that we'd like to discuss is disagreeing with others. This can present itself in any situation—meeting with your boss, meeting a stranger at a cocktail party, participating in a group conversation, stating your opinion during a water-cooler conversation at work, and so on.

Many people are concerned about expressing their views in situations where others might disagree. It's easier to talk about neutral subjects rather than discuss views that could be somewhat controversial. People also often worry about disagreeing with someone else's opinion. Do you ever worry that you'll seem offensive, rude, unlikable, different, or unpleasant if you say something controversial or disagree?

We'd like to help you develop the confidence to express your views, stand up for yourself, and, when necessary, disagree assertively with people in ways that will help you achieve your personal or professional objectives. There is a continuum of appropriate disagreement and expression of views. On the one end, people are passive and do not speak up. On the other end, they are aggressive and force their views on others or put people down for having views different from their own. We want you to be in the middle, where you are assertive and able to preserve or enhance your relationships by assertively expressing your thoughts and opinions. Here are some tips:

1. *Realize the appropriate time and place.* When expressing potentially controversial viewpoints and disagreeing with others, there is always an appropriate time and place. The first time you meet a new boyfriend's or girlfriend's parents, for example, is not necessarily the time to discuss your opposing views on politics. A friendly debate among friends, on the other hand, is a great time to express your views. We'd like you to feel comfortable to state your views when it's important and to your benefit to do so. You may be tempted to tell yourself that it is never the appropriate time and place, and so avoid expressing your views and opinions. Be cautious about this because it can increase anxiety and make you appear meek and passive. Push yourself to say what's on your mind. Taking some risks can pay off.

   It's important to feel out your audience. Some people like to have conversations that remain on a nice, polite, surface level. They're not interested in getting into discussions about

potentially controversial topics. Know that the response you
are likely to get will depend in part on who is giving you the
response. Of course, you never want to compromise your
integrity or values and remain quiet about something critical to
you, even if other people may not like it. But you can couch
your disagreement in terms that they're likely to relate to,
respect, and listen to.

Begin to practice expressing different views about relatively
neutral topics, such as the weather, a recent movie, or the food
at a local restaurant. Save discussing highly emotionally
charged, controversial topics until you have a positive
relationship with someone.

2. *Respectfully disagree.* Equally important to *when* you express
your views is *how* you do so. Remember that your goal is twofold
(assuming that you like the person with whom you're speaking
and want to further the conversation). First, you're working on
overcoming anxiety by doing what makes you uncomfortable.
Second, you're working on creating a favorable impression.
Expressing your views and opinions is critical in making a
favorable impression because it shows that you're a person of
depth and interest.

When you disagree with something someone said, don't
come off too strongly in your disagreement. If someone says,
"I don't agree with the erection of a parking structure across
from the schoolyard. It will contaminate the air, be loud and
noisy, and take away some of the beautiful green area our city
has left," do *not* respond by saying, "How could you not want
more parking in this city—the parking is ridiculous!" Instead
say something like, "You raise a good point, and I agree that
there are some downsides to the parking structure. I'm in favor
of it because it will give the teachers and administrators a
close, safe place to park and will attract more shoppers to that
area and boost the economy." Many people try to temper their
disagreement by saying. "With all due respect, I disagree . . ."
Phrases like this are a bit clichéd, but they are okay as long as

you then actually follow through and express your views in a respectful manner.

The keys to appropriately disagreeing include:

- Acknowledge other people's viewpoints and do not make them feel wrong for having the opinions they have.
- State your view and give some *specific* reasons to support your idea.
- Defuse any tension by your verbal and nonverbal responses. It's not necessary to say, "I respectfully disagree." Phrases like these seem trite and can put people on the defensive because they often precede an attack. It's more powerful to *show* that you respectfully disagree. It's like saying, "I'm a nice person," rather than proving it with actions. So instead, express genuine interest in other people's points of view to show your respect them and then state why you disagree.

3. *Practice assertiveness skills.* Gaining some general practice with assertiveness will help you assertively communicate your beliefs. You can practice assertiveness by requesting help at work or at home, saying no to projects and commitments you're unable to or uninterested in taking on, asking questions, and making requests. An example of the latter is when you go out for dinner, request a specific table, and then ask the server several questions to be sure you select the entrée you'd most enjoy.

   Assertiveness has to do with not being bullied or feeling pressured to say or do things you do not truly want to say or do. When you gain practice with these skills, you'll be better able to express important views, even if they're controversial or in contrast to what others say.

4. *Have courage and take some risks—people find this attractive in others.* Remember that, as a rule, people like and respect those who show courage and confidence, and who are willing to take some small risks. It shows that you have backbone. This will also make it less likely that people will attempt to take

advantage of you in business or in your personal life. When you speak in a manner consistent with your values and beliefs, you will attract people who you actually want to be around. Allow yourself to take some risks, and they're sure to pay off for you in terms of valuable lessons.

We have now gone through all kinds of speaking situations, and we have discussed the fears that arise in them. Next, we'll address some other concerns—those that arise specifically for men or for women. But first, take a moment to download one of our free special reports to further help you build confidence and attract friends and business relationships through speaking. Go to www.TheConfidentSpeaker.com and download "How to Use Speaking in Public to Attract Clients, Friends and Unlimited Business Opportunities" and "The 10 Secrets to Magnetic Confidence—Feel Great and Attract Others Every Time You Speak." Once you have these in hand, you're ready to move on to our final chapters on navigating specific speaking situations and finding opportunities to practice and polish your skills.

15

———

Techniques Specifically for
Men and Women

———

Karen is halfway through what she thought was sure to be a brilliant and rousing speech to her colleagues, and she feels herself panicking, certain that she's losing her audience. The few women in the audience are nodding absently, but the men's faces are inscrutable and Karen doesn't think she has their attention. Worried that she's coming across as too assertive, she changes her tack. She adds tags and disclaimers to her thoughts using the phrases "in my opinion" and "wouldn't you agree?" Now no one is nodding and everyone's eyes seem to have glazed over. Worse, when she wraps up her speech and takes questions, Karen quickly finds that she has lost the floor. Her male peers dominate the question-and-answer session with long-winded questions and interrupt her answers. She is exhausted when she's finished and wonders what went wrong.

Speaking to an audience of peers can be difficult if you don't understand the differences in the communication styles of men and women.

Understanding gender and cultural differences in speech and body language can help you both read your audience and adjust your speaking style depending on whether you are speaking to men or women. Whether you're presenting a formal speech to a large audience or leading an informal brainstorming session, knowing how to communicate effectively to both genders can help your personal life and your career.

To succinctly describe the research on gender differences in anxiety and communication, we simplify terms in this chapter to "feminine" and "masculine." Please recognize that, as with any generalization, there are many individual differences: To varying degrees, men employ feminine communication styles and women employ masculine communication styles. According to social researchers, men tend to use language to preserve or assert status, power, and authority. Women, on the other hand, are inclined to use language as a means of building and cementing relationships. The difference of goals — power versus intimacy — is what determines the style of speech. Both styles, feminine and masculine, are relevant to different situations, and neither is better or worse than the other. The trick is knowing when to use which style and developing the ability to alternate between the two.

A commanding use of both feminine and masculine styles of speech, conformed to the situation, can make both men and women more effective communicators. Fluctuating between styles gives the speaker the ability to effectively engage both genders. This requires a comprehension of the differences in word choice and presentation inherent in these two styles. However, it's important to note that the speaker's gender does not dictate his or her style of speech. Speaking with a feminine or masculine style is a choice that can be made and embodied by an educated and astute communicator.

Feminine Speaking Style

Sociologist Carol Gilligan asserts that linguistic differences begin to occur between boys and girls at about age four. As boys reach this age, they begin to separate from their mothers and enter the realm of other boys, a world dominated by sports and other activities that are the basis for building friendships. Girls, on the other hand, submerge themselves in intimacy and empathy. Conversation begins to become the currency of relationships and friendships. Although there can be varying degrees of feminine and masculine styles of communication in individuals, for the most part it is this early experience that determines one's normal style of speech.

The feminine style of speaking is warm and inclusive, often involving storytelling and the insertion of self into communication. Feminine style can also be tentative and less assertive, using tags and disclaimers and making requests through questions instead of commands. The feminine style often involves the use of more positive words and less discussion of money and numbers, as well as less use of swear words and long words. These are generalities, of course, but they represent the basis of what is considered a feminine speaking style.

Another important component to keep in mind is that women are more likely than men to focus on negative aspects of themselves. This doesn't mean that men don't do this, but in general woman show more negative self-focus and distress. As a result, women are more likely to tune in to themselves and become uncomfortable. When people become self-focused, they are more likely to engage in overcompensating behaviors and not be themselves. This means that women, when nervous, often neglect their natural abilities to connect and empathize with others. On the other hand, when women tune in to others (instead of themselves), they not only capitalize on their natural strengths, they also reduce self-consciousness and anxiety.

We mentioned that a speaker's gender does not dictate the speaking style he or she may use. Harrison estimates that his typical speaking style is approximately 60 percent feminine and 40 percent masculine. He easily adjusts his style, however, based on his on-the-spot assessment of whether a mostly feminine style or mostly a masculine one will get his message across best with a particular audience.

There are many other examples of men who typically use the feminine style of speech. Former President Bill Clinton, for example, tends to work stories into his speeches and to include personal examples. His style is also predominantly feminine, whereas Senator Hillary Clinton tends to use a more assertive, masculine style of speech. George H.W. Bush, in his 1988 acceptance speech at the Republican convention, spoke of a "kinder, gentler America." This moment in the speech was markedly feminine in style compared to his normal masculine style. There are times when the warm and inclusive feminine style of speaking can be very effective, especially for men. However, feminine style can have liabilities as well.

Liabilities and Assets of Feminine Speech

Girls are socialized to reduce conflict and please others. Boys are reinforced for independence and risk-taking. As a result, girls and women sometimes experience greater difficulty communicating assertively and disagreeing with others. A people-pleasing style of communication can preclude speakers from getting their needs met and from projecting confidence.

The feminine style of speech is softer and can easily be interpreted as ineffectual, especially when used by women. Men are likely to be perceived as making an effort to be more accessible when using the feminine style. Women, however, can be considered unsure and lacking confidence when using this style.

There are several things women should consider when using the feminine style of speaking. First, it is best not to apologize as a means of demonstrating empathy. Men interpret this as women taking responsibility for problems even if they had nothing to do with their causes or the outcomes. Men often don't understand that "I'm sorry" is a ritual statement frequently made by women. When women say "I'm sorry" in response to a disaster, they really only mean, "That's a shame." It's best to avoid this misunderstanding altogether.

Women should also try to avoid overuse of tags and disclaimers. The social structure of female relationships in many global cultures demands that women be self-effacing and not make themselves appear better than others. This translates to women adding tags of "don't you agree?" and disclaimers such as "I'm no expert, but ..." Women typically respond well to this style of including the audience and leveling the playing field. Men, however, frequently interpret this style as lacking in confidence and will dismiss the speaker. In some settings, both genders are likely to dismiss this style of feminine speech. After all, how much confidence would you have in a president who said, "I'm no expert, but maybe we should go to war. Don't you think?"

Masculine Speaking Style

Masculine and feminine styles of speech are very different. Generally, women grow up with peers and adults who expect them to not boast, to downplay their achievements, and to not assert themselves. A girl who uses a masculine speaking style to tell a girlfriend what to do is likely to be labeled "bossy" and excluded from the group. Boys, on the other hand, are expected to be bossy. There are always boys who are higher up on the totem pole, and being bossed around by them is to be expected. Boys also learn to downplay their weaknesses and to emphasize their accomplishments as a means of surviving and working their way up the group hierarchy. These experiences are the core of the masculine style of speaking.

The masculine speaking style is often characterized as the "informational style," as opposed to the "relationship style" of feminine speech. Men tend to use language specifically to share information rather than to build relationships. They're more likely to use conversation as a negotiating tool, a way to achieve status and preserve their independence, rather than as a means of establishing a connection. Consider that men use about 7,000 words a day, whereas women use upward of 20,000.

Masculine speech can frequently be more straightforward and to the point. Rather than telling anecdotes and sharing information about themselves, a person using a masculine style of speaking is more likely to share facts, numbers, and statistics to prove a point. The language is more direct, and the speaker may present himself or herself as an expert rather than a peer.

Liabilities and Assets of Masculine Speech

Masculine speech is frequently effective for men speaking to a group of men. Men respond positively to a speaker who comes across as confident, powerful, and knowledgeable. This style may also convince the women in the audience of the speaker's expertise and leadership ability. A male speaker using powerful language is more likely to be perceived by both genders as competent, intelligent, and trustworthy. Using a masculine style that's too strong, however, can make some of the audience feel excluded. Women, especially, may ultimately respond more favorably to a male speaker who mixes some of the feminine style into his speech, making them feel more included, especially in a smaller group setting.

One of the biggest challenges and risks for a man with a masculine style of speech is his difficulty reading the emotions of his audience or the person with whom he's speaking. Thus, men who use a strong masculine style may not only come across as lacking compassion, but may also not take the time to gauge others' reactions.

Women in an audience frequently won't ask questions if they're upset, and therefore won't give the speaker a chance to smooth things over and clarify or better express his opinions and positions. As a general rule, it is critically important for a speaker to be aware of audience feedback and recognize signs of confusion or upset, and to try to address those nonverbal cues immediately, especially when speaking to smaller groups.

Using masculine speech when you're a woman can be a difficult road to navigate. Women who use direct language with men may find themselves less influential. While a masculine style of speech may make a woman appear more competent, studies have shown that men will find a woman who speaks with a more direct style less trustworthy and likable. Thus, using a very strong masculine style of speaking can backfire for a woman speaking to a room full of men. Sometimes women can also be turned off by a woman using the masculine style of speaking. Practicing primarily a feminine style of speech can undermine a woman's authority and expertise, while depending primarily on a masculine style can make the audience perceive a female speaker as unlikable and therefore ineffectual. However, for both genders, comprehending the two styles and learning how to switch between them can greatly enhance a speaker's effectiveness.

Sociolinguist and author Deborah Tannen notes in a 1997 interview with *Training & Development* that "developing awareness that people have different styles is important. Try to raise your own sensitivity to the kind of responses you get so that you can gauge: This seems to be working well with this person, I'm okay. Or, this person isn't reacting well: What can I do differently?" Understanding these two styles is the first step to using them effectively and to learning how to present yourself successfully.

The second step is to look at your objective in a conversation or presentation. In general there are three types of objectives: relationship, outcome, and informative. In a relationship objective, your goal is to create, preserve, or improve the relationship with those to whom you're speaking. In an outcome objective, you seek to be assertive and make requests of others or convince them to align with you in some way. With an informative discussion, your primary goal is to educate the other party or parties. As a general rule, relationship focus is critical when you meet someone new. When someone likes you and trusts you, he or she will be much more receptive to your outcome or informative communication styles.

Presentation and Body Language

Body language and choice of personal presentation, as we've learned, can have just as big an impact for both men and women as can style of speech. For both, paying attention to effective body language can add significant impact to your presentation and possibly negate the negative effects of either a masculine or feminine speaking style. What you wear, as well as your posture and stance at the podium, can have a profound effect on how the audience perceives you.

Research has shown that women tend to be more sensitive than men to other people's facial expressions. A woman speaker may look at what is going on around her (at the facial expressions of the audience, for instance) and then use this audience feedback to make a determination about how she feels. For example, a woman speaker may read a facial expression as negative (even if it's not) and conclude that she is (or should be) nervous because her audience isn't responding well. Therefore, she might jump to inaccurate conclusions that create anxiety. And once anxiety exists, she is more likely to draw further inaccurate conclusions. Many men look to others to determine their emotions as well, but it's a characteristic more common to women. Whether the men in an audience "like" a female speaker weighs heavily on whether they will be influenced by her.

Choosing a "high task" nonverbal style or a "social" nonverbal style of presentation can also effect audience perception. High task style is defined as rapid speech and firm tone in conjunction with upright posture, calm hand gestures, and a high amount of eye contact. A more social style involves less eye contact, a friendly facial expression, and a more pleading tone of voice. A woman who speaks in a more masculine manner but presents herself using a social style is more likely to gain the acceptance of male audience members. Men tend to be put off by a high task style of presenting. If the situation calls for hard facts and a powerful point of view, speakers of either sex might find more favor with the audience if they moderate their tones, use friendly facial expressions, and avoid using too much eye contact, thereby seeming confrontational.

It is important as well to understand that body language also differs between genders. Understanding this difference can help a speaker more easily gauge her audience and know if the audience understands and agrees with what she is presenting. For example, head nodding means something different in men and women. A woman nods her head to let the speaker know that she understands. When a man nods his head, he means that he agrees with what the speaker is saying. The women in the audience may be nodding, smiling, and trying to relate to the speaker rather than hearing what is being said. The facial expressions of men, on the other hand, may not be as friendly, but if they're taking notes and seem attentive, they are probably hearing your words and considering how to take action. Take note of the gender differences when scanning a crowd.

The gender differences in how one should dress when giving a presentation are also skewed in favor of men.

Men, in a way, are "unmarked." A nice haircut and a standard suit, tie, and dress shoes are all perceived as neutral and make no surprise statement about the speaker. If a man appears on stage in his standard business attire and with conservative grooming, people are not likely to make critical judgments about his trustworthiness or expertise based on his appearance.

Women, on the other hand, don't have a standard haircut or dress style or shoes that should be worn. Even a woman's choice of makeup can strongly influence perceptions about who she is and how she wants her audience to relate to her. Women may therefore want to carefully consider how they want to be perceived; the challenges include trying to appear respectable but not too bland, attractive but not too sexy. Particularly in a more formal setting, it's a good idea to wear your hair off your face when speaking, otherwise your audience might perceive you as uncomfortable or trying to hide something.

Always consider the basics of appearance when giving a presentation. There are certain truths that apply when it is important to appeal to both genders. You are expected to stand tall, look up from your notes and into the audience, speak clearly, and appear both confident and enthusiastic about your message. You are also likely to have a better chance resonating across genders if you come across as professional, well-groomed, and articulate. And the more comfortable you feel in your own skin on stage, the easier it will be to handle any curveballs the audience throws at you.

Emotional Push Buttons

Perhaps it goes without saying that men and women handle emotions and emotional situations differently. However, an awareness of the difference and why we react to situations as we do may help us deal with surprise situations coolly, calmly, and professionally. It is also important to understand how the two genders perceive emotions in order to react appropriately and effectively in a variety of situations.

It is frequently noted that women are the more emotional gender, but this is not exactly true nor is it necessarily detrimental. The ability to perceive emotions can be a definite asset to a speaker. While women tend to more easily recognize feelings in others and themselves, men traditionally have a more difficult time recognizing emotional clues, unless the clues are uncomfortably obvious, such as crying or yelling. Studies show that women have much higher brain activity when it comes to remembering emotional events. Male speakers are therefore advised to attune their perceptual acuities to the emotional cues of the audience in order to respond appropriately to the audience's mood, while women are encouraged to effectively utilize their natural gift of emotional intelligence when interacting with their audiences.

It must be acknowledged that men are just as emotional as women, even if they're less apt to see the emotions in their colleagues and peers. But men are also less in tune with their own emotional states than women are, meaning that while men experience the same emotions, their ability to recognize them can be lower. The positive aspect to this is less negative self-focus and attention to distress while speaking; that is, men are less likely to express and act on their emotions than women. This is where women can get themselves in trouble. It's important for women to understand that the emotions that arise in highly charged situations, such as speaking to groups, are common to everyone. Ultimately it is how the emotions are handled that will determine favorable or unfavorable audience perceptions and feedback, thereby affecting a speaker's impact and effectiveness.

Understanding what causes you to react to particular stimuli in certain ways can save you in uncomfortable situations. If someone attacks you verbally during a talk and you recognize the internal emotional response for what it is (i.e., a common emotional reaction that can be dealt with), it's less likely that you will be caught off-guard, and you'll probably be able to respond reasonably and with a clear head. Therefore, if you can keep your composure when under attack and deal with the emotions as you respond, you'll stand a good chance of increasing audience support.

Similarly, any situation that would stimulate an emotional response, particularly in a presentation situation—such as the loss of one's train of thought, defective audiovisual equipment, hecklers, a hostile audience, or the introduction of a controversial topic—needs to be dealt with effectively in order to preserve status and credibility. In order to create positive perceptions in the audience, a speaker must appear unflappable, even maintaining a sense of humor in the face of the unexpected. This may be easier for men, although recognizing that an emotional reaction is natural and can be effectively managed is good news for female speakers too.

Knowing how to deal with criticism when giving a talk is also an important aspect of dealing with one's emotional push buttons. Women are more likely to take criticism as a personal assault than men. Understanding that criticism is nothing more than an opinion can help women deal with reacting to criticism. If the commentary is harsh and unfair, try to detach yourself emotionally, and consider the source of the criticism and possible underlying motives that may color the critic's opinion. By doing a quick analysis of the situation, you'll be in a better position to dismiss the comments rather than take them personally. If you find that there's something to be learned from the criticism leveled at you, extract what you think is useful and discard the rest. In all cases, thank the audience member and move on.

Women can also benefit from watching men engage in discussions of opposing viewpoints without taking the argument as a personal affront. Men, in most cases, can argue a point heartily without any hard feelings when the debate is over. Women, on the other hand, are more likely to take an argument personally. Arguing can often result in pushing emotional buttons rather than in finding the truth and an appropriate solution. Although arguing during a question-and-answer session at the end of a speech may not be appropriate as far as time and place are concerned, a woman who has practiced effective debate won't be rattled by an argumentative questioner.

The key to handling one's emotional push buttons is the anticipation, rehearsal, and preparation for a potentially contentious issue. The better you know your material from all angles and viewpoints, the more likely it is that you will prevail and succeed when the unexpected occurs. Being mentally and emotionally flexible, as well as knowing your material inside and out, will enable you to manage any emotionally charged situation that may otherwise derail your confidence and lessen your impact before an audience.

Part of this process is repetition. Repetition of effective methods builds confidence, which, among other things, helps develop a positive self-image.

If a negative self-image or a social phobia represents one of your emotional push buttons, get expert feedback and incorporate it into your speaking practice. If you know your limitations and address them constructively, you're well on your way to becoming the confident, influential speaker you deserve to be.

Tips for Women Talking to Men

No matter what your style of speaking, having a number of options to more effectively communicate with the opposite gender can effectively boost your working relationships. It's also relevant when mingling or networking with an audience before or after you give a presentation. Women should keep in mind that men respond best to conversation that is succinct and to the point without being abrupt. Being straightforward about accomplishments and current projects is expected and is not considered by men to be bragging. Feel confident about sharing your vision and avoid disclaimers and tags.

Men don't usually respond well to expressions of highly charged emotions or to personal disclosure and problems. Remember that men bond through activities and not through conversation the way women do. Presenting men with a problem for discussion spurs them to come up with a solution rather than empathy. Men are trained to be problem solvers from a young age and are more likely to think you are dumping your problems on them than that you're including them in the process.

Women are more likely to allow themselves to be interrupted and to miss natural pauses in conversations as jumping-in points when men are speaking. If you're running a question-and-answer session, don't let yourself get run off the floor. There is no reason to be rude to someone who is monopolizing the Q&A session, but learn to politely interrupt. If you lose control at the end of your presentation, you may negate the good work that you did during the main part of your speech.

Tips for Men Talking to Women

The feminine style of communication is soft and warm, characteristics that men often mistake as a sign of incompetence. Chances are that the woman you are speaking to is far from incompetent; she just has a different style of communication. Try adding a little of her style to your own to gain her attention and support. Add more details to your speech and be personable. Adding personal disclosure to your conversation will make a woman feel you trust her and value her friendship. Adding *please* and *thank you* to your requests can also go a long way.

Keep in mind that although women tend to talk more, they generally talk about themselves; however, they volunteer their opinions less often than men do. Women think that if you want to know their opinions, you'll ask. And if you want them, you should do so. Pay attention to the accomplishments of the women you speak with and congratulate them for what they have achieved. It is unlikely that they will point out their accomplishments to you. Try not to interrupt, and use active listening skills when communicating with women.

Not Better, Only Different

Don't forget that different isn't worse or wrong. It's just that: different. Men and women can learn a great deal from each other's differences, and they can utilize them in their own communication styles. Understanding what makes you and your peers tick will go a long way toward making you a more confident and successful speaker.

Again, one style of communication isn't better than another. There is only effective and ineffective communication, all of which depends on the context, the message, and the senders and receivers of the message. Businesses may mainly communicate in a masculine style, but only because many companies were founded with their creators communicating in that style. There are, nevertheless, several modern companies that have been built and run by women who normally communicate in the feminine style. Either can benefit from the inclusion of both styles within their organizations, just as most speakers can benefit from utilizing both styles in their presentations. Thinking that all women will respond best to a feminine style of speaking can be just as detrimental as speaking to all women as if they were men.

The important thing is to find the style that works for you. This will take practice, keen observation, and empathy. Many successful male speakers use a mix of masculine and feminine communication styles. There are also very successful women who have found the most effective way to give a talk is by limiting themselves to a masculine style or even to an ultrafeminine style of speaking.

In your quest to reach your objectives with any audience, male or female, you'll benefit from continuously monitoring and adjusting the style and content of your communication. Never stop considering the vast amount of nuanced intelligence available to you that can be used on your next audience. By striving to understand your listeners on a deeper level and adjusting your style so that they can perceive you according to their communication model of the world, your message has the best chance for resonating with your audience.

Beyond Gender

Even when you have mastered the effective use of both feminine and masculine styles of speech, you'll find that gender isn't the only consideration in communication.

People have their own styles of communicating, constantly shaped and developed under the influence of many environmental and cultural factors. The best way to communicate, persuade, and influence people, therefore, is to adapt your style directly to theirs. While this is critical knowledge to consider when communicating in your own cultural environment, it's even more important when you're speaking to audiences outside of your culture, whether you are communicating in your native language or not. Cultural, ethnic, and individual differences can present formidable obstacles when trying to communicate with cross-cultural audiences.

Ignorance is not bliss. Before you speak to any audience or give a presentation to a company you're not familiar with, do your homework. Don't talk to strangers; instead, get to know who you will be addressing. This is critical intelligence in formulating your style of speech. Knowing if your audience is predominantly male or female is important, but gender, ethnicity, and class are all intertwined. Consider, for instance, that in some Asian cultures disagreement and opposition are considered inappropriate by both genders. Other cultures, such as those of Western Europe and North America, commonly engage in confrontation and opposition as part of their communication in business dealings. The better you understand the cultural idiosyncrasies of your audience, the more effective you'll be in communicating with them and engaging their hearts and minds.

Whether you are presenting to an executive board or sharing your ideas at the local PTA meeting, it pays to maintain a certain amount of professional detachment.

◆ ◆ ◆

People communicate in many nuances, and you should not be rattled by a critical question or a heated conversation. Keep your emotions under control and your head clear. If someone offends you, it may have been unintentional or due to a cultural misperception. Emotional outbursts serve only to undermine your authority and perception of professionalism. Use wit, reason, and your developing ability to communicate in your audience's style to establish strong rapport and influence their perspectives.

16

Recovering from a Speaking Crisis or Blunder

Crisis Communication 101

How do we know when we're having a speaking crisis? For some people the awareness of a crisis hits while they're in full panic mode. At that point it's hard to make clear, level-headed decisions that can turn an unpleasant event around and improve the situation. Often, the key to getting out of a crisis quickly is to anticipate it beforehand. Let's first look at what constitutes a crisis.

A crisis is an event that has spun out of control, energized by any number of environmental influences such as competitors, the media, technology, friends, business partners, product flaws, software glitches, injuries, death, scandals, people, airline delays, weather, and any other outside influence that can cause a deviation from an anticipated or planned course. When a crisis occurs, the stakeholders' initial communication is often a reaction to runaway fast-moving events as opposed to being the driver of the situation.

Key characteristics of a crisis are that they are typically unexpected, that some consequences are inevitable, and that stakeholders are forced to make quick and smart decisions under increased pressure in an attempt to normalize the situation.

Since there are innumerable possible crisis scenarios, we can't give you a patent recipe for dealing with the unexpected. We can, however, outline some helpful considerations that will give you a general idea of how to react vis-à-vis an impending or current crisis.

1. *Anticipation.* One of the most important steps in dealing with a crisis is anticipating it. When preparing for an event, speakers and meeting planners must consider worst-case scenarios and provide resources as well as alternate plans for them.

2. *Awareness.* Once the first signs of a crisis occur, denial and wishful thinking can take the place of quick thinking and determined decision-making. In any high-stakes situation, particularly when a crucial outcome hinges upon the delivery of an important speech, talk, or communication situation, stakeholders must be on high alert for the first signs of trouble on the horizon and act immediately.

3. *Responsibility.* When the unexpected happens, people often reach for excuses and scapegoats. It's important that every stakeholder in the process has a clearly defined role and responsibilities. Then, once things go awry, accountable key players can be contacted to take charge and work on correcting the situation.

4. *Rehearsal.* A potential crisis situation should be rehearsed mentally as well as physically. If a PowerPoint projector breaks down in the middle of a presentation and the show must go on, a presenter must be able to pick up where the slides left off and bring the scheduled talk to a successful conclusion without the audiovisuals. Being prepared and rehearsing situations like this under realistic circumstances will ensure that everyone's objectives can still be met and a bigger crisis averted.

5. *Composure.* Even when all the proverbial *i*'s are dotted and the *t*'s are crossed, things can still go wrong. When that happens,

panicking is like pouring gasoline on a fire, causing a small crisis to quickly escalate into a bigger one. The more "moving parts" a particular situation has, the more potential there is for a glitch somewhere along the line. And sometimes it isn't just one problem that pops up, but a series of interconnected problems that can lead to a disastrous domino effect. This is where cooler heads will prevail. By maintaining composure and quickly analyzing the situation, a presenter can confidently tap into the resources and planning that were put into place for a crisis situation. If no plan exists for a particular crisis, rational thinking and quick decision-making by the stakeholders will contribute constructively to devising an on-the-spot alternative. Remember that handling a crisis with composure will increase your credibility.

What to Do When You Face a Hostile Audience

When you're faced with a hostile audience, the first thing to do is ask yourself: "How do I *know* that this audience is hostile?" Remember that when people are anxious they interpret neutral information as negative. In research studies, anxious people are more likely to pay attention to negative feedback and to think that neutral feedback is negative. For example, when we're nervous, we're more likely to believe that someone is laughing at us rather than that they're laughing at something funny or laughing with us.

So before you assume that the audience is hostile, tell yourself to look at the situation objectively. Are people speaking while you're in the midst of saying something? Are people rolling their eyes at you? Are they demeaning you or asking questions to embarrass or stump you?

If you find that objective criteria for hostility are met, then you can assume you have a hostile audience. If these objective criteria are not met, then work on releasing the belief that your listeners are hostile.

Another factor to consider is whether you have a hostile audience or a hostile audience member. A single person can make you feel on edge. This one person can make you feel as though you're being attacked.

How do the other people present respond to the hostile person? If they're not saying anything to defend you, do not assume that their silence means that they agree with the heckler or aggressor. It may be that the rude individual holds a higher level of power in the organization or situation than they do, and that they are intimidated by the individual. Recognize whether you are truly facing several hostile people or if only one is aggressive.

With just one hostile audience member, you have several choices. You can choose to ignore him or her and remind yourself that no one can please everyone. Instead, focus your attention on the positive verbal or nonverbal feedback from others in the audience or group. Another choice is to do some research ahead of time. If you hear that there is a challenging person in the group, you can learn about this person and his or her common objections and then address the objections in the group. For example: "Some of you may be wondering how this point could be true — let me tell you . . ." You can also try to engage this person in the conversation and defuse tension by asking him or her for ideas or for answers to questions.

Another potential scenario to consider is whether the general tone of the audience is hostile because of a ringleader. Often a charismatic ringleader can influence others to a particular point of view and initiate "group think," which occurs when a point of view becomes contagious and spreads from a powerful leader to others. Group think is typically an emotionally charged type of thought process, so the best way to defuse the tension is by pointing out facts and relating to people's rational thought processes. Group think occurs when there is no room for dissenting opinions, so find a way to get some other ideas on the table. Ask people to play devil's advocate and come up with alternative explanations.

Cardinal Rule of Thumb: Don't Be Defensive

Whatever way you choose to handle hostile audience members, the key rule to keep in mind is to not get defensive. When your response is defensive, you lose control of the situation and lose credibility. People no longer see you as an expert or authority figure, and you lose esteem.

Most important, defensive responses do not endear people to you. It's hard to like and feel connected to someone who responds defensively, because a defensive response sets up an adversarial relationship. It becomes a "me against them," "win-lose" scenario. What you want is a "win-win" sentiment whenever you're communicating with others.

Think about a time when someone responded defensively toward you. How did you feel? What was your initial reaction? You probably became defensive as well and clung more strongly to your position. When people defend their positions, both sides end up clinging more strongly to their original positions. No resolution is reached, and both parties are frustrated and disappointed.

If someone disagrees with you, a defensive response would be: "No, that's not true. It's really like this . . . " or "As I said earlier [then repeat your original statement]." A nondefensive and more helpful response would be: "Okay, I can appreciate your question. Thanks for raising that point. Now, help me understand which part concerns you the most."

In the event that someone asks a truly inappropriate question, do not get defensive or try to fumble through an answer. Simply say something like: "That's not a topic I'm qualified to address," or "I don't take personal questions such as that one," or "I'm not the appropriate source to respond to that question."

What to Do When You're in the Hot Seat

The higher the stakes and the more critical the outcome of any communication situation, the more likely it is that a speaker can find himself in the proverbial "hot seat." More often than not we are merely spectators to others in the uncomfortable situation of being grilled by a hostile questioner at a national news conference. President George W. Bush, for example, is perceived by the media as trying to avoid the "hot seat" as much as possible by limiting his participation in press conferences and other forums that expose him to critical inquiries and that force him to take positions and defend his policies. You don't have to be the president, however, to find yourself put on the spot, having to answer to a critical audience that will analyze every nuance of your verbal and nonverbal communication. From business executives who must respond to allegations of corporate impropriety to spouses who accuse one another of marital infidelity, the hot seat is not only an uncomfortable place to be, but how you handle yourself when you're in it can determine others' perception of your credibility, competence, and trustworthiness.

While it's always good to keep a cool-headed perspective when communicating with others, it's downright imperative when you're communicating under pressure.

One effective method of dealing with being in the hot seat and having to defend yourself before one or several hostile questioners is to behave in a strategically counterintuitive way that inhibits the escalation of an emotionally charged exchange of words and actions.

When someone shouts at us, for instance, our first instinct is to shout back. When someone tries to rush us, we start to become anxious and to hurry. When someone interrupts us, we tend to do the same to maintain control of the conversation. When someone acts hostile toward us, our tone may become equally sharp, and we switch into fight-or-flight mode.

Unfortunately, these methods of behavior rarely serve to benefit us or the situation in any constructive way, other than to perhaps temporarily let off steam. On the contrary, this type of behavior often causes the escalation of an already tense situation into an even more explosive one.

By acting counterintuitively, however, and using communication to deescalate a situation, we maintain credibility by keeping our emotions in check. It further allows us to maintain a clear perspective of the contentious situation, responding to it rationally rather than being manipulated into behavior that can cause us to lose control and negatively influence the audience's perceptions of us.

Resolve to use these deescalating behaviors the next time you find yourself in a pressure-cooker situation. If someone keeps interrupting you when you speak, don't compete by doing the same. Rather, take a moment and ask in a calm, friendly tone, "May I finish?" or say, "I would like to answer your question if you would let me."

If someone acts in a hostile manner toward you, stay composed, and with utmost sincerity counteract the person in a warm and friendly way. Separate the other person's message from the emotions you perceive. Respond to the content of the message rather than to the hostile behavior.

Likewise, when someone asks you a question you perceive to be unfair, don't jump to a defensive answer. Instead, ask the questioner to clarify or rephrase the question. Then, if you still perceive accusation in the query, address the underlying message you deem to be unfair before you answer the question. Now you have not only taken the momentum from the questioner but you have also gained a few moments of reflection to allow yourself to respond effectively to the disguised attack within the question.

People may use oppositional questions or antagonistic behavior to get a reaction from you. Don't play their game. Stay level-headed; listen closely to the core message and counter their manipulative attempts, verbal or nonverbal, with deescalating behavior and language that allow you to maintain control of your response and take the power out of their attacks.

Practice Exercises

1. Get experience handling challenging personalities. Seek out people who are opinionated and not warm and fuzzy in their interactions. Have conversations with them and learn that even if the conversations don't go well, it may not be because of you. Practice your poise and grace under fire when in a stressful speaking situation.

2. Practice disagreeing with people and expressing controversial points of view. You'll see that a disagreement does not necessarily mean that someone doesn't like or respect you.

3. Spot your assumptions. Be on the lookout for assumptions that you make about people who judge you or what you have to say. Question these assumptions and realize that they may not be true.

How to Recover Gracefully from Memory Lapses

We've all forgotten things from time to time. Someone comes up to you and says, "Hey, it's so great to see you!" and you have no idea who the person is. Someone asks you a question about something you were speaking with them about earlier that day and you can't even remember the conversation. Larina recently had an experience like this when she was being interviewed for a magazine. The writer said, "Hey, that part that you just said was really wonderful, can you say that again?" Larina had no recollection of what she'd just said (but she was glad it sounded good the first time!) and couldn't repeat it. It's common to pay little attention to yourself as you speak, and in fact it is a good thing, because self-focused attention increases anxiety. If you're focused externally on a conversation, you're likely not to feel nervous, but a problem can occur if someone asks you to repeat something.

Believe it or not, memory lapses can be a great thing when you handle them with grace. Everyone has experienced memory failure— some of us more than others! The wonderful thing is that people can relate to it and will find it funny if you're honest about it. When Larina forgot what she was talking about in her press interview, she simply said, "Oh, I have no idea what I just said!" and laughed. The reporter laughed too. Respectful of the reporter's tight deadline, Larina then said, "Let's go on to your next point, if that's okay, and it'll come back to me." If she had engaged in an overcompensating behavior and tried to come up with an answer she did not have, her response would not have been good. She could have damaged not only her chance of being quoted but also her relationship with the interviewer.

If you're in a new social situation and want to remember people's names and avoid a memory lapse later, there are some tricks. The key to remembering something is to find a way to relate it to something else you already know. Let's say that at a party you meet a man named Jeffrey, and he is wearing a shirt that is pool blue. You remind yourself that the person who cleans your pool is named Jeffrey, and then you're more likely to remember the new Jeffrey's name. This process is called elaborative rehearsal, which means that rather than just rehearsing the person's name by saying, "Jeff, blue shirt, Jeff," you're tying the new information into previous memories: "Jeff, pool blue." By doing this, you'll greatly decrease your memory lapses.

A great deal of research shows that anxiety can impair memory, and the results of Larina's dissertation research indicated that depressed feelings can do the same. If you're anxious or blue, you may be more likely to experience memory difficulties. Plan for this and don't rely on memory alone during times of pressure and stress. Keep your conversations grounded in the present tense so that you're not reliant on memory.

We've discussed memory triggers such as note cards and PowerPoint slides for presentations. If you're prone to forgetfulness when under stress (which most people are), then do not create additional pressure for yourself by overrelying on your memory when giving a speech. Create a couple of solid memory triggers for yourself. Always have a Plan B in case you forget something important during a formal presentation.

What to Do If You Feel as Though You're Going to Cry

Most people fear "breaking down" in situations where they need to speak or to participate nonverbally. One of the worst fears we've heard people express is the fear of crying in front of others. Some people are prone to crying when they're overwhelmed or nervous. Have you ever worried about this? Has it ever happened or come close to happening? It's a horrible feeling, but there are some things you can do about it:

- Figure out how close you are to actually welling up with tears. If the tears are already in your eyes or you've started to cry, quietly excuse yourself from the situation for a few minutes to gain your composure. Crying is like a ball rolling down a hill—it's hard to stop it once it's in motion. But you can stop it as it's rolling along the top of the hill before it plummets down. We'll tell you how in the next few steps, but first let's return to the idea of excusing yourself if you're beginning to cry.

  When you excuse yourself, it's important to regain your composure quickly so you don't return to your social situation all puffy-eyed or wait for 30 minutes before returning. Do not use the time to go through all the things that are making you upset because that will exacerbate the cycle. Instead, realize that you're justified in being upset, but focus on some positive aspects of the situation or some upcoming pleasant events to help change your emotion.

- If you notice yourself becoming emotional but have not actually started crying, challenge yourself to say something. Yes, it's probably the last thing that you want to do in this situation, but in fact it is very effective because you'll get your mind off your worries and get engaged in a conversation with others. You will also teach yourself the valuable lesson that you can control your emotions with your actions.
- If possible, chew some gum or eat a snack. It is difficult to cry when you're chewing. Try this—pop in the saddest movie you've ever seen and then chomp on a big piece of bubble gum. You'll find that it's difficult to chew and cry at the same time.

Even if the worst-case scenario occurs and you do show some tears or signs of a distressed emotion, remember that most people are empathetic and will assume that you're going through something difficult. Most social or speaking blunders or crises are not huge deals if they happen just once in front of people who see you regularly. These people already have a favorable impression of you, and one incident will not tarnish it. If, on the other hand, these crises happen more frequently, such as once a month in your staff meetings, negative judgments are more likely to occur. If expressing emotions (crying, angry outbursts, or other behaviors that aren't appropriate in specific situations) is a problem, consider seeking therapy or counseling.

How to Recover from a Verbal or Nonverbal Blunder

Imagine these embarrassing scenarios:

- You stammer over your words during the interview for your dream job and can't get your thoughts out.

- You're at a critical lunch meeting and you get spaghetti sauce all over your crisp white button-down shirt.
- You call your neighbor "Jerk" instead of "Jack."
- You're giving a speech and you trip and fall over the microphone cord.

These all sound like minor crises, right? They certainly could be, but here's an important point to remember: The way you respond to a crisis situation is more important than the crisis itself. Handling a crisis with poise can score you more points with audiences and other people than you'd get in a situation with no problems.

Ask yourself how noticeable the mistake or blunder was to others. People often draw more attention to themselves when they try to cover something up than they would if they let it go unnoticed. If something is completely obvious or funny, you may want to respond to it and briefly acknowledge its occurrence. Otherwise just let it go and keep speaking or listening to others.

If you're quick-witted and have a funny joke to make, go for it. If your joke is likely to bomb and be worse than the original blunder, then don't make the joke. Try to avoid self-deprecating humor and don't make a huge fuss.

If you accidentally insult or offend someone, offer a sincere apology. Don't go on and on saying, "I can't believe I said that! That's sooooo embarrassing . . ." If you have a legitimate reason why your brain is under-performing that day, you can offer it. For example, if you've just arrived at a conference and said something embarrassing, you can say, "I got in to the hotel at 4:00 a.m. last night. I guess the sleep deprivation is catching up with me!" Just remember not to overdo your explanations and apologies.

People are generally empathetic and nonjudgmental about faux pas. We've all done something silly and embarrassing at some point in our lives. If we laugh at others, it's often because we're glad it didn't happen to us and we feel badly that it happened to them. Laughter is rarely motivated by spite, judgment, or cruelty. And if a person is motivated by these things, we need to ask ourselves if we should care about the opinion of someone who is so judgmental.

How to Respond When You Don't Know What to Say

It's a horrible feeling to be in a situation or be asked a question and your mind is totally blank. Do you know this feeling? It's pretty bad, isn't it?

You may have been caught in the midst of spacing out and thinking of other things. Or maybe what the other person said made no sense to you. Or perhaps you simply have nothing to say about that topic. Regardless of the cause, it's a bad feeling to have all eyes on you and not know what to say. Here's what to do:

- First, ask yourself if you've adequately heard the question or statement to which you'll respond. If not, it's absolutely fine to ask for a clarification or repetition. Now, you don't want to be a perfectionist and make sure you completely understand the question by asking five questions to clarify the question. But it's certainly all right to ask someone to repeat or clarify one time.
- Second, it's time to think on your feet! Give yourself some credit; you probably know more than you think you do. If you aren't the best at thinking on your feet, practice. When you're not under the gun, get some experience with free associating about important topics in your life. Make a list of several key conversational topics you discuss regularly. Use concepts from your job, neighborhood, family, and hobbies. Take five pieces of paper and write a topic on the top of each. Then take one topic at a time and write freely about it. Don't censor yourself; just write whatever comes into your mind. For more on this process of free writing, read *The Accidental Genius: Revolutionize Your Thinking Through Private Writing* by Mark Levy.
- Third, never feel pressured to discuss something you aren't interested in discussing or qualified to discuss. However, don't shy away from a topic simply because it makes you uncomfortable. We've discussed the importance of expressing your views and not allowing anxiety to hold you back from speaking up and saying what's on your mind. On the other

288 ◆ The Confident Speaker

hand, there will be times when you don't have a view to express.
It may not be anxiety, but instead that you simply have no
inspiration to speak on a particular topic. If that's the case, give
yourself permission to take a pass and say that you don't have a
comment.

- Fourth, remember that most of the impact of what you say is
  often in *how* you say it, not what you say. If you don't think you
  have a wonderful answer but you want to make your point with
  impact, consider using some of the nonverbal and verbal
  techniques we've discussed in this book. If you need to pause for
  a moment to think, use your time to pause as a drama-creating
  moment. Maintain good posture and look people in the eye to
  show your confidence. Don't fidget or show that you're
  uncomfortable with the topic.

- Finally, realize that you can always say that you don't know
  something. As we've discussed throughout the book, honesty is
  the best policy. It's almost always better to say that you don't
  know than it is to fabricate an answer. When people see you as
  honest and genuine, they like you. And when people like you,
  they interpret your actions favorably. There's something in
  psychology that is called the "halo effect." When people have a
  favorable impression of you, they tend to view all of your
  behaviors with a positive halo. If you lie or fudge your way
  through something, you might get a negative halo, which could
  follow you like a black cloud into other speaking situations. So
  when in doubt, don't cover up what you don't know. Be honest
  and trustworthy first and foremost.

Practice Exercises

1. Make some minor blunders and learn that people often don't
   even notice them. If you're worried about saying something
   silly, do it. You'll see that it's nowhere near as big a deal as you
   thought it would be. Then the next time (and there will be a
   next time; we all do and say silly things from time to time),
   you'll react with poise and confidence.

2. Practice the process of free writing. For about five minutes per day, without censor, jot down whatever thoughts come into your head. You'll train your brain to think spontaneously and creatively.

3. Say you don't know the answer to something. You'll probably see that people appreciate your honesty.

4. Pick some times when you don't have something to say and choose to ask some questions. Instead of forcing a comment, ask someone to clarify a point, ask a question of your conversation partner, or ask your audience for an idea or comment.

Now that you can handle any speaking situation—even a blunder or crisis—you're ready to go out there and get as much practice as possible. The more practice you get, the more you'll hone your speaking skills and be confident to speak anywhere, anytime, in front of anyone. Read on for tips on getting more practice and polish.

17

Finding Speaking Opportunities for Practice and Polish

As with any new skill you learn, chances are you want to "road-test" your oratory talents as quickly and as often as you can. After all, what good is it to learn performance competency that can virtually skyrocket your professional and social status virtually overnight when you don't know how and where to practice your developing skills? Plus, as you've learned, to overcome a fear, the more you practice, the less fearful you'll be.

In this last chapter we'll help you find opportunities to practice and polish your speaking skills and become a truly spectacular speaker. Remember that the best way to practice is to begin with something just outside your comfort zone where the stakes are relatively low, gain practice and confidence, and then work your way up to the high-stakes speaking engagements.

Places to Practice Your New Skills

Fortunately, there is no shortage of opportunities to practice becoming a spectacular speaker. We will go into situations and places where you can continually hone your public speaking skills with audiences of all sizes and backgrounds, numbering anywhere from one to thousands. As you read through this section, rate how difficult speaking at each of the situations would be for you, on a scale of 0 to 10, with 10 being the most difficult. Begin practicing with anything that is a 6 or lower and then work your way up to more challenging situations.

Staff Meetings

Every company has meetings, either daily, weekly, or monthly, and all too often the same people speak up to give their views on what is and isn't working. Why not take notes before such a meeting and list your ideas so that you can present them the next time the boss asks for feedback from the group?

Learning Annex

In some cities these are called "Free Universities." It's where adult learners can take classes in everything from Bird Watching to Salsa Dancing, and from Professional Mediation to How to Market Professional Services. You can also do a Google search for "adult education programs" to find these classes. University catalogs are filled with hundreds of topics that "experts" are teaching. The classes can be anywhere from 90 minutes to five hours in length, and they often require from their teachers little more than rudimentary knowledge and experience in a topic.

If you have a hobby or passion about which you could teach a class, contact one of those free universities or learning annexes in your hometown or nearest larger city to see if they're interested in having you present a regularly scheduled program. The practice you get from speaking in front of an audience eager to learn your hobby is invaluable. Plus, the stakes are low, and when you mess up, you get immediate feedback from the audience in the form of class evaluations at the end of each session. They can give you valuable insight into your effectiveness as a speaker and presenter, allowing you to continuously adjust and improve your style until the evaluations are consistently filled with the highest marks. In addition, you get paid as much as $8 to $16 per student for teaching these programs, depending on the length of your class. Talk about a great way of getting paid to learn!

Elevators

That's right. We're talking about the little vessels that shuttle small groups of managers and worker bees from floor to floor in America's office towers. They give you a captive audience for an impromptu, albeit brief, chat about nothing in particular with quasi-strangers. What's the benefit? Just asking a simple question of someone from a different department or floor can train your speaking ability in front of groups and help desensitize you from feelings of anxiety when you speak in a more formal setting. Asking a colleague in a crowded elevator how her project is going or how her recent vacation went can go a long way in taking you out of your comfort zone and gently pushing you in the direction of where the movers and shakers stand and speak up.

PTA Meetings

If you're a parent and you go to this type of meeting at your children's school, you have a perfect opportunity to speak up the next time an issue arises that is of concern to you and other parents. If you do this on a regular basis, you may eventually be seen as a spokesperson and champion for others who share your views and concerns.

Book Clubs

These little informal gatherings are organized in virtually every neighborhood. Many are advertised in your local newspaper or on the bulletin board of your grocery store. At a book club, you read a book that will subsequently be the topic of discussion at a follow-up get-together with other members. You'll be able to practice your speaking skills by giving your perspectives on and perceptions of what you've read, initiating a lively discussion with the group that can also test your question-and-answer abilities and sharpen your senses in argumentation.

Toastmaster Groups

These organizations have been around for decades and have a number of chapters in cities large and small across the world. You'll find their contact and location information in your daily paper's community calendar listings. Their meetings are typically held in the mornings before office hours or conveniently during the lunch hour. As a member, you get ample opportunities to give short talks on virtually any topic, with other members providing you with immediate feedback on distracting verbal and nonverbal habits like uttering too many "ahhhs" and "ums" or fidgeting with pens and other items you like to hold on to as security blankets while you speak.

Their quick drills and immediate audience feedback on your speaking can make a big difference in your comfort and proficiency level with audiences in your professional and social environment. Go to http://toastmasters.org/ to find a group near you. If you're just getting started and are especially nervous, go to a group that is not in your local area so that it's very unlikely that you'll know anyone.

Parties and Networking Events

At these events, as you go from waiting to be approached by others to making the first move in engaging conversation partners and "taking the floor" in group discussions, you can practice your storytelling and public speaking skills. These situations give you a perfect chance to leave the protective cocoon of your comfort zone and thrust yourself into the public spotlight by taking a stand on the issue at hand, or you can simply tell an amusing anecdote from your day, week, or life, depending on the circumstances and appropriateness of the situation.

Here too you can gauge the audience's reaction for immediate feedback and guidance on what worked and what didn't. Did they laugh at your funny story? Are they asking follow-up questions to an interesting fact you told? Do people try to engage you in conversation immediately after you made a point? How have their attitudes changed toward you after you spoke? The answers to these questions will help you adjust or reinforce your techniques in the quest to become an impressive communicator and speaker.

Dinners and Weddings

Giving a toast is a wonderful way to practice speaking in public. You can give a brief 30-second toast at a birthday dinner for one of your friends, or an extended toast at a wedding. Don't wait to be invited somewhere. Host a holiday dinner or a dinner just for fun and give a toast to your guests, thanking them for coming. Or give a quick description of the menu you prepared.

Opportunities in Daily Life

There must be hundreds of opportunities in an average day where the chance to speak to others arises. Whether at work, the grocery store, with strangers at a party or acquaintances at the gym, wherever there are people in groups or alone, we can practice speaking on a variety of topics and situations. By choosing to see these situations as learning opportunities, we can continually practice our skills and polish our style and delivery, as well as more effectively select the content of our speaking efforts, based on the invaluable feedback and reactions we get from our unsuspecting practice audiences.

The opportunities to practice are in front of us, we just have to recognize and seize them for our benefit, perhaps enriching the lives of those around us in the process. Remember that the more you purposefully seek out opportunities to confront your anxiety, the more you will be in control of the anxiety, rather than the anxiety being in control of you. Make a concerted effort to find an opportunity to practice speaking up every day.

Take It a Step Further: Become a Professional Speaker

With an arsenal of new skills at your disposal, you may be ready to take your speaking skills up a level and become a professional speaker. All you need is an area of expertise and passion and the desire to share it with many people. Professional speaking is a wonderful way to share your knowledge, market your products or services, help people who would not otherwise have access to your ideas, *and* earn a good income. To give you a sense of how possible this is, consider Harrison's story of how he got his start as a professional speaker.

How Harrison Got Started as a Professional Speaking Coach

Harrison's desire to become a professional speaker grew gradually, beginning with an inability to speak in front of groups larger than two. Though painfully shy as a kid and even more so as a teenager, he always had a strong sense of humor and a natural ability to make people laugh. From this talent and a secret yet strong desire to stand out and be recognized and accepted by people came the desire to perform. But while harboring fantasies of greatness, he still couldn't get himself to actually stand up in front of a crowd and give any kind of speech or presentation that wasn't cut short by a severe case of stage fright.

After college, Harrison took a job as a sales manager for an Austrian commercial real estate firm based in Vienna, the heart of Europe. There, he interacted frequently with clients from many surrounding European countries as well as with a large number of sales executives in the office. His ability to communicate grew stronger as he observed and learned from the various styles of presenting and speaking used by clients and staff members alike. He chose to emulate and learn from what he liked and improve upon what didn't produce much impact.

He began to devour any kind of literature that dealt with the topics of social science, human interaction, styles of communication, and speaking and presentation skills. He was fascinated by the vastly different results various communication styles would yield from people. Most of the books he found had been around forever, but they nevertheless gave him enough of an education on the subject to make him want to do his own research. He was taken by some speakers' ability to captivate an audience, throw them into some sort of spell, and make them hang on every word. What was it about their way of communicating that made them stand out from the crowd? His curiosity led him to study the phenomena of "personal magnetism," as it's also called, and the more he understood the ability to communicate with charisma and literally shape the thoughts of an audience, the more determined he was to make his future in professional speaking and in teaching others to speak with impact, purpose, and clarity.

It was through this passion that he came to form the institution GuruMaker—School of Professional Speaking. The faculty of Guru-Maker is comprised of some of the top communication specialists in the world. Together, the GuruMaker team helps professionals who speak for a living communicate with power, clarity, and maximum impact.

When Harrison first started his speaking business, he spoke for free whenever he had a chance. He called every association he could find and asked them if they had any meetings coming up. If they did, he asked if he could speak at them. Since he didn't know the process for getting an engagement, he figured he would just be straightforward and tell them he wanted to speak to their members. If they asked what he spoke on, he would ask back, "What do you need?" Sometimes this drew a chuckle, other times pregnant pauses, and still other times, he would be told that they were all set for speakers, be thanked for calling, and be hung up on.

Learning from his lack of results, he changed his approach and started tailoring his proposed speech to the association or trade group's likely topics of interest. When calling the American X Association, for instance, he would tell the meeting planner that he had a program called X. Similarly, when calling the Y Association, he would change the title of his topic to Y. He was not playing a game with them or using them for his own benefit, but in getting his foot in the door, he fully intended to give his future audiences the best speech they'd ever heard. Of course, he had to adjust his entire program for a particular group and not just manipulate the title. It was a great exercise.

Though rough around the edges at first, he always made sure that his programs were a good fit for the audience and that his enthusiasm shone through so that the audience could feel that he cared about them and wanted them to succeed—the reason he was hired in the first place. Inevitably, he would receive standing ovations every time he finished his programs. People would come up to him, thanking him for making them feel better, for letting them know they were appreciated, and for giving them the tools they needed to enjoy their jobs and lives a little more than they had prior to his presentation. For Harrison, that's what it's always been about—helping people live a better life, knowing people will be better off because of something he gave them. He still says there is no better feeling than this.

Larina's Journey from Timid Public Speaker to Energetic Professional Speaker

As a 19-year-old sophomore in college, Larina remembers the day she sat frozen in horror upon learning that "Oral Communications" was a requirement for her college major. Her mind raced to dozens of potential excuses for why she could not possibly take the class. Alas, she realized that none of these excuses would fly, so she unhappily registered for the course.

She recalls sitting in class on the first day, her heart pounding, calculating how many awful minutes she'd need to speak during the semester. She told herself, "No more than 35 minutes total. I guess I'll survive." True to her expectations, her first speech did not go very well. By the end of the class, however, she had gained a small amount of confidence as a public speaker, and she almost actually enjoyed speaking before her audience.

Fast forward several years to when Larina needed to give a presentation to the eminent faculty at the University of Pennsylvania as part of the interview process for a faculty job. Those familiar butterflies swiftly returned. And to make matters worse, she was speaking to some of the world's foremost experts on anxiety. Her first thought was, I better not look nervous in front of them! Her second thought was, Maybe that job isn't right for me (because she was looking for a way to get out of the job talk). She then reminded herself that she had the choice of whether to make her anxiety a help or a hindrance. Using her anxiety as a source of energy, she gave a speech that resulted in the renowned anxiety expert Edna Foa saying, "Great lecture," and Larina was offered a position that changed the course of her professional career.

More recently those old butterflies made a resurgence when Larina experienced several technical failures while speaking to an audience of around 600 people. The room layout was not what she expected; she had to carry (and of course trip over) a long cord for a microphone; and the microphone didn't work properly. Ironically, Larina's talk was about how to embrace fear and failure as your friends. Larina said to her audience,

"When you have a powerful message to share, nothing can hold you back. Not the intimidation of a large audience. Not the pounding heart and sweaty palms you experience. Not your fears of making a fool of yourself. Not a microphone failure … nothing. Remember that your message can change people's lives—but only if you share it with them. So get out and share your message with as many people as possible!"

Now, whenever speaking jitters threaten to distract Larina, she focuses on what she and others stand to gain from her presentation. On her seminar days she pops up in the morning, not with fear, but with eager anticipation because she knows that there's a good chance that people will use the information they learn that day to change their lives.

Opportunities in the Speaking Industry

The Good News

While the speaking industry is international in scope, observers have noted that it's rooted in the quintessential American ideal of boundless individual promise. The impulse to formulate and share proven methods of success goes back at least to the time of Benjamin Franklin and continues today in the romantic advice of John Gray and in the motivational spectacle of a Tony Robbins infomercial.

The speaking industry caters to an abundance of groups and individuals who are willing to gamble sizable fees for the chance to hear just the right message, from boosting sales to jump-starting love lives. Twenty or so years ago, corporations thrived on a growing economy and management styles that emphasized the power of a select few over lower-level employees. The recession of the last decade changed all that. Companies had to figure out ways to continue growing even when the economy was less than hospitable. They also had to deal with the changing nature of their employees. The increasing number of women and minorities in the workforce required a new way of seeing management and employee relations. The prospect of staying at one job for an entire lifetime was now a thing of the past. Businesses had to think of ways to maintain profits and employee morale. Meanwhile, speakers were called in to offer motivating insights and practical skills that companies could use to survive.

Prospects for speakers were by no means reduced during the technology boom of the late 1990s. With new technologies came the need to train employees and produce a return on companies' investments. Though the boom hasn't lasted, today's corporations are still in need of advice on how to stay competitive. In fact, the corporate or business market represents a virtual "all-you-can-eat" buffet of paid speaking, training, and presentation opportunities for aspiring and veteran speakers alike.

The pursuit of personal goals is another large market for public speakers. The best-seller list often includes the latest nonfiction titles on how to improve relationships or physical and mental health. In 1997, *Writer's Digest* published a list of promising self-help markets. These included engendering creativity on the job or at home, time management, spirituality, and improving quality of life. The list suggests priorities shared by many and promising subjects not just for books but also for self-help programs.

The demographics of the speaking industry are also changing. Women are increasingly being hired to talk about how to achieve success, cope with depression, devote time to family, and develop fruitful relationships between business and technology. And then there are speakers who tackle issues particularly relevant to minority business leaders. One of them is Dennis Kimbro. At one time a business professor, Kimbro started his new career as a successful author with *Think and Grow Rich: A Black Choice.*

Speaking fees depend on the speaker's experience and celebrity. Colin Powell can get $75,000 for a keynote speech, while a single appearance can earn Tony Robbins $175,000. In comparison, former President Bill Clinton reportedly earns at most a mere $150,000 for an appearance.

Whether you're a seasoned celebrity or a speaker just starting out, prospects for public speakers have never been more promising. Currently, corporations invest around $64 billion a year for training and motivational programs for their employees, while *Newsweek* has reported that individuals spend about $2.5 billion on books, tapes, and programs devoted to self-help. And with steadily rising numbers of women and minority speakers, the industry has grown increasingly diverse.

At the same time, speakers have had to adjust to the reality of tougher economic times. Topics like "How to Start Your Own Business," "How to Learn New Job Skills," and "How to Make a Successful Career Change" are particularly relevant to the speaker who wants to motivate an audience facing an unstable economy.

The Bad News

With the increasing competition in business today, businesses in the market for a speaker are a lot savvier about getting their money's worth. And they're less willing to spend money—even on a celebrity—if the investment does not yield tangible results, such as an increase in productivity, improved employee morale, higher sales, and so on. The speaker who hopes to flourish in the lucrative corporate speaking world must have more than a motivational message that temporarily rallies the troops and boosts morale. Today's corporate meeting planners demand that speakers have real-world experience relevant to the industry, and the ability to connect with an audience. Since the performance of meeting planners is judged by the success of the events they organize, a few bad choices when it comes to presenters can jeopardize their relations with upper management. So it's in the speaker's best interest to make the meeting planner a hero. If the speaker succeeds at this, his or her chances of being rehired for the next convention or program are excellent. Everyone wins.

The desire for results fits with the ambivalent image of professional public speakers, particularly so-called motivational speakers, in the popular media. Common sense suggests that change cannot be effected by words alone, much less words spoken at an event where the luxury locale is potentially more memorable than the keynote speaker. Is one hour or even one week of motivational speaking and exercises going to turn around a lifetime of bad management or personal habits?

Art Levine, writing for *U.S. News & World Report* in 1997, decided to test the promises of a Tony Robbins television ad and purchased a 30-day program for $200. When his financial and romantic prospects failed to improve after a month, Levine decided to confront Robbins after a one-day seminar in Charlotte, North Carolina. Hearing of Levine's failure to make tangible improvements, Robbins dismissed the reporter's complaints, telling him that "you're in no-man's-land . . . You don't feel bad enough to change."

Of course, public image should not be the deciding factor in your choice of career. If you're committed to your topic and have the skills to help people, you can produce tangible change as a professional speaker and have an impact on the lives of many. But the prevailing skepticism of what a public speaker can do for businesses and individual consumers is a sobering reminder that showmanship is only one part of becoming a successful speaker. Your message must provide some kind of positive result, whether it is visibly seen by your clients or knowledgeably projected by your own research and experience in the field.

The Good News About the Bad News

With businesses and individuals trying to make motivation more cost effective, there's more room for those speakers who may not have the celebrity of a Colin Powell or a Bill Clinton but who do have proven expertise. These days, companies care more about results than about boosting morale by hiring the most famous coaches and political figures. In these leaner economic times, new speakers lacking celebrity may still impress major clients on their own specific, professional terms.

Of course, corporations and businesses aren't the only potential markets for aspiring professional speakers who are looking to enter the circuit. There are many opportunities to speak professionally and go from "free to fee" by offering your services to universities, networking groups, and some of the thousands of associations that hold regular conferences for their members, as well as self-help groups and churches, and even major cruise lines that hire speakers to entertain and educate passengers during ocean voyages. Dottie Walters, a veteran in the speaking industry and founding member of the National Speakers' Association, and her daughter Lilly Walters, are a wonderful resource for additional opportunities in the world of professional speaking. Their best-selling book, *Speak and Grow Rich*, is a must-read for aspiring speakers. It offers solid advice, from topic development to speaker marketing and working effectively with speaker's bureaus.

Professional speakers are inevitably subjected to intense public scrutiny, and this applies particularly to those speakers who talk the talk but can't convincingly show that they walk the walk. If a speaker preaches "The 12 Principles of Financial Success," he or she better be able to show evidence of financial wealth. Likewise, if a presenter has never been in a position of leadership, it's not likely that an audience will give his or her programs any credence. And without credibility, there is no market.

Having said that, there will always be "fast-buck artists"—speakers whose abilities to charm, combined with a certain eloquence and flair for showmanship, will give audiences the equivalent of a major sugar high: a couple of hours of hyperactivity followed by an empty feeling soon after. Such fast-talkers will always be around. Fortunately, you can avoid their influence by holding yourself to a simple but essential standard: Speak only about those things that you have earned the right to speak about, whether through experience or study.

What It Takes to Be a Professional Speaker

It takes knowledge, experience, practice, and a flair for the dramatic. Successful professional speakers have backgrounds as eclectic as their client lists. Some have advanced degrees, like well-known speaker Danielle Kennedy, who has a master's degree in writing from USC, which she earned after making a name for herself selling real estate. Then there's Les Brown, whose background includes stints in sales, radio, and politics. And Patricia Fripp, a speaking veteran whose early seminars were spin-offs from her career as a hair stylist. Denis Waitley is known for his understated approach to topics like winning and competitive management strategies, and he has a Ph.D. in human behavior and has used his dissertation to develop his best-selling program, "The Psychology of Winning." On the other hand, Tony Robbins does not have a bachelor's degree, and Brian Tracy didn't even finish high school.

As you can see, you don't need a Ph.D. to be a successful speaker. But while successful speakers may not share the same levels of formal education, they do share certain qualities honed in the course of their respective careers:

- *Enthusiasm.* The speakers who regularly pack large auditoriums bring an enthusiasm to their presentations to which audiences respond. They can project passion for the topics they are presenting. They know how to use humor, storytelling, and physical movement to engage a crowd and make their presentations more memorable.
- *Credibility.* Regardless of your specialty as a speaker, your audience needs to know that your advice is backed up by proven success in the area you're addressing—and an ongoing effort to develop your knowledge and presentation skills in this area.
- *Action.* The central issue all speakers deal with is fostering change. Change is impossible without taking action. Many of today's most successful speakers have managed to survive challenging circumstances in both their personal and professional lives. Les Brown struggled in his early years of school and was thought to have a learning disability until his high school drama teacher convinced him otherwise. Tony Robbins has described the squalid living conditions he endured—doing his dishes in the tub of his kitchenless Venice, California, apartment—before making it as a motivational speaker. On stage, successful speakers not only empathize with the difficulties experienced by their audiences, but often share similar universal experiences that they were able to successfully overcome to arrive where they are today.
- *Compassion.* Savvy speakers are good at promoting what they can contribute to a company's or an individual's growth. But the great ones stress the importance of their audience's success over their own personal gains. They enter public speaking to help others, and they emphasize that this goal must ultimately come first.
- *Business sense.* Those who want to have long careers in this increasingly competitive industry must have an eye toward the practical side of the business. They must know how to expand their business without becoming overwhelmed by substantial overhead, bad time management, or other administrative problems. Professional speakers must also know their audience and their audience's needs well enough to anticipate necessary

changes to speaking programs or to products for sale at the back of the room. Compassion should get you into the speaking profession, but only with good business sense will you stay in it. Part of business sense is marketing savvy. You need to be able to effectively package your services, give them a great name, and market them to those who can benefit from them. If you don't have marketing skills, you can hire someone who does.

- *Flexibility.* In addition to the pressures of marketing themselves and their businesses, professional speakers wear many hats when on stage. Their success depends on shaping the core of their message to a wide range of individual and corporate audiences, sometimes right on the spot. They must wrestle with the logistics of constant air travel, over- (or under-) heated hotel rooms, faulty audiovisual equipment, and the challenge of keeping to the allotted time during programs featuring multiple speakers. The contingencies that can make or break a program require a speaker to adapt to unanticipated problems.

- *Stamina.* Professional speaking requires a certain degree of physical stamina, especially if you want to compete with the onstage antics of a Tony Robbins. Don't worry—you don't have to be a seven-foot giant with the physical training of a triathlete, as Robbins is. But the rigors of frequent traveling, hotel food, and the intensity required by public performance demand that you look after yourself physically as well as mentally. Getting sick in this industry may mean missed engagements worth thousands of dollars, not to mention the scorn of meeting planners hoping to impress a client during a big meeting. Planners and organizers are left to scramble for a suitable replacement who may not be found in time. The success of an entire event may be jeopardized, and the meeting planner will be the scapegoat.

Remember what we said earlier: As a speaker, it's your job to make the meeting planner look like a hero. Getting sick before a big event where you're scheduled to speak is a sure way to lose a client and risk your reputation for reliability. This, in turn, might result in fewer bookings in the future, since meeting planners trade experiences and gossip with one another, just as professionals in other industries do.

And speaking of mental health: Speakers can develop depression after an intense period of presenting. *Training & Development* covered this in an article detailing how diet, exercise, and other techniques can combat the "post-presentation blues." This is just one example of how successful speakers have to know how to take care of themselves and their audiences.

- *Self-teaching.* The fact that some very successful professionals lack academic credentials by no means implies that learning is unnecessary to becoming a better speaker. What was not learned in the classroom was often picked up through intense self-instruction. Brian Tracy's ideas on success were shaped in part by his independent readings in philosophy and other disciplines. A young Les Brown memorized dictionary entries in order to expand his vocabulary. Of course, one should not overlook the art of speaking itself. A developing professional learns the most by spending time behind the lectern, getting a realistic picture of strengths and weaknesses.

While there is no distinct curriculum for becoming a professional speaker, there are plenty of guidelines, suggested courses of action, and insider tips. Nevertheless, how you learn the trade and the amount of time you're willing to invest in your professional growth is ultimately up to you.

When and How to Grow Your Speaking Business

Let's say you've begun to speak on a regular basis to anyone who will listen to your topics of choice. How do you know when it's time to expand a personal interest or special business knowledge into a thriving speaking business?

Patricia Fripp provides a good rule of thumb in Michael Jeffreys's *Success Secrets of the Motivational Superstars*, a book of interviews with industry leaders. Fripp suggests that after training as a free speaker, you can move to paid engagements by listening to your audience. The more you get asked about how much you charge, the more you know that you've reached the level where people are willing to pay to hear you.

However, the decision to set up your own speaking business involves more than figuring out how much to charge an audience. You also have to consider the logistics of running a profitable business. You can work from home, but even a home office can be a significant investment. Computers are ubiquitous in business and are a necessity at the outset, as are the basic tools for business communication, which include phone, fax, and Internet access. In a recent report, *Entrepreneur* magazine estimated that a seminar promotion office based at home can cost anywhere from $5,000 to $25,000, depending on the quality of your equipment. You are selling a service, so as you're planning to promote your speaking talents, you need to invest in office supplies, equipment, and a considerable amount of time and perhaps money in marketing.

Developing your speaking skills will not generate much income—at least not at first. Experienced professionals often start by making short presentations to Kiwanis, Rotary, or other local clubs and associations. If you deliver consistently excellent programs, the word-of-mouth generated can lead to your first paid engagements.

Figuring out what you should be paid depends on your experience, reputation, and the type and length of the program you present. It would be reasonable to expect (and accept) a fee in the low hundreds for your first paid speech. Hold off on dreams of early retirement from your first speaking fees and continue to work on your strengths and weaknesses. The better you are at promoting yourself and your program, the more well-known you'll be and the more prospective clients will want to pay to have you speak to their groups.

Top professional speakers get fees that average in the lower four figures per day. You can expect more if you're an in-demand celebrity or business guru. If you've developed books, tapes, or other educational products related to your specialty, your prospects as well as the fees you can demand as a speaker increase significantly. Besides raising your status as a professional and expert on your topic, such products can be sold at seminars, workshops, or other engagements, and result in considerable profits. The controversial real estate trainer Mike Ferry is legendary for generating product sales of $750,000 in a single day. How do you think he slept that night?

While your public speaking might start off as a passion, it could ultimately end up as a business. If that happens, experts recommend that, as business increases and you get busier, you could benefit from the support services provided by a staff. Ferry, interviewed in *Success Secrets*, suggested that speakers should delegate certain administrative duties to a personal assistant, an accountant, and, if possible, an aggressive marketer. Delegating these distracting but essential responsibilities will give a speaker more time to work on his or her programs and presentation skills. Patricia Fripp's staffing suggestions are more modest. She recommends having someone around to answer your phone so that prospective clients won't be missed. As you can see, the approaches to the business side of the speaking profession are as varied as the speakers' personalities.

When Harrison first started, he worked as a one-man show, without any staff or even a secretary to answer the phones. It's tough to pay a staff when you're speaking for free to get your name out in front of people.

Harrison had to be creative, so he took advantage of one of those great American ideas of using outsource help and rented a "virtual" office, often listed under "Executive Suites" in your local yellow pages. Many larger cities have companies that offer these services, so if you can't find them in your hometown, look at the big city nearest you. For just a couple of hundred dollars a month, Harrison got a package deal that included professional answering of his own personal line by a real-life, flesh-and-blood person. That wasn't all, though. This deal came with a professional mailing address in a prestigious zip code, office space whenever he needed it, and all the copying and faxing his new business venture required. The only thing left to do was craft an airtight marketing plan, design and print brochures of his programs, and let the world know he was ready to do business.

What happens when you decide you're ready to earn more per speech or engagement, providing, of course, that you can justify this increase with your speaking and other professional experiences? Successful speakers have rules of thumb for this. Negotiation expert Roger Dawson, for instance, recommends having a fee structure for the different kinds of programs you present and sticking to it once it's set up. Rather than lowering your fee to get a job, he advises in *Success Secrets*, you should offer value-adding extras such as books, tapes, or other products. Or you can offer to do two presentations or breakout sessions for the price of one. You'll already be at the location, it will just take an extra 40 or 60 minutes of your time, and planners can justify a higher fee for two presentations.

If you can afford it, you should also be willing to say no to a presentation if you can't get what you ask for. Once you start charging for your speaking services, your fee will suggest the value of the information you provide; the lower the fee, the less likely an organization is to hire you, due to the perceived lack of value of your program.

Dawson adds that you should review your fees annually and, if appropriate, raise them in order to maximize your earnings while minimizing the frequency of your appearances. As you grow and develop as a speaker, this is potentially a fair way to consistently garner higher fees while giving your audiences increasing value.

Despite the challenges of a troubled economy, the professional speaking industry continues to offer a promising forum for companies and individuals in search of self-improvement. For the person with the right combination of compassion, enthusiasm, and business savvy, professional speaking offers a way to turn personal interests into a long-term career.

Final Thoughts

You may still be in school, planning your course in life; or maybe you're already a seasoned professional in your industry. Perhaps you're simply a person who is ready to contribute your ideas, thoughts, and opinions to the discussions and interactions at parties, work, and virtually anyplace where humans gather for a purpose. With the advice and information in this book, we hope we've shown you how you can thrive in all kinds of interpersonal communication situations by embracing and working with your anxiety, not fighting it. We also hope that you will use the new speaking skills you've learned to get out there, speak up, and share your ideas and dreams with the world around you.

While both of us, at the beginning of our professional speaking endeavors, experienced significant anxiety, we found ways to overcome the debilitating feelings of presentation reluctance and performance apprehension. Using the techniques and tools we've developed and presented to you in this book, we learned to make anxiety our friend and incorporate its presence into the enthusiasm we feel for training and coaching the future confident speakers of the world. Our journey as professional speakers and trainers, and the ability to speak confidently to thousands of audiences, has presented us with wonderful opportunities and introduced us to fascinating people from across the globe. You should expect nothing less in your quest to become a confident speaker.

Endnotes

Chapter 1

5   *How severe is your public speaking anxiety?*
    —This proprietary assessment was developed by Larina Kase specifically for use within this book.

12 *Shy people are often more likely to feel anxious about speaking than their less shy peers.*
    —M. M. Antony and R. P. Swinson, *The Shyness and Social Anxiety Workbook.* Oakland, California: New Harbinger Publications, 2000.

15 *Cognitive therapists such as Dr. Aaron Beck, known by many as the "father of cognitive therapy," have studied the type of thinking that occurs with anxiety and written about it extensively.*
    —A. T. Beck, *Cognitive Therapy and the Emotional Disorders,* reprint edition. New York: Plume, 1979.

18 *In fact, the latest research reveals that these behaviors are largely responsible for public speaking anxiety.*
    —J. D. Huppert, D. A. Roth, and E. B. Foa, "Cognitive-behavioral treatments of social phobia: New advances," *Current Psychiatry Reports* (2003) 5: 189–96.

Chapter 2

22 *One of Larina's colleagues from the University of Pennsylvania is fond of saying, "Even sea slugs habituate."*
    —Quote by Shawn P. Cahill, Ph.D., Assistant Professor, Center for Treatment and Study of Anxiety at the University of Pennsylvania.

30 *Did you know that some social blushing is actually interpreted as a good thing?*

—M. R. Leary, T. W. Britt, W. D. Cutlip II, and J. L. Templeton, *Psychological Bulletin* (1992) 112 (3): 446–60.

Chapter 3

33 *In this chapter we'll cover the top 10 situations that most frequently cause people anxiety.*
—The list of the top 10 situations is based on Larina's clinical and coaching experiences and Harrison's training experiences with clients.

Chapter 5

85 *You don't even need to believe your positive image for the technique to be effective.*
—S. E. Taylor, *Positive Illusions: Creative Self-Deception and the Healthy Mind.* New York: Basic Books, 1989.

Chapter 6

89 *The solution to breathing problems like shallow breathing is to take deep, diaphragmatic breaths.*
—E. B. Bourne and L. Garano, *Coping with Anxiety: 10 Simple Ways to Relieve Anxiety, Fear and Worry.* Oakland, California: New Harbinger Publications, 2003.

91 *Another way to relax your body and beat both stress and anxiety is through muscle relaxation.*
—D. Bernstein, T. Borkovec, and H. Hazlett-Stevens, *New Directions in Progressive Relaxation Training: A Guidebook for Helping Professionals.* Westport, Connecticut: Praeger Publishers, 2000.

97 *Research has shown that people who are nervous about giving presentations tend to more readily recall negative descriptions about themselves before giving a speech.*
—W. Mansell and D. M. Clark, "How do I appear to others? Social anxiety and processing of the observable self," *Behaviour Research and Therapy* (1999) 37: 419–34.

98 *There is evidence that people who are socially anxious engage in extensive processing once speaking events are over.*
—S. Rachman, J. Gruter-Andrew, and R. Safran, "Post event processing in social anxiety," *Behaviour Research and Therapy* (2000) 38: 611–17.

Chapter 8

126 *The approach we present to you has been validated by empirical research with people who are likely to have much more significant social anxiety and speaking phobias than you.*
—J. D. Huppert, D. A. Roth, and E. B. Foa, "Cognitive-behavioral treatments of social phobia: New advances," *Current Psychiatry Reports* (2003) 5: 189–96.

126 *Clinical research and treatment at world class centers for the treatment of anxiety, such as the Center for Treatment and Study of Anxiety at the University of Pennsylvania under the leadership of internationally renowned anxiety expert Dr. Edna B. Foa, have shown this cognitive-behavioral approach to be extremely effective.*
—E. B. Foa and M. J. Kozak, "Emotional processing of fear: Exposure to corrective information," *Psychological Bulletin* (1986) 99 (1): 20–35.

128 *Trying to suppress a thought typically results in the thought coming up more.*
—J. S. Abramowitz, D. F. Tolin, and G. P. Street, "Paradoxical effects of thought suppression: A meta-analysis of controlled studies," *Clinical Psychology Review* (2001) 21: 683–703.

138 *Your attention plays a highly important role in how anxious how feel. The more you focus on yourself, the more you will be self-conscious.*
—D. M. Clark, "A cognitive perspective on social phobia," in *International Handbook of Social Anxiety: Concepts, Research, and Interventions Related to the Self and Shyness*, W. R. Crozier and L. E. Alden, eds. New York: John Wiley & Sons, 2001.

146 *Professional speaking expert Lilly Walters recommends that those who experience dry mouth picture in their minds a juicy lemon and*

then lightly bite the inside of their cheek or press their tongue to the top of their mouth.
—L. Walters, *Secrets of Successful Speakers*. New York: McGraw-Hill, 1993.

Chapter 9

150 *When others look at us for an extended amount of time, even just a few seconds, our sympathetic nervous system gets a jolt . . .*
—D. B. Givens, *The Nonverbal Dictionary*. Spokane, Washington: Center for Nonverbal Studies Press, 2002.

162 *A study conducted during the 1984 presidential campaign tells of the late ABC News anchor Peter Jennings's tendency to smile more when he spoke on the air of incumbent president Ronald Reagan than when he spoke of his challenger, Walter Mondale.*
—D. B. Givens, *The Nonverbal Dictionary*. Spokane, Washington: Center for Nonverbal Studies Press, 2002.

162 *During the latter part of the 1990s, U.S. supermarket chain Safeway Corp. mandated that its employees smile at each customer they made eye contact with.*
—*USA Today*, "Safeway's Mandatory Smiles Pose Danger, Workers Say," 1998.

163 *Researchers have found that during a real or genuine smile, we activate a number of facial muscles.*
—D. B. Givens, *The Nonverbal Dictionary*. Spokane, Washington: Center for Nonverbal Studies Press, 2002.

163 *Now there is a school of thought that says that you can actually* feel *a certain way by* acting *a certain way first.*
—D. B. Givens, *The Nonverbal Dictionary*. Spokane, Washington: Center for Nonverbal Studies Press, 2002.

Chapter 10

174 *This idea takes its inspiration from a school of acting instruction known as the* Meisner technique, *favored by actors such as Robert Duvall, Tom Cruise, Diane Keaton, and Jeff Goldblum.*
—Wikipedia, "Meisner Technique," accessed August 27, 2006.

175 *As Crystal said in an interview with the* Milwaukee Journal Sentinel, *"It's almost like creating a football playbook with options. We bank thousands of jokes — and then, hopefully, you don't need any of them. The best ones are the ones that just arise spontaneously."*
— J. Weintraub, "Ready for more Oscar moments: Wisecracking Crystal will return to host Academy Awards gala," *Milwaukee Journal Sentinel Online,* January 2004.

176 *"Conveying information in a story provides a rich context, remaining in the conscious memory longer and creating more memory traces than information not in context."*
— A. Bennet, *The Use of Storytelling in DON.* U.S. Department of the Navy, December 2000.

176 *"A relaxed, happy relationship between storyteller and listener is established, drawing them together and building mutual confidence."*
— E. M. Pederson, "Storytelling and the Art of Teaching," *Forum,* March 1995, vol. 33, no.1, 4.

177 *"Consider the CEO of a biotech start-up that has discovered a chemical compound to prevent heart attacks."*
— R. McKee, "Storytelling That Moves People: A conversation with screenwriting coach Robert McKee," *Harvard Business Review* (2003) 81 (6): 51–55.

Chapter 11

185 *Aristotle, often considered the father of persuasion and public speaking, wrote in the fourth century B.C. that ethos, or one's character, is the foundation of a person's credibility and his ability to persuade others to a point of view.*
— W. Braden, *Public Speaking: The Essentials.* New York: Harper & Row, 1966, 90.

198 *"Even if you are not looking to make a sale, to gain a contract or change audience member's minds, you are still attempting to persuade them to listen to you, and to accept your information."*

—Lawrence Tracy, *The Shortcut to Persuasive Presentations.* Alexandria, Virginia: Tracy Presentation Skills, 2002, 30.

Chapter 12

212   *Stop focusing on yourself. Getting your attention onto your coworkers will help you feel less self-conscious.*
—D. M. Clark, "A cognitive perspective on social phobia," in *International Handbook of Social Anxiety: Concepts, Research, and Interventions Related to the Self and Shyness,* W. R. Crozier and L. E. Alden, eds. New York: John Wiley & Sons, 2001.

215   *Also, a good deal of research shows that people who are afraid of critical evaluation interpret ambiguous social cues as negative.*
—E. B. Foa, M. E. Franklin, K. J. Perry, and J. D. Herbert, "Cognitive biases in generalized social phobia," *Journal of Abnormal Psychology* (1996) 105: 433–39.

216   *An optimistic attitude is strongly correlated with a successful outcome.*
—M. Seligman, *Learned Optimism.* New York: Knopf, 1991.

Chapter 13

229   *Public speaking is humanity's number one fear, but like all fears, it can be faced and conquered, even if it involves large audiences.*
—Susan K. Jacobson, *Communication Skills for Conservation Professionals.* Washington, D.C.: Island Press, 1999, 258.

232   *Audiences have a limited capacity for what they remember, so make sure the gist of what you're trying to say is obvious and repeated appropriately throughout your talk.*
—Eric Matson, "Now That We Have Your Complete Attention . . ." *Fast Company,* February 1997, 124.

235   *Authors of* How to Persuade People Who Don't Want to Be Persuaded *Joel Bauer and Mark Levy refer to a physical illustration of a point through the use of props as a type of "transformational mechanism."*

—J. Bauer and M. Levy, *How to Persuade People Who Don't Want to Be Persuaded.* New York: John Wiley & Sons, 2004.

237 *Generally speaking, it's best to keep your talk under 45 minutes, if possible.*
—Susan K. Jacobson, *Communication Skills for Conservation Professionals.* Washington, D.C.: Island Press, 1999, 258.

237 *The law of primacy and recency says that people remember most what is said at the beginning and the end of a talk.*
—Lawrence Tracy, *The Shortcut to Persuasive Presentations.* Alexandria, Virginia: Tracy Presentation Skills, 2002, 52.

Chapter 14

257 *There is a continuum of appropriate disagreement and expression of views. On the one end, people are passive and do not speak up. On the other end, they are aggressive and force their views on others or put people down for having views different from their own.*
—R. J. Peterson, *The Assertiveness Workbook: How to Express Your Ideas and Stand Up for Yourself at Work and in Relationships.* Oakland, California: New Harbinger Publications, 2000.

Chapter 15

263 *The feminine style often involves the use of more positive words and less discussion of money and numbers, as well as less use of swear words and long words.*
—R. B. Slatcher, et al., "Winning words: Individual differences in linguistic style among U.S. presidential and vice presidential candidates." *Journal of Research in Personality,* Austin, Texas: Elsevier, 2006, 1–13.

263 *Another important component to keep in mind is that women are more likely than men to focus on negative aspects of themselves.*
—N. Mor and J. Winquist, "Self-focused attention and negative affect: A meta-analysis," *Psychological Bulletin* (2002) 128(4): 638–62.

265 *Consider that men use about 7,000 words a day, whereas women use upward of 20,000.*
—L. Brizendine, *The Female Brain*. New York: Morgan Road Books, 2006.

266 *Sociologist and author Deborah Tannen notes in a 1997 interview with* Training & Development *that "developing awareness that people have different styles is important. Try to raise your own sensitivity to the kind of responses you get so that you can gauge: This seems to be working well with this person, I'm okay. Or, this person isn't reacting well: What can I do differently?"*
—Quoted from R. Koonce, "Language, Sex and Power: women and men in the workplace," interview with author Deborah Tannen, *Training & Development*, American Society for Training and Development (1997) 51(9): 34–40.

267 *Research has shown that women tend to be more sensitive than men to other people's facial expressions.*
—J. W. Pennebaker and T. Roberts, "Toward a his and hers theory of emotion: Gender differences in visceral perception," *Journal of Social and Clinical Psychology* (1992) 11(3): 199–212.

267 *Whether the men in an audience "like" a female speaker weighs heavily on whether they will be influenced by her.*
—L. L. Carli, S. J. LaFleur, and C. C. Loeber, "Nonverbal behavior, gender, and influence," *Journal of Personality and Social Psychology*, 68 (1995) 1030–41.

269 *Studies show that women have much higher brain activity when it comes to remembering emotional events.*
—"Sexes handle emotions differently," BBC News, July 23, 2002, http:// news.bbc.co.uk/1/hi/health/2146003.stm

269 *But men are also less in tune with their own emotional states than women are, meaning that while men experience the same emotions, their ability to recognize them can be lower.*
—J. W. Pennebaker, "Psychological factors influencing the reporting of physical symptoms," in *The Science of Self-Report: Implications*

for *Research and Practice*, A. A. Stone and J. S. Turkkan, eds.
Mahwah, New Jersey: Lawrence Erlbaum Associates, 2000, 299–315.

Chapter 16

278 *In research studies, anxious people are more likely to pay attention to
negative feedback and to think that neutral feedback is negative.*
—D. M. Clark, "A cognitive perspective on social phobia," in
*International Handbook of Social Anxiety: Concepts, Research,
and Interventions Related to the Self and Shyness*, W. R. Crozier
and L. E. Alden, eds. New York: John Wiley & Sons, 2001.

283 *Larina recently had an experience like this when she was being
interviewed for a magazine.*
—M. Villano, "Recovering a Fumble at the Flip Chart," Career
Couch column, *New York Times*, August 20, 2006.

287 *For more on this process of free writing, read* The Accidental Genius:
Revolutionize Your Thinking Through Private Writing *by Mark Levy.*
—M. Levy, *The Accidental Genius: Revolutionize Your Thinking
Through Private Writing*. San Francisco: Berrett-Koehler Publishers,
2000.

Chapter 17

299 *Speaking fees depend on the speaker's experience and celebrity.
Colin Powell can get $75,000 for a keynote speech, while a single
appearance can earn Tony Robbins $175,000. In comparison, former
President Bill Clinton reportedly earns at most a mere $150,000 for
an appearance.*
—B. Straub, "Clinton in high demand as speaker abroad," *Rocky
Mountain News*, July 28, 2001, 4A.

306 *In a recent report,* Entrepreneur *magazine estimated that a seminar
promotion office based at home can cost anywhere from $5,000 to
$25,000, depending on the quality of your equipment.*
—L. Tiffany, "How to Start a Seminar Production Business,"
Entrepreneur.com, June 14, 2001.

Index

About the Authors

Harrison Monarth is the founder and president of GuruMaker—School of Professional Speaking, a high-impact communications consulting firm that counts Fortune 500 executives, professionals, and political candidates as clients. Through GuruMaker, he has assembled a select team of coaches, trainers, and behavior change experts, who work together to help clients overcome their most challenging communication issues and to influence important events through the skill of public discourse. Dubbed "The Speakinator" by one of his enthusiastic clients, Harrison has been a sought-after authority in the field of confidential executive presentation coaching for more than a decade. He has helped executives and corporate leaders from top companies throughout Europe and the United States prepare and deliver crucial business presentations. As a specialist in persuasive communication and in the reduction of conflict and stress through effective interpersonal communication, he is frequently called upon when the stakes are high and audiences need persuading. Harrison has personally coached senior corporate leaders from top companies such as Merrill Lynch, Intel Corporation, Cisco Systems, and Northwestern Mutual, as well as members of the U.S. Congress. Learn more about how to become a persuasive speaker at www.gurumaker.com

Larina Kase, PsyD, MBA, is a licensed psychologist and the president of Performance & Success Coaching, an organization specializing in peak performance skills and anxiety and stress management for executives and entrepreneurs. Through her popular seminars entitled Diversity for Workplace Creativity, Control Stress—Achieve Success, and Be the CEO of Your Career, she has provided coaching to dozens of small businesses, universities, professional organizations, and Fortune 500 companies. Dr. Kase is regularly quoted in publications such as *Entrepreneur* magazine and the *New York Times*, and she is the author of several books, including *Anxious 9 to 5: How to Beat Worry, Stop Second Guessing Yourself, and Work with Confidence*. Get more information and dozens of free resources including the seven-week e-course 7 Steps to Career Success at www.pascoaching.com.

◆ ◆ ◆

Did you enjoy the ideas in this book? Want more? We've put together several free resources to further help you. Go to www.TheConfident Speaker.com where you'll find a collection of special reports, including:

- "The 10 Secrets to Magnetic Confidence—Feel Great and Attract Others Every Time You Speak"
- "Powerful Storytelling Techniques for Executives"
- "How to Use Speaking in Public to Attract Clients, Friends and Unlimited Business Opportunities"

You can take a 50-question self-assessment called "What's Your Charisma Quotient?" Personal charisma and magnetism are the keys to a mesmerizing speaker. Our quiz will help you discover how captivating you are and how you can become even more charismatic. Just go to www.TheConfidentSpeaker.com to get your special reports and charisma quiz now. They're free!